Beginning Windows® 7 And Microsoft Office® 2010

Kiel Emerson

Author: Kiel Emerson
Editor: Chris Emerson

ISBN: 1489540857
ISBN-13: 978-1489540850

First Printing June 2013
For ordering and other information, contact:
Compare Computers L.L.C.
P.O. Box 1211
Hays, KS 67601
support@comparecomputers.net
www.comparecomputers.net

DEDICATION

For my Sarah

Introduction

With Windows 7, Microsoft has worked to improve a number of features from previous versions of the operating system. Windows 7 features faster boot up times and faster overall performance than Windows Vista. The User Account Control, added after Windows XP, adds an additional defense against malicious software and unauthorized changes. Internet Explorer 10 provides support for HTML5 and CSS3.0, as well as numerous security enhancements. Those familiar with previous versions of Windows will find many familiar elements in Windows 7, and after reading this guide, be aware of the new features and how to comfortably work with them on a daily basis.

In this book we will explore the layout and features of Windows 7, explain how to perform common tasks in the OS, and get an overview of Office 2010 and other programs commonly run on Windows 7.

KIEL EMERSON

Chapter 1 - Getting Started and the Boot-Up Process

Before we can begin to use Windows 7, we will need to be sure the computer is connected properly to the display, power, and any peripheral devices. In the following section we will take a look at the physical ports on a desktop and laptop, and make sure the correct cables are connected to the computer before powering on the PC.

Physical Ports on the PC

On the chart that follows, you will find the physical ports on many desktops and laptops, and the common uses for each port.

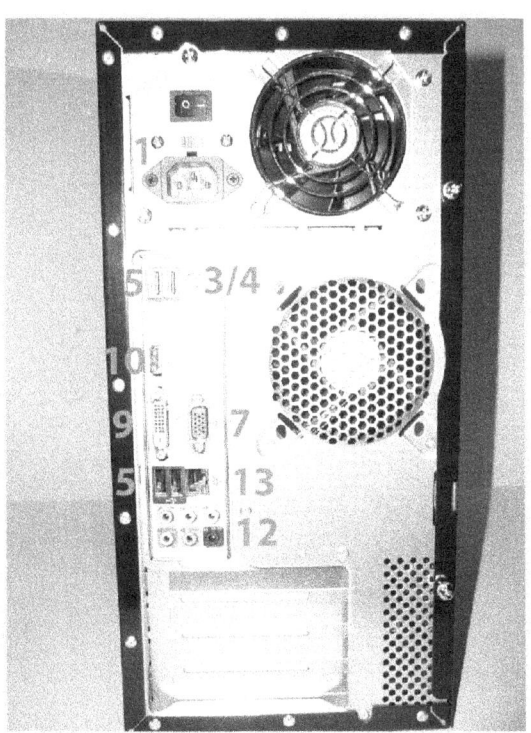

Figure 1.1: Desktop Ports

Figure 1.2: Laptop Ports

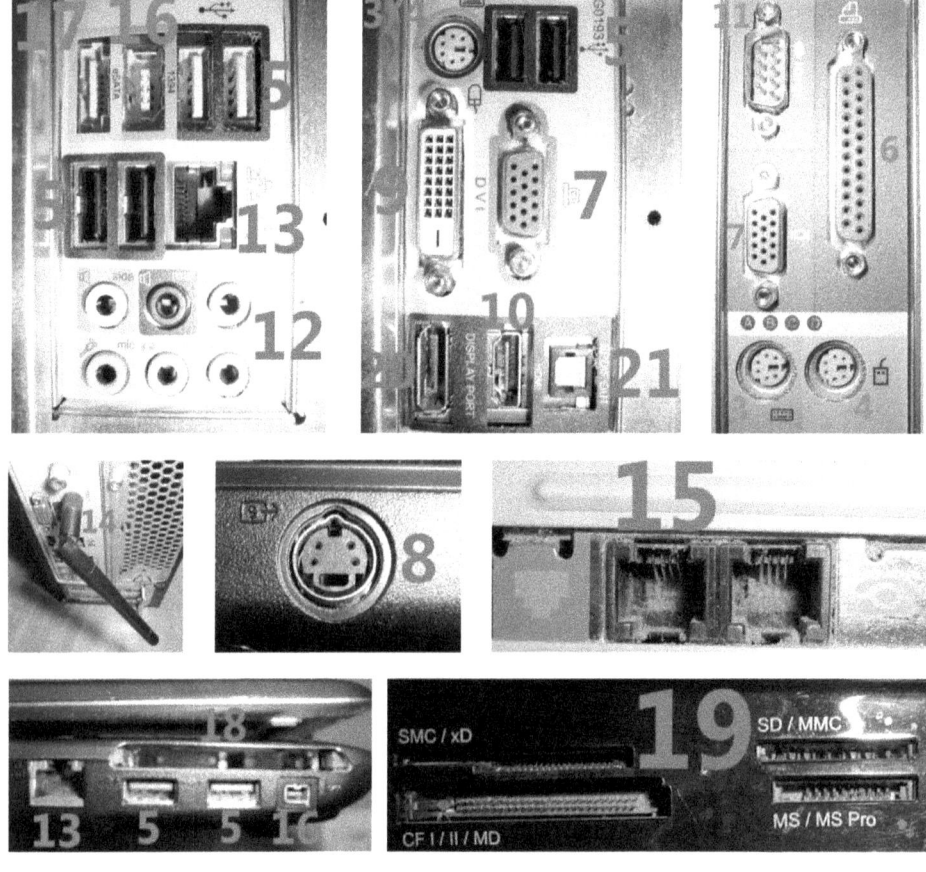

Figure 1.3: Computer Ports

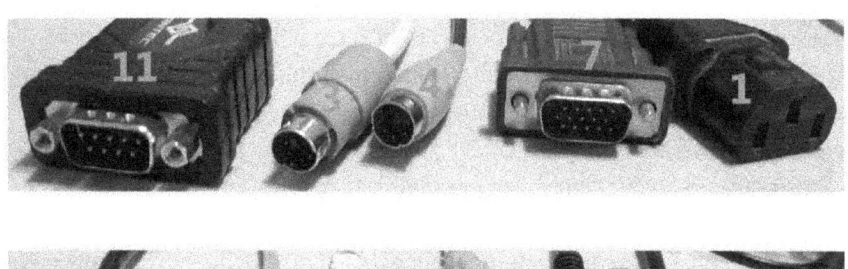
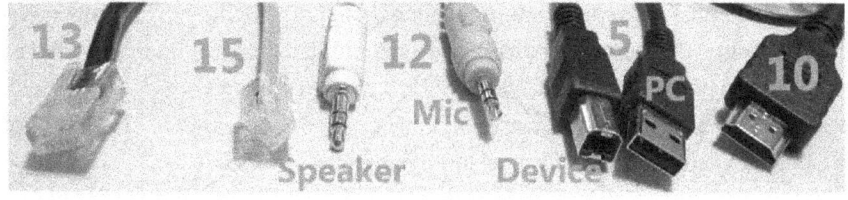

Figure 1.4: Computer Cables

1. **Desktop Power Connector** - This is the electrical power connector that plugs into your wall outlet.
2. **Laptop AC Adapter Power Connector** - This port will vary by brand and model, but connects to the AC power adapter that runs and charges the laptop.
3. **PS/2 Keyboard Connector** - This port (usually purple) is used only for a PS/2 type keyboard connector.
4. **PS/2 Mouse Connector** - This port (usually green) is used only for a PS/2 type mouse connector.
5. **USB Port** - This port is used by a large number of devices, from USB keyboards & mice, to printers, cameras, and mp3 players. The order that devices are plugged into these ports does not matter. Some devices may require drivers to be installed before a device can be recognized and used.
6. **Parallel Port** - This is a legacy connector that is no longer common on new PC's. In the past, it was primarily used as a connection to printers and scanners.
7. **VGA or D-Sub Video Port** - This is the most common video connector to an external monitor or TV. This is likely the connector that your monitor uses, and the connector has been common for many years.
8. **S-Video Video Port** - This video connector is rarely used to connect to an external display or TV, and lacks the video quality that other video connections provide.
9. **DVI Video Port** (varies by type) - There are several types of DVI ports and cables, and not all are compatible with each other. This video port is used to connect to an external monitor or TV.
10. **HDMI Video & Audio Port** - Many new systems include this all-in-one, high definition video & audio connector, used to output video & audio to an external monitor or TV.
11. **Serial Port** - This legacy port was used mainly to connect to older legacy hardware for communication. It is no longer common to find this connector on many desktops & laptops.
12. **Surround Sound Audio/Line-in/Speakers Out/Microphone Port** - The layout of the 1/8"

5

audio jacks will vary, and depend upon stereo or surround sound output capabilities. On most PC's, there are three audio ports: Line-in (usually blue), Stereo Speaker Output (usually green), and Microphone In (usually pink).

13. **Ethernet Port** - This port looks like an oversized phone jack. An Ethernet cable plugs into this port for use with your high speed internet connection.

14. **Desktop Wireless Card Antenna** - The wireless card antenna connects to your wireless router to establish a high speed internet connection.

15. **Dial-up Modem** - This legacy port/card was used primarily for dial-up internet access in the past, but is rare now due to the ubiquity of high speed networks.

16. **1394/Firewire Port** - This port is not commonly found on current PC's, but was used as a data connector for video cameras and some peripheral devices.

17. **eSATA Port** - The eSATA port is an external serial ATA port used as a high speed connection to external hard drives and similar devices.

18. **PCMCIA Port, Laptop Expansion Ports** - Laptop expansion ports will vary depending on the age of the system, but these ports are primarily used for add-on cards. Add-on wireless cards and mobile broadband cards are one commonly used PCMCIA card.

19. **Card Reader Slots** - These ports vary on each system, and are only compatible with specific types of cards. These ports allow you to plug in a camera memory card and access pictures stored on the device. Memory cards show up as a removable device in Windows Explorer.

20. **DisplayPort** - This port is usually used to output video and audio to a monitor or external display. DisplayPort has a similar functionality to HDMI, but is not compatible with HDMI without a specific adapter.

21. **SPDIF Out (Sony/Philips Digital Interconnect Format)** - This digital audio port is usually used to output sound to external audio equipment, such as a surround sound stereo receiver.

On a desktop PC we need to be sure that at least the keyboard, mouse, monitor video cable, and power for both the monitor and tower are all connected. You may also have speakers, an Ethernet cable, and other peripheral devices connected. On a laptop you will need the AC power adapter connected, as well as any peripheral devices you wish to use. We can proceed to the next section once the required cables are in place.

Powering On the Computer

To begin, we first need to power on the computer. While every computer will vary in design, generally the power button will tend to be on the front of a desktop tower or above the keyboard on an open laptop (Figure 1.5). Generally the power button may have a symbol with a circle and a line through it.

Once you have located the power button, give it a quick press to power on your system if it is not already powered on.

Figure 1.5: Desktop & Laptop Power Button

The first screen you may see will likely be the BIOS POST screen or a screen with the computer manufacturer's logo. Following that screen, you will likely see the Windows 7 splash screen (Figure 1.6) with four orbs of light that form the Windows logo. This screen shows that Windows is booting up.

Figure 1.6: Windows 7 Splash Screen

First Boot Initial Setup

If this is the first time you are powering on your Windows 7 PC you will likely see the initial setup screens that follow. The screens you will see may vary from one system to the next. Each of these steps will configure settings on the computer and allow you to personalize the system with the settings you select.

The first screen you will likely encounter is one prompting you to enter in a user name and a computer name. I recommend that you use your own name or simply enter the name "owner" if you do not want to use your own name. Click next when you have entered the required information.

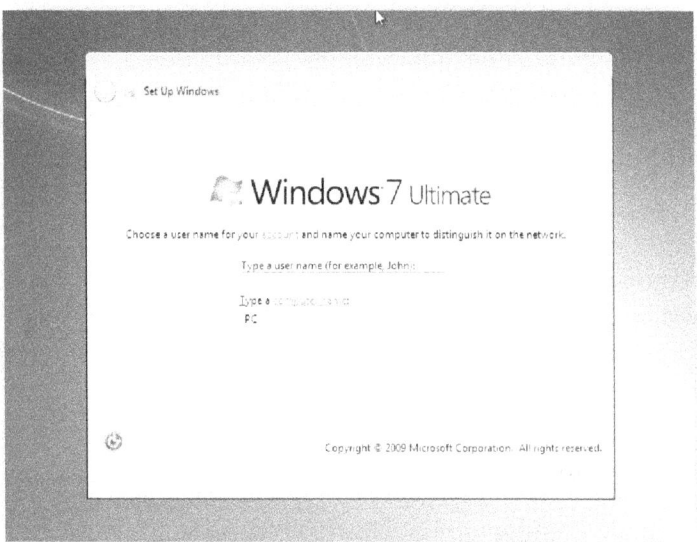

Figure 1.7: Windows 7 Setup Step 1

The next screen you will see will be asking you for a password and a password reminder for the user account that you just created. If you do not wish to enter a password at this time, you can simply leave the fields blank and click the Next button.

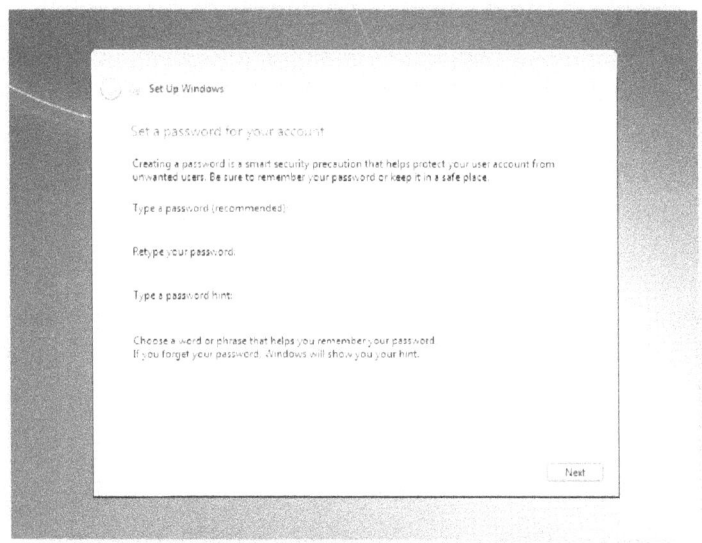

Figure 1.8: Windows 7 Setup Step 2

The next screen you may encounter may prompt you to enter your Windows Product Key. In most configurations the initial setup will not prompt for the product key, as it will usually be saved on the system hardware or entered earlier during a disc-based installation. If you do see this screen you will need to locate the product key sticker and type in the 25-digit key listed. This sticker will often be on the side or back of a desktop computer. On a laptop it is often located on the underside or in the battery compartment.

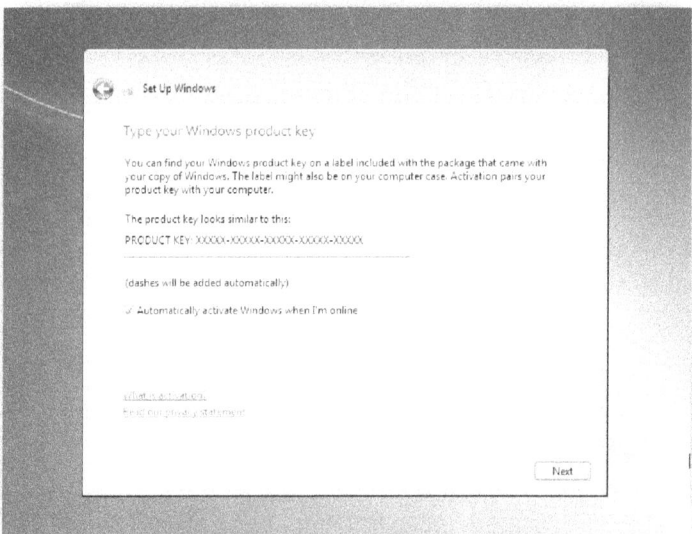

Figure 1.9: Windows 7 Setup Step 3

The following screen gives you options for keeping the computer up-to-date, secure, and allows the system to check online for problem solutions. We suggest that you use the top Recommended Settings option.

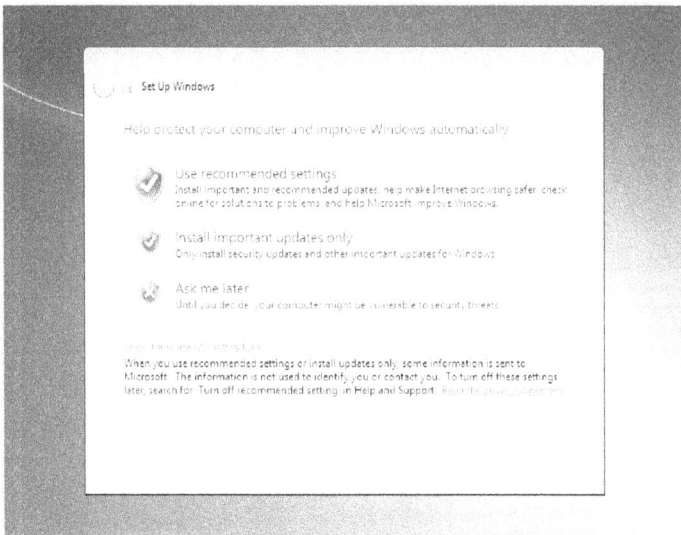

Figure 1.10: Windows 7 Setup Step 4

 Select Use Recommended Settings option for the preferred system settings.

In the next screen, you will be prompted to choose your time zone and set the date and time. Click the Next button to continue after configuring your settings.

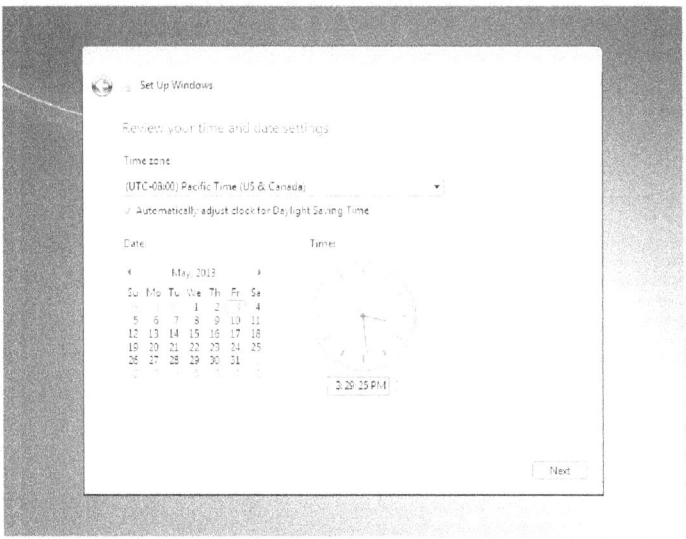

Figure 1.11: Windows 7 Setup Step 5

Once the previous steps have been completed, Windows will show a progress bar while your settings are finalized. This step may take several minutes to complete while the computer is being set up.

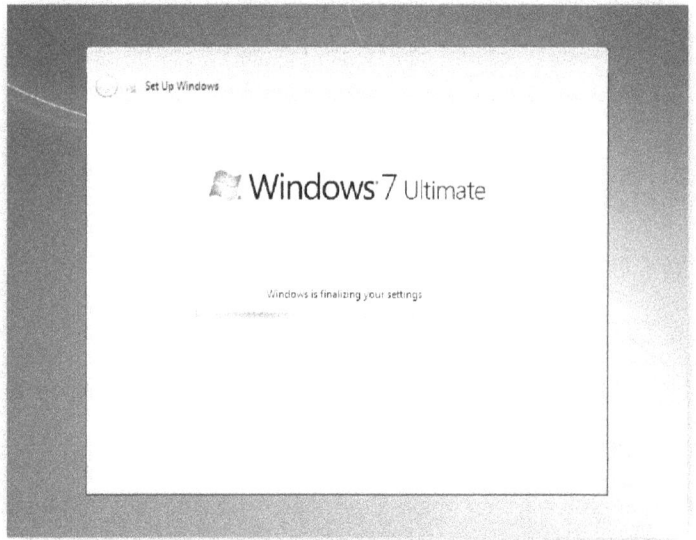

Figure 1.12: Windows 7 Setup Finalizing Settings

After this step the computer may restart, and then the computer will boot into Windows 7 and load the Windows Desktop. If you created a login password you will be required to enter the password before booting into the desktop.

Windows Login and Login Screen

When you power on your Windows 7 PC, it may boot directly to the Windows Desktop, or to a Login screen. If you see the Login screen with user accounts listed, click the user account you wish to use. If there is a password for the account, you will be required to enter it. Accessibility options are available with the button on the left side of the screen and shutdown options are available with the button on the right side of the screen.

Figure 1.13: User Account Login Screen

If you only have a single user account and it does not have a password, then your PC will continue to boot up and immediately load the Windows Desktop. Once all the startup programs have loaded, you will find a screen similar to Figure 1.14.

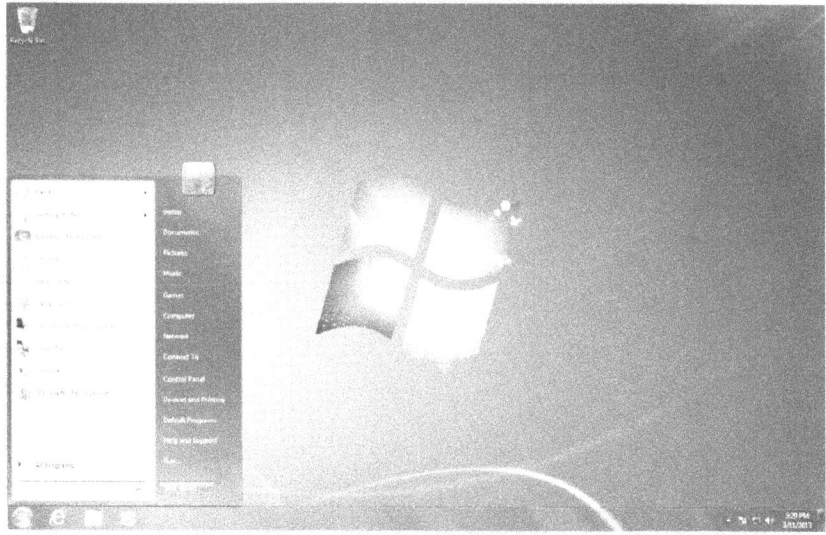

Figure 1.14: Windows Start Menu

Now that the initial Windows 7 setup and configuration is complete, we can start learning and exploring the many new features in Windows 7. In the sections that follow we will walk through the different parts of the Windows Desktop and provide an overview of how to use each feature.

Chapter Review Questions:

1. Identify the ports on your computer and describe the purpose of each port.
2. During the initial setup of a new Windows 7 computer, what is the first screen you are likely to see that requires input from you?
3. What screen will you likely see when your computer completes setup if you have a single user account without a password?

Chapter 2 - Windows 7 Primary Components

In Windows 7 there are three primary components to the operating system. The first item is the Windows Desktop which contains icons for programs, files, and folders located on top of the background wallpaper image. The second item is the Windows Taskbar that runs along the bottom of the screen. Clicking the Windows Orb icon in the lower-left corner of the screen will open the Start Menu, which is the third Windows 7 component we will discuss. In the following sections I will walk you through the each part of the Windows desktop and provide an overview of how to use each feature.

Windows Desktop

The Windows Desktop is the traditional interface for working with files and desktop applications. The Windows 7 Desktop is similar to the desktop that was available in previous versions of Windows.

You will notice several main components on the screen while looking at the Windows Desktop. Desktop icons for programs, files, and folders are located on top of the background wallpaper image. You also can store files and shortcuts on the Windows Desktop.

Figure 2.1: Windows Desktop and Taskbar

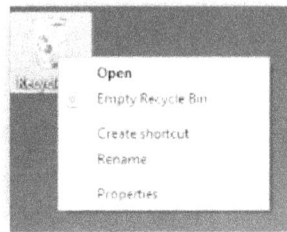

Figure 2.2: Empty Recycle Bin

The next primary Windows component that we will examine is the Windows Start Menu.

Windows Start Menu

The Windows Start Menu is one of the primary interfaces in Windows 7. The Start Menu icon is located on the Taskbar in the lower-left corner of the screen. The Windows 7 Start Menu layout is very similar to the Start Menu in Windows Vista.

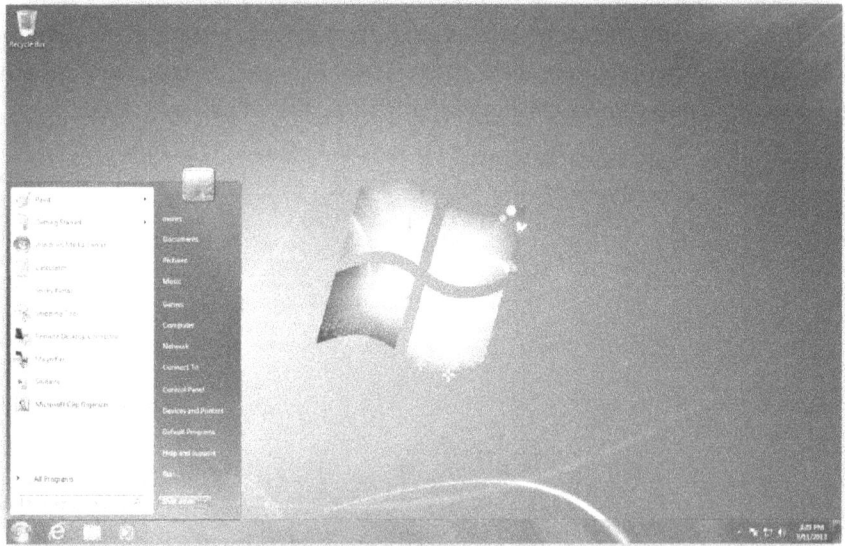

Figure 2.3: Windows Start Menu

When you click the Windows Orb icon on the taskbar the Start Menu will open. Along the left side of the Start Menu are commonly used programs. Along the right side of the Start Menu are links to various locations and items. Below I have outlined the most common links on the right side of the Start Menu, and what those links do:

- **User Profile Folder** – this folder's name will vary depending on the account name that was created when the computer was first set up. It may be your own name, it may be "owner", or it could be something arbitrary – the main point being that when you click it, it takes you to the folder where the majority of your files (documents, pictures, music, etc.) all reside.

- **Documents Folder** – This link takes you directly to the current user's documents library, which for now we'll say is equivalent to the current user's documents folder. This folder generally contains only documents (such as word documents, excel spreadsheets, and other data files saved there), and not pictures, music, or other files.
- **Pictures Folder** – This link takes you directly to the current user's pictures library, which for now we'll say is equivalent to the current user's pictures folder. This folder generally contains only images (such as photos and saved pictures), and not documents, music, or other files.
- **Music Folder** – This link takes you directly to the current user's music library, which for now we'll say is equivalent to the current user's music folder. This folder generally contains only audio files (such as mp3's, wma's, and other audio types), and not documents, pictures, or other files.
- **Computer** – The computer link opens a Windows Explorer window showing the drives in your computer, such as "C:\" or "Local Disk", DVD+/-RW DVD Burners, USB Storage Devices, Camera Cards, and other storage devices. Double clicking on available drives will open the drive, allowing you to explore the contents and files.
- **Control Panel** – The Control Panel is a group of programs that allow you to change various settings on your PC. Settings ranging from user accounts, to security configuration, to background wallpaper and screen saver can all be configured here.
- **Devices and Printers** – This item allows you to see devices connected to your computer such as a webcam, printers, mp3 players, phones, and Media Center Extenders. From the device and printers center, you can view properties and see actions available for specific hardware.
- **Default Programs** – This link allows you to access settings that pertain to default programs used to open certain file types. You can also manage the default autoplay options for media on the PC, like CD's and external storage.
- **Help and Support** – This link launches the Windows Help and Support program, which can be used to search for answers to questions and access online help topics.
- **Shut Down/Restart/Sleep/Hibernate** – Clicking this link will take whatever default action is listed. By clicking Shut Down, the PC will immediately start shutting down. To choose options other than the default, click or hover over the arrow just to the right and the alternate options will appear.

On the bottom left-hand corner of the Start Menu, there is a link for "All Programs". If you hover over that link, or single left-click the link, it will expand to a list of all available programs and folders. If you right-click a program in this list, you can choose to pin the program to the Start Menu, pin the program to the taskbar, or send a program shortcut to the desktop (Send To option, then "Desktop (Create Shortcut)").

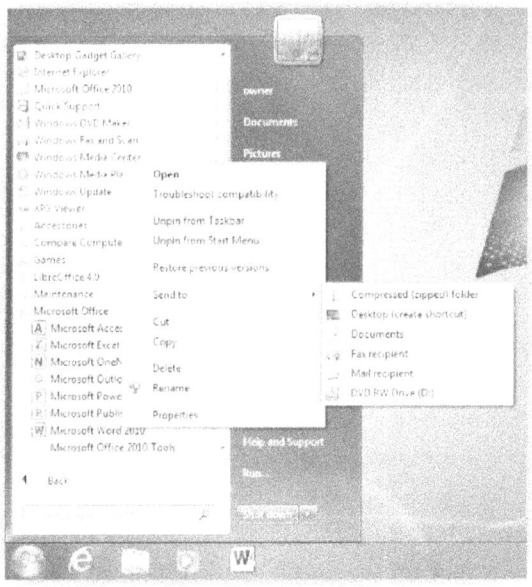

Figure 2.4: Create a Desktop Shortcut

To create a desktop shortcut, right click a file, folder, or icon and then select the "Send To" option, followed by the "Desktop (Create Shortcut)" link.

Just beneath the "All Programs" link in the lower left corner of the Start Menu, you'll find a search box. By typing the name of a program, file, or option, you can see a list of results appear as you type. You can then click the item you wish to use thereby quickly accessing that resource.

Figure 2.5: Start Menu Search Box

Some programs pinned or listed on the Start Menu will expand out into the right side of the Start Menu. These programs may list recently opened files or may offer program specific actions, such as running an antivirus scan or opening your e-mail inbox.

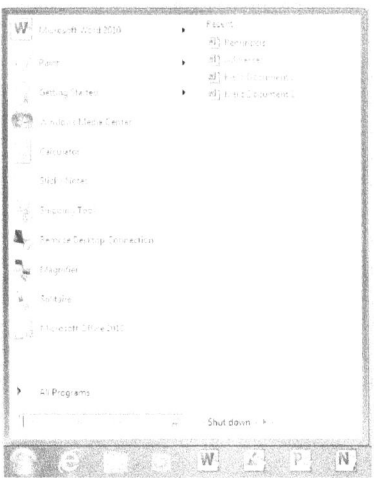

Figure 2.6: Start Menu Expanding Right Pane

The next component we will discuss is the Windows Taskbar running along the bottom of the Windows Desktop.

Windows Taskbar

In the lower left corner of the Windows Desktop there are usually several programs pinned to the Taskbar. Usually you will find at least the Taskbar links shown in Figure 2.7, but other programs may be pinned to the Taskbar as well.

Figure 2.7: Windows Taskbar

By default, the first item to the right of the Start Menu icon is Internet Explorer. This web browser can be used to view websites and access internet resources. To the right of Internet Explorer is Windows Explorer. Windows Explorer is a file manager that is used to view files, folders, and drives that are accessible to your system. The next icon is Windows Media Player. Windows Media Player is a program for playing music, videos, and DVD's. Icons to the right of the Start Menu will vary from system to system. Icons on the taskbar can be added, removed, and sorted any time you choose.

When you right-click on programs pinned to the Taskbar, you will see what is known as a Jump List. A Jump List provides quick access to common features or files, and allows items to be pinned to the list. The Jump List for Internet Explorer will list frequently visited websites or sites that you have pinned for faster accessibility. The Jump List for Microsoft Word will list recently opened documents and any documents that you have manually pinned. To pin an item to the Jump List, open the Jump List and click the thumbtack icon next to the listed file name.

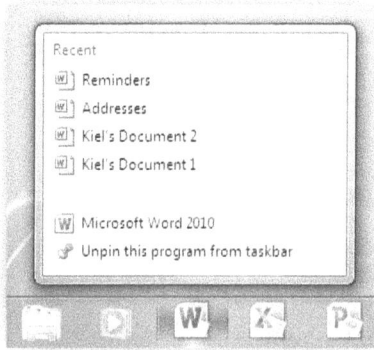

Figure 2.8: Jump Lists

A **Tip** Pin commonly used files to the Jump List by pressing the thumbtack icon next to the filename in the Jump List.

When you have a window open, hovering your cursor over the taskbar icon for that window will display a thumbnail image. This makes it easier to view the open windows you want to access while you have multiple windows and applications running at the same time.

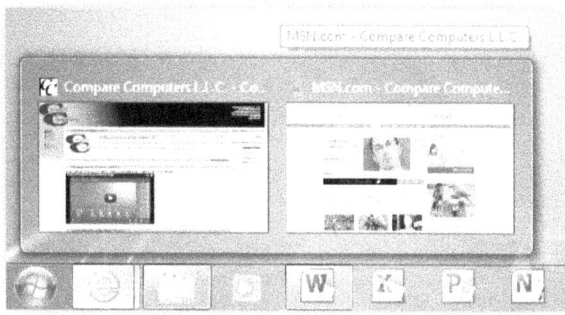

Figure 2.9: Open Program Thumbnails

The desktop area is the area on top of your background wallpaper where icons, folders, and files can be located. Many programs place a shortcut on the desktop during their installation in order to make it easier to run the application. You can save files to the desktop, but I recommend grouping files by type (images, music, videos) in their respective folders located in Windows Explorer for consistency. Many programs will look for specific files in those folders – for instance, Windows Media Player will search your Music folder for any audio files, and will automatically import the songs into the program, making them available for listening all in one place.

It can be difficult managing multiple program windows that are open at the same time. There are a few options available for easily accessing the specific window that you want to work with. On the far right corner of the taskbar is a thin bar icon called Show Desktop. If you hover over this icon all windows on the screen will minimize until you move the cursor off of the icon. This feature is known as Windows Peek. If you click Show Desktop, it will minimize all windows, even if you move your cursor off of the icon. By clicking it again, you can restore all previously minimized windows to the way they were.

Figure 2.10: Show Desktop

To the left of the Show Desktop icon on the taskbar, the notification area is where some background programs and alerts will appear. Windows 7 has made improvements to the notification area in an attempt to make it not interfere with normal everyday tasks. In previous versions of Windows, pop up alerts in this area lead to distractions and other problems. With Windows 7 the majority of those issues have been resolved. The Action Center now handles many of the critical alerts relating to system security and maintenance. When issues need to be resolved, the Action Center will alert you with a flag with a red circle and "X", along with an alert balloon. Clicking on the balloon or Action Center icon will provide you with more information on the issue and how to resolve the problem.

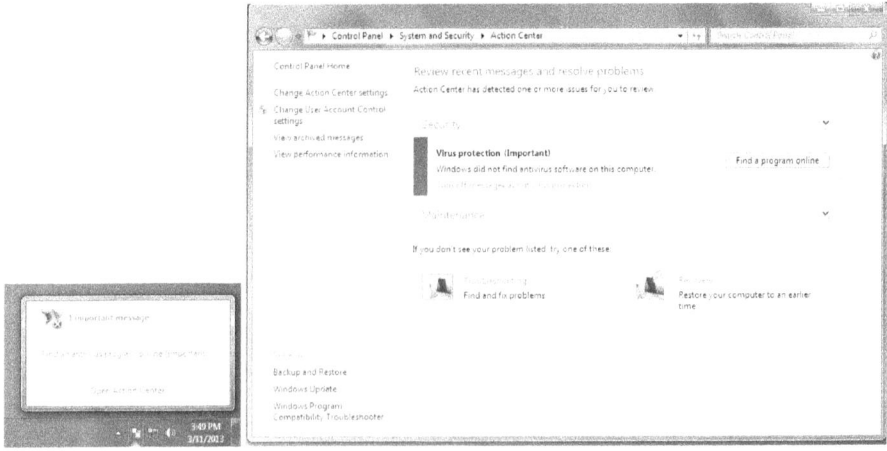

Figure 2.11: Action Center

Desktop Window Management

If you are working with two windows and wish to easily resize them so they both occupy half of the screen, Windows 7 has an easy to use feature called Windows Snap. Windows Snap allows you to drag the Title Bar (very top of program window) of one program to one side of the screen edge to automatically resize the program to half of the screen. Dragging the other program's Title Bar to the opposite side of the screen edge resizes it to the other half of the screen. This feature makes it handy to read information on one screen and type in the other window, without having to minimize either screen.

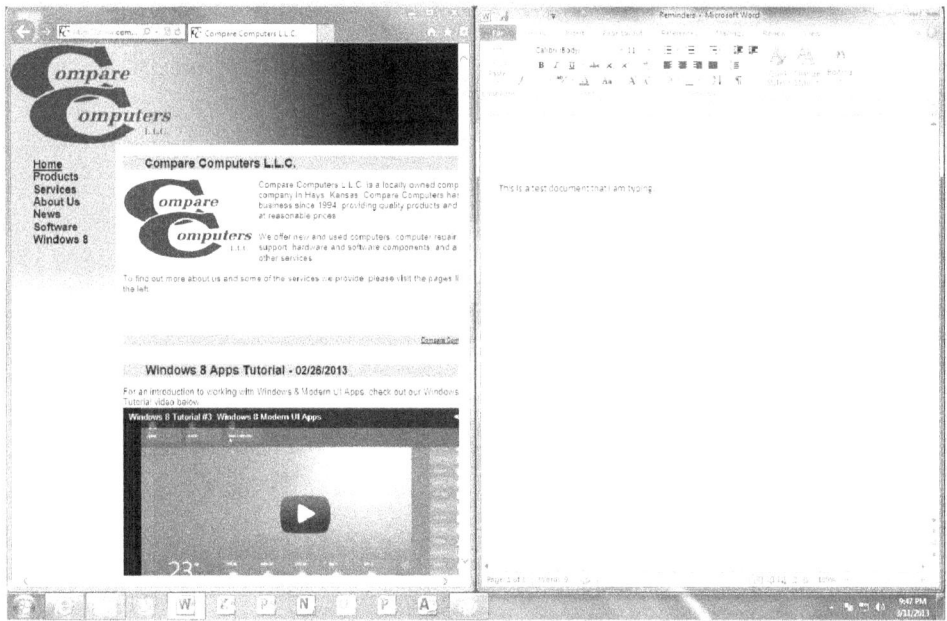

Figure 2.12: Windows Snap

Window Shake is a Windows 7 feature that allows you to minimize all windows except the one you want to work with. Simply click and hold the Title Bar of the open program you want to work with, and shake your cursor on the screen. All other windows will minimize. If you repeat the process, all windows will restore back again.

A simple keyboard key combination is another option for easily moving between open windows. On your keyboard, hold down the Alt key (usually located next to the spacebar on your keyboard). Then click the Tab key on your keyboard. You should see a window that displays all of the open program windows on your computer. By continuing to hold the Alt key, and tapping the Tab key, you can cycle through the open programs. Release the Alt key to select the window you wish to open. You can also use the Windows Key on your keyboard in place of the Alt key to cycle through open programs in 3D.

To change your desktop wallpaper, theme, screen saver, and other options, right-click on a blank area of the desktop and click Personalize. This will open the personalization section of the control panel. Clicking the four items at the bottom of the window (Desktop Background, Window Color, Sounds, and Screen Saver) will allow you to adjust those settings. In the Desktop Background section, you can select multiple images that will cycle through as the wallpaper at the selected interval.

In Chapter 3, we will explore the Windows Desktop in more detail by learning about traditional desktop applications and their interfaces.

Chapter Review Questions:

1. What are the three primary components in Windows 7?
2. Describe the functions of each item listed on the right-side of the Start Menu.
3. Describe how you can quickly open a file with the Jump List feature.
4. What are some of the notices you may see in the Action Center?
5. How are Windows Snap and Window Shake used?

Chapter 3 - Exploring Desktop Application Windows & Windows Explorer

Application Interfaces

Every application window layout will vary depending on how it was designed. However, many applications have similarities in their design and layout, which we will review in the following section.

Figure 3.1: Application Window Layout

The Title Bar is the uppermost portion of an application window that usually contains the name of the running application. To the right of the Title Bar in the upper right corner of the window, you will usually find three icons for managing the open window. The bar icon on the left is the Minimize button, which will keep the window open, but minimize it to the taskbar. The middle icon with a picture of either one or two squares is the Maximize/Restore button. Clicking it will either maximize the window to full screen, or restore it to a smaller size on the screen. The red "X" icon on the far right is the Close button. Clicking this button will exit the current application or window.

Beneath the Minimize, Maximize, and Close buttons on some application windows, you may find a Search Box. This search box allows you to search for files, folders, and settings within the current window. There may be an Address Bar to the left of the Search Box in some windows. The Address Bar may show the current page, website, folder, or other location that you are currently accessing.

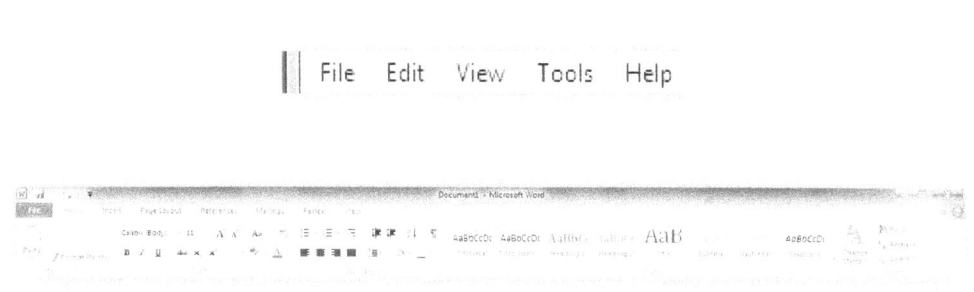

Figure 3.2: Menu Bar & Ribbon Bar

Below the Title Bar many programs also have a Menu Bar or ribbon user interface. The Menu Bar contains drop down menus that perform actions for that program. Usually you will find drop down menus for File, Edit, View, Tools, and Help. The Menu Bar generally contains options for creating and opening files, saving files, printing, editing, and configuring layout. Programs using the ribbon user interface, such as Microsoft Office 2007, 2010, and 2013, are becoming more commonplace. Ribbon UI's offer a clear visual representation of various functions and tend to be more touch-friendly on touch screen monitors. Ribbon UI's have tabs, similar to the tabs on a paper file folder. Under each tab are icons for functions relevant to that tab.

Next we will look at Windows Explorer-the file management tool in Windows 7.

Windows Explorer

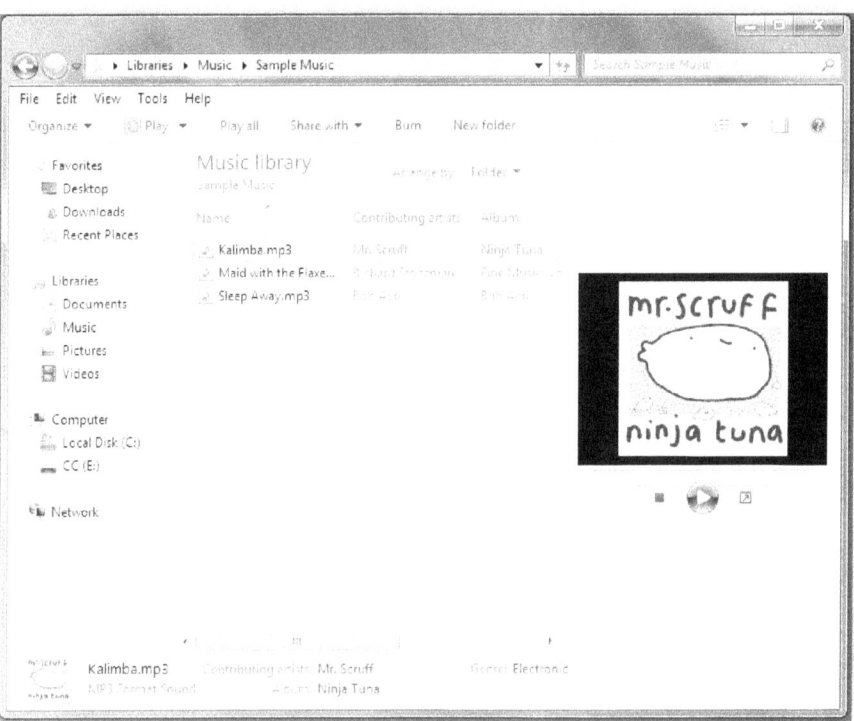

Figure 3.3: Windows Explorer Layout

By default, the Windows Explorer program window will have a Title Bar, Address Bar, and Search Box. The Minimize, Maximize, and Close buttons will be located in the upper-right corner of the window. Below the Address Bar are six sections to the main window: the Task Menu, the Navigation Pane, the Library Pane, the Details Pane, the Preview Pane (disabled by default), and the File List.

The Task Menu's contents will change depending on the files selected and the contents of the currently open folder. Some of the options in the Task Menu allow you to organize and change the layout onscreen, share files, create new folders, and burn files to disc, among other features. The Navigation Pane provides quick shortcuts to folders, drives, libraries, and network paths. The Library Pane displays information about the currently open library, and has a link to view, add, or remove library folder locations. The Details Pane displays details of the currently selected file, folder, or drive, such as size, sharing status, modification date, and creation date. The Preview Pane (when enabled) allows you to see a preview of selected documents and other supported files, without having to open the file. Supported audio files can be played directly from the Preview Pane without needing to open a media player program.

The file list is the main section of the Windows Explorer window. It lists the file and folder names of objects in the current path. You can adjust the size of the icons in the file list by clicking on the "change your view" option in the Task Menu. Click the button, or click the arrow and more the slider, to adjust the size of icons or thumbnail pictures on the screen.

When you open Windows Explorer, usually you will see the Favorites, Libraries, Computer, and Network links on the left pane. Below you will find some basic information on these links and some other common file paths.

- **Favorites Folder** – Users can add commonly used folders to this list so that they show up in Windows Explorer favorites list.
- **Documents Folder** – This link takes you directly to the current user's documents library, which for now we will say is equivalent to the current user's documents folder. This folder generally contains only documents (such as Word documents, Excel spreadsheets, and other data files saved there), and not pictures, music, or other files.
- **Pictures Folder** – This link takes you directly to the current user's pictures library, which for now we will say is equivalent to the current user's pictures folder. This folder generally contains only images (such as photos and saved pictures), and not documents, music, or other files.
- **Music Folder** – This link takes you directly to the current user's music library, which for now we will say is equivalent to the current user's music folder. This folder generally contains only audio files (such as mp3's, wma's, and other audio types), and not documents, pictures, or other files.
- **Computer** – The computer link opens a Windows Explorer window showing the drives in your computer, such as "C:\" or Local Disk, DVD+/-RW DVD Burners, USB Storage Devices, Camera Cards, and other storage devices. Double-clicking on available drives will open the drive, allowing you to explore the contents and files.
- **Network** – This link allows access to any shared network folders and networked computers.
- **User Profile Folder** – This folder's name will vary depending on the account name that was created when the computer was first set up. It may be your own name, it may be "owner", or it could be something arbitrary – the main point being that when you click it, it takes you to the folder where the majority of your files (documents, pictures, music, etc.) all reside. Typically the path to the user profile folder is in "C:\Users\".

Windows Libraries

A new feature in Windows 7 are the locations called Libraries. These Libraries are a collection of files and folders that are physically stored in separate locations on your PC. The Documents Library normally contains files and folders from two different locations – the current user's Documents folder, and also the Public user account's Documents folder. So by opening the Documents Library you can see the contents of both folders in a single location.

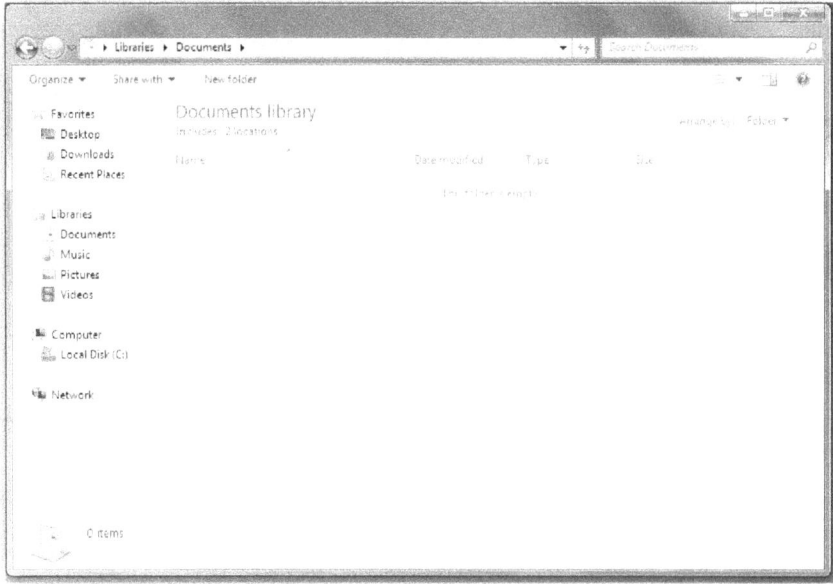

Figure 3.4: Documents Library Window

⚠ Keep in mind that files and folders that appear inside your Libraries folders may be located in an area other than the current user's profile folders.

You can add additional folders to a Library by clicking on the "Includes: # Locations" link while a Library is open. This will open the Library Locations window. In this window you can add and remove folder locations associated with the currently open Library.

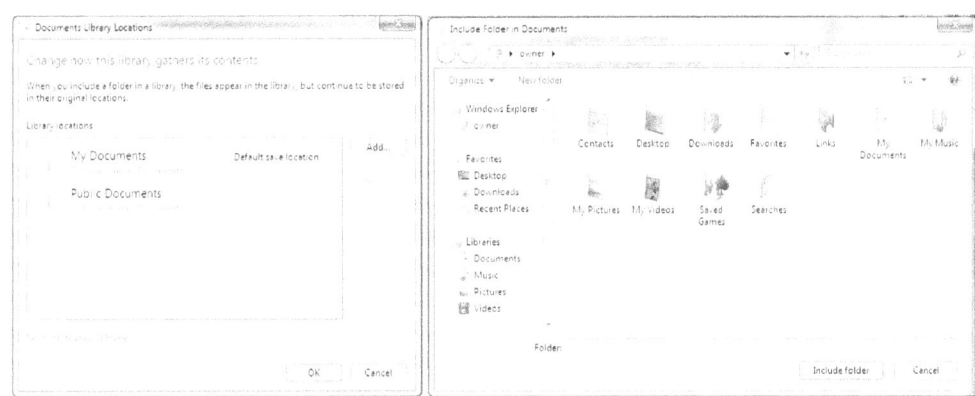

Figure 3.5: Add Folders to Library

Click the Add button to browse for additional folders to add into the currently open Library. You can also add folders from other computers and devices on the network into your Library.

There are four default Libraries in Windows 7 – Documents, Music, Pictures, and Videos. To create a new custom Library, click the New Library button on the Task Menu bar while the Libraries folder is open.

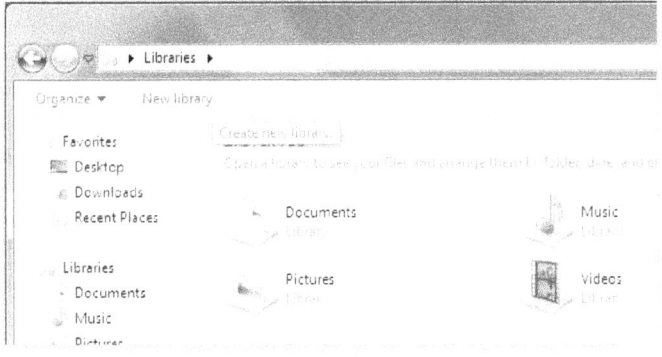

Figure 3.6: Create New Library

Choose a name for your new Library folder and press Enter. The new Library folder will be added to your list.

Figure 3.7: Name New Library

To add folder locations for the newly created Library, simply open the new Library, click the "Includes: # Locations" link, and then add desired folders to the new Library collection.

In chapter 4 we will briefly look at the file system in Windows 7. We will also review how to work with files and folders.

Chapter Review Questions:

1. Name three programs that use a Ribbon UI interface instead of a drop-down menu.
2. Describe the process of creating a new Library and adding locations to the Library.

Chapter 4 - Getting to Know the File System

Drives, Partitions, Folders, and files

When you open the Computer link in Windows Explorer, you will see a listing of the drives on your computer. Usually this will include at least your system drive (usually "C :\"), and an optical drive (usually your DVD Burner "D :\"). Your hard disk is the physical hard drive inside your computer where your data is stored. This drive may be divided into multiple partitions, which may appear as separate drives in Windows Explorer, even though they are stored on the same physical device. When you double-click on the system drive ("C :\") you will find a number of files and folders. To keep the concepts of drives, folders, and files straight, think of a filing cabinet. The cabinet is like a drive. The paper folder is like a folder on the drive containing single files storing data. To create a new folder, right-click in a blank space in the file list area, and choose New, then Folder. You can then type the name that you would like to use for the folder, followed by the Enter key on your keyboard. The folder will then be renamed.

Cut, Copy, Paste, and Delete

There are many ways to copy and paste files: keyboard shortcuts ("ctrl + c", "ctrl + v"), dragging and dropping the file, using menus ("File Menu – Edit – Copy/ Paste"), and right-clicking the file and choosing Copy or Paste. Usually the easiest method for most people to start with is to right-click on the file you wish to copy and click Copy from the context menu. To copy multiple files in the same location you can hold the "Ctrl" key and left-click on the files you want to select. When your selection is complete you can right-click on one of the selected files and choose Copy from the context menu. Browse Windows Explorer to the destination path you desire, right-click in a blank area of the file list, and choose Paste from the context menu. To delete a file, right-click the file name, and choose Delete from the context menu. Confirm the file delete confirmation window if you are certain you wish to move the item to the recycle bin.

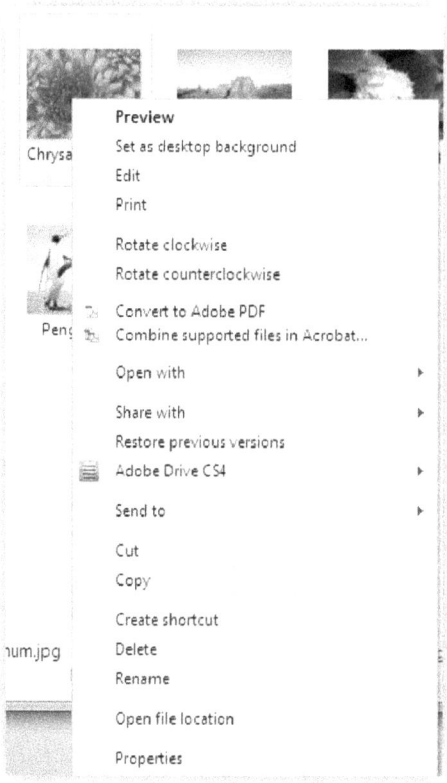

Figure 4.1: File Right-click Context Menu

Right-clicking on a file or folder allows you to Cut, Copy, or Delete. Right-clicking on a folder or blank area in Windows Explorer allows you to paste copied files.

Now that we have reviewed working with files and folders, we will turn our focus to working with some common desktop applications in Windows 7.

Chapter Review Questions:
1. Describe the differences between a drive, a partition, a folder, and a file.
2. Describe three different ways to copy and paste a file into a folder.

Chapter 5 - Web Browsing

Today, much of what we do on our computers relies upon accessing the internet-be it for news, e-mail, shopping, or for work. There are several popular web browsers that help us to securely accomplish these tasks.

Internet Explorer 10

Internet Explorer is currently the most widely used PC web browser. Windows 7 was released with Internet Explorer 8. At present the newest version of Internet Explorer for Windows 7 is version 10. Internet Explorer 10 can be downloaded for free through Windows Update. Internet Explorer 10 sports a minimal user interface, leaving a large amount of screen space for the page you are viewing. The program includes numerous security improvements and support for HTML5 – the new standard for many newly designed websites.

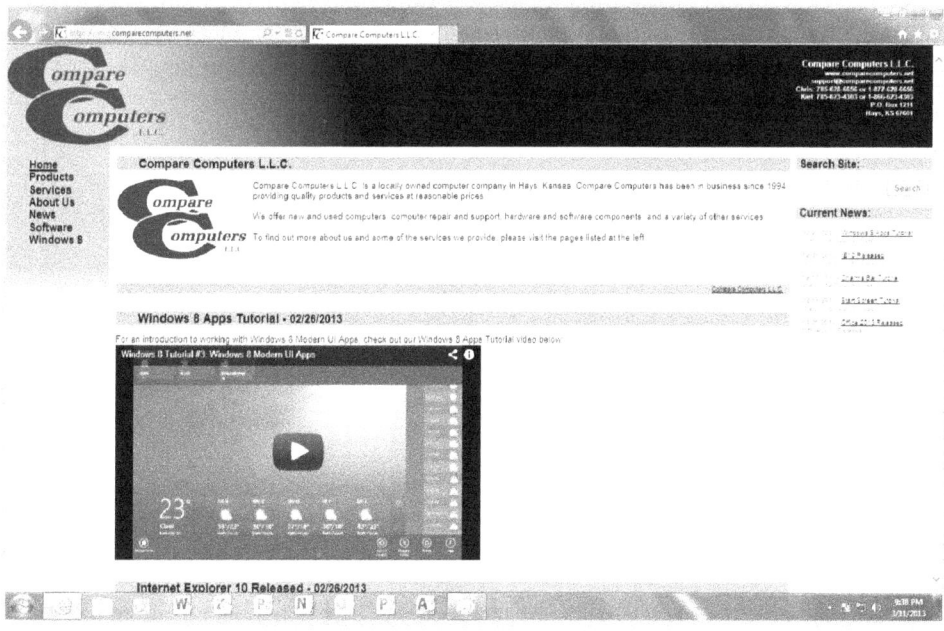

Figure 5.1: Internet Explorer 10 Address Bar

Internet Explorer 10 Window Layout

Internet Explorer 10 has several primary components to the program window. The Title Bar is the uppermost portion of the window. Located underneath the Title Bar and on the left side of the window, the Address Bar shows the web address of the current page, and is used to type in an address for a site you wish to visit. You can also use the Address Bar to perform a web search using the default search engine for the browser. For instance, you would type either the web address www.microsoft.com or type the word "Microsoft", and hit enter on your keyboard. This action will then search using your default search engine, using the search term "Microsoft". As you type in the Address Bar, you will see a list of websites that match the keys typed in the Address Bar, as well as favorites and sites you have visited matching the search term.

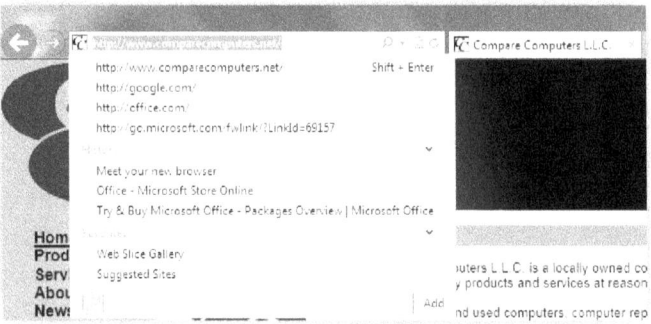

Figure 5.2: Address Bar Results

To the left of the Address Bar are the Back and Forward buttons. These buttons can be clicked to navigate to recently visited websites. You can right-click the button to see a list of recent sites to navigate to.

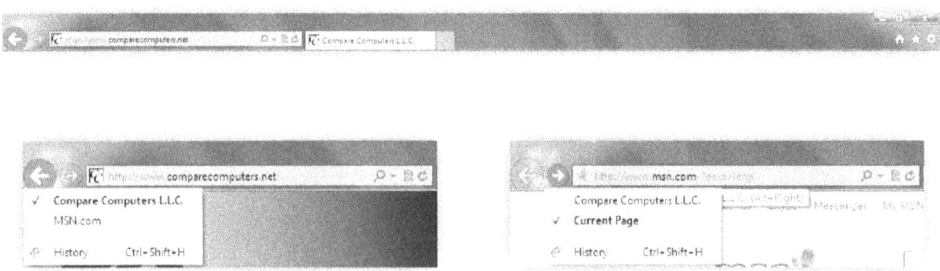

Figure 5.3: Internet Explorer 10 Forward & Back Buttons

The Compatibility View button is located between the Search and Refresh buttons on the Address Bar. This button can be used to reload a webpage that was designed for an older web browser that may not be displaying correctly.

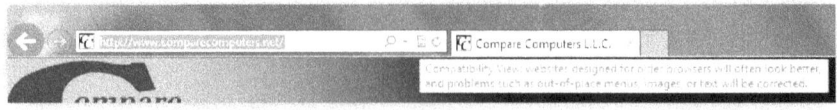

Figure 5.4: Compatibility View Button

On the upper right side of the screen you will see the Minimize, Maximize/Restore, and Close buttons that have been previously discussed. Beneath those buttons you will find three icons: The Home button, the Favorites button, and the Tools button. The Home button will take you back to your homepage, or if you right-click it, you can add or change your homepage.

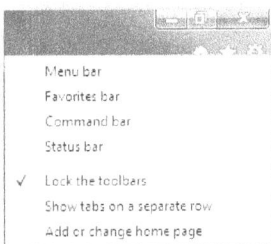 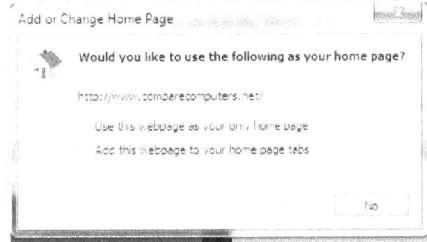

Figure 5.5: Change Home Page

The Favorites button will open your list of saved favorite websites (as well as subscribed newsfeeds and browsing history). The Favorites menu also provides a button to add the current page or current tabs to your favorites list.

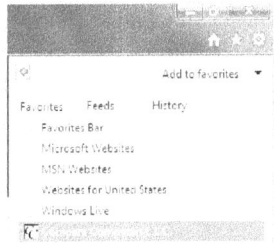 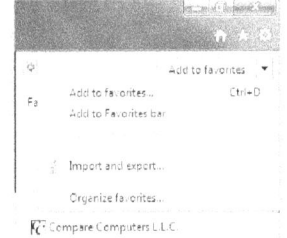 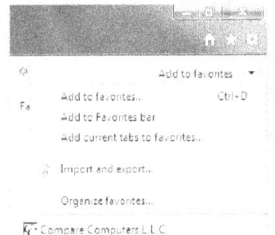

Figure 5.6: Favorites Button

The Tools button has options for printing, safety options, zoom options, and various other configuration options. Safety options include deleting browsing history and InPrivate Browsing mode. You can also adjust the SmartScreen Filter settings and website checking features.

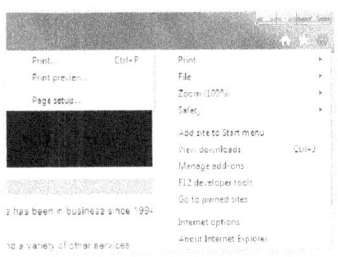 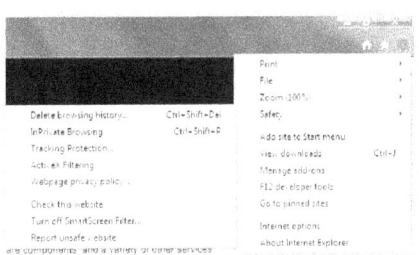

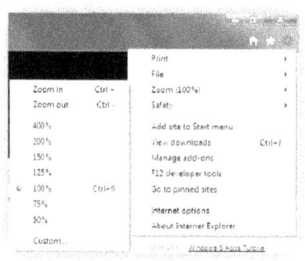

Figure 5.7: Tools Button

To configure a number of Internet Explorer settings, click on the Tools button and select Internet Options. This will open the Internet Options window. From this screen you can adjust security settings, internet connections, and manage browser add-ons and settings.

On the General Tab you can type in a homepage address, delete browsing history and related files, and adjust the appearance of Internet Explorer. The Security Tab allows you to adjust the security level for several zones. The Privacy Tab is used to manage the privacy level, control the pop-up blocker settings, and set various other privacy-related settings.

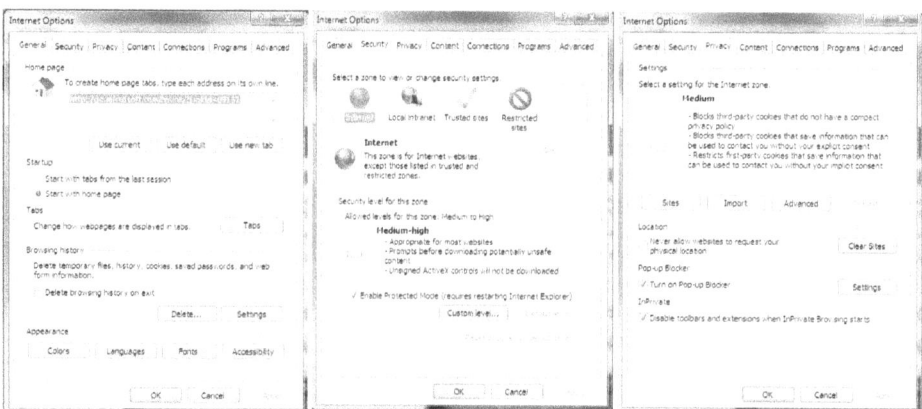

Figure 5.8: Internet Options

The Content Tab is used to control the Family Safety settings for web browsing, and also manages site certificates, AutoComplete settings, and RSS Feed settings. The Connections Tab is used to add manual internet connection settings. The Programs Tab can manage browser add-ons and toolbars. This tab can also configure default programs used with Internet Explorer.

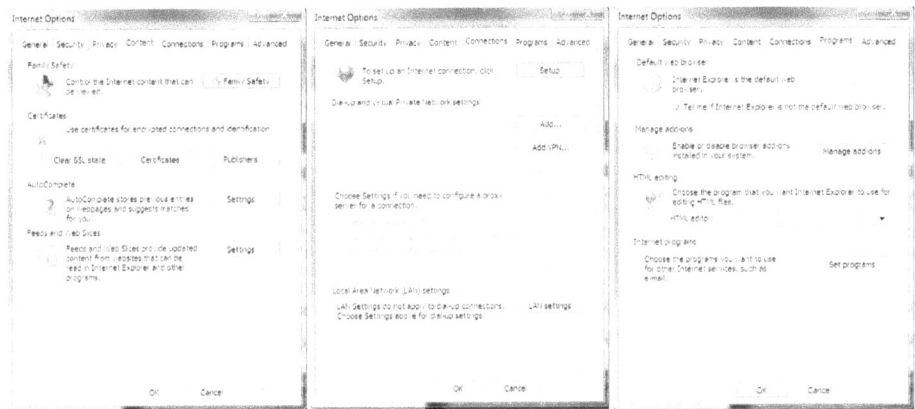

Figure 5.9: Internet Options

The Advanced Tab controls a number of settings for the browser. From here you can adjust accessibility options, browsing options, and security options for web content. I recommend leaving these settings with their default values unless a specific issue needs to be addressed.

Figure 5.10: Internet Options

Clicking the Manage Add-ons button under the Programs Tab will open a new window for adjusting Internet Explorer add-ons. Under the Toolbars and Extensions option, you can enable and disable toolbars and extensions that have been installed. Under the Search Providers option, you can adjust the order of search engines and set your desired default provider. The Accelerators options allows you to adjust the service used for the Internet Explorer Accelerators feature. Tracking Protection and Spelling Correction options let you choose lists for the provided features.

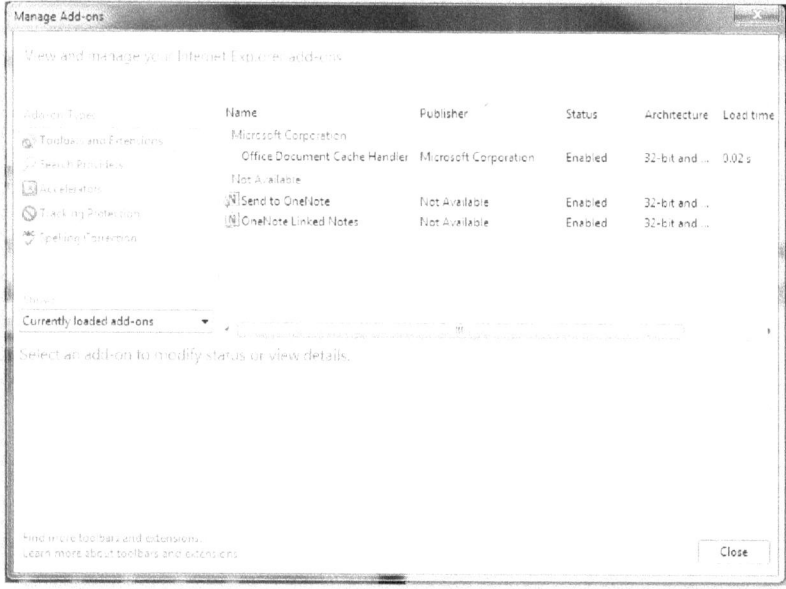

Figure 5.11: Manage Add-Ons

With Internet Explorer 10 you can have multiple tabs open. Each tab can contain a different webpage-all from within the same window. Simply click the new tab button, type the address you wish to visit, and click on the tab to switch back and forth between screens.

Figure 5.12: Open a New Tab

Opening a new tab will display commonly visited websites in the blank tab. You can either click on one of the listed sites or type in an address in the Address Bar.

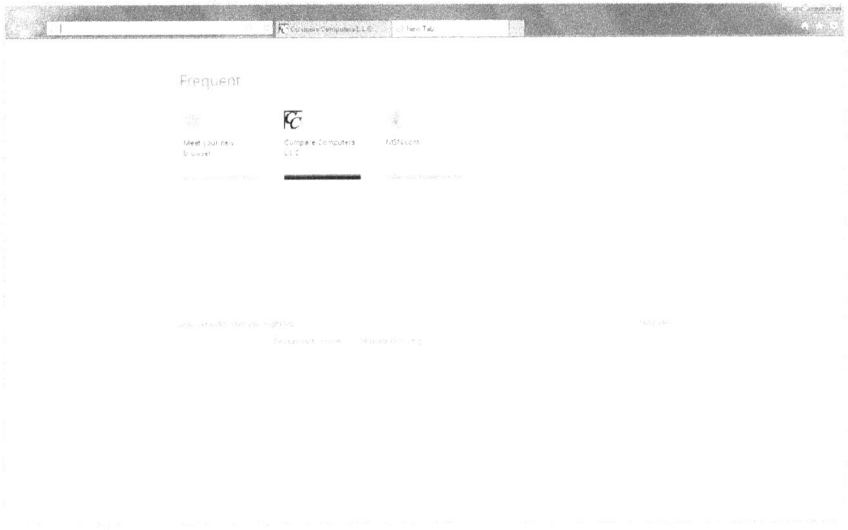

Figure 5.13: Frequent Websites

If the computer is not connected to the internet, or if there is another network related issue, you may see the screen in the example below with the message "You're not connected to a network". If you see this screen, check your network connections, devices, and settings. You can also click the Fix Connection Problems button to attempt to troubleshoot the issue.

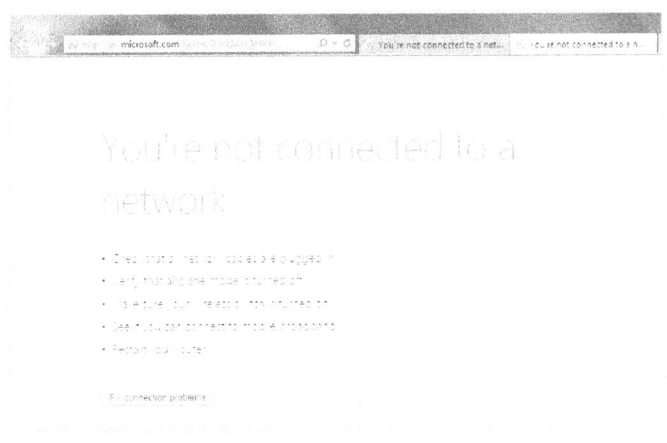

Figure 5.14: Connection Message

Downloading Files In Internet Explorer 10

One of the most common internet tasks is downloading a file – be it a picture, document, or installation file. Before clicking on a download link be sure the site and the content of the link are known and from a trusted source. Viruses and malware often are unknowingly downloaded by clicking on a link expecting one thing, and instead being tricked into downloading a malicious program.

 Use caution when downloading files for installing content from the web.

When you click on a download link, you will notice a small yellow bar at the bottom of the webpage prompting you to Run, Save, or Cancel. In many cases you will want to click the save button.

Do you want to run or save **Firefox Setup 19.0.2.exe** (19.6 MB) from **download.cdn.mozilla.net**?   Run   Save ▼   Cancel

Figure 5.15: Download File Dialog Box

You can click the View Downloads button to view the progress of the download. By default, downloads will be saved to the Downloads folder inside of your user profile directory (ex. C:\Users\Owner\Downloads). The download will progress until complete, and will then offer the choices to Run or Open, Open Folder, or View Downloads. Current download progress can be seen by using the Download Manager via the View Downloads button.

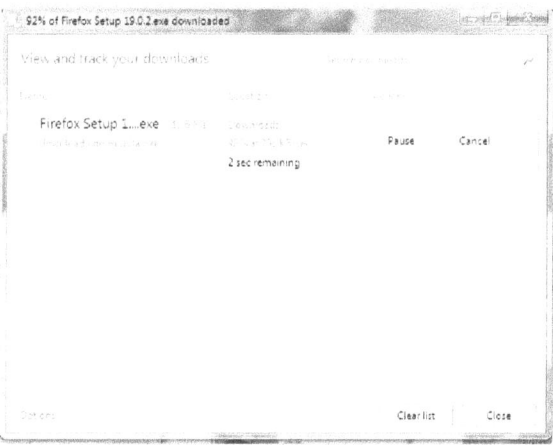

66% of Firefox Setup 19.0.2.exe downloaded   9 sec remaining   Pause   Cancel   View downloads

Figure 5.16: Download Complete Dialog Box

If you wish to run or open the file you can do so at this time, or you can navigate to your download folder and open the file at a later time. You may want to scan any downloaded files prior to opening them if your antivirus program does not automatically scan files downloaded from the internet.

Printing In Internet Explorer 10

To print a webpage in Internet Explorer 10, click on the Options button in the upper left corner of the window. Expand the Print option and select either "Print..." or "Print Preview..."

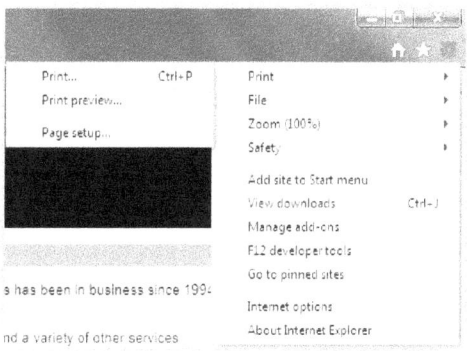

Figure 5.17: Print Menu

The Print Preview option will allow you to see a preview of how the page will be printed.

41

You can adjust settings on this screen to modify the way the document will print.

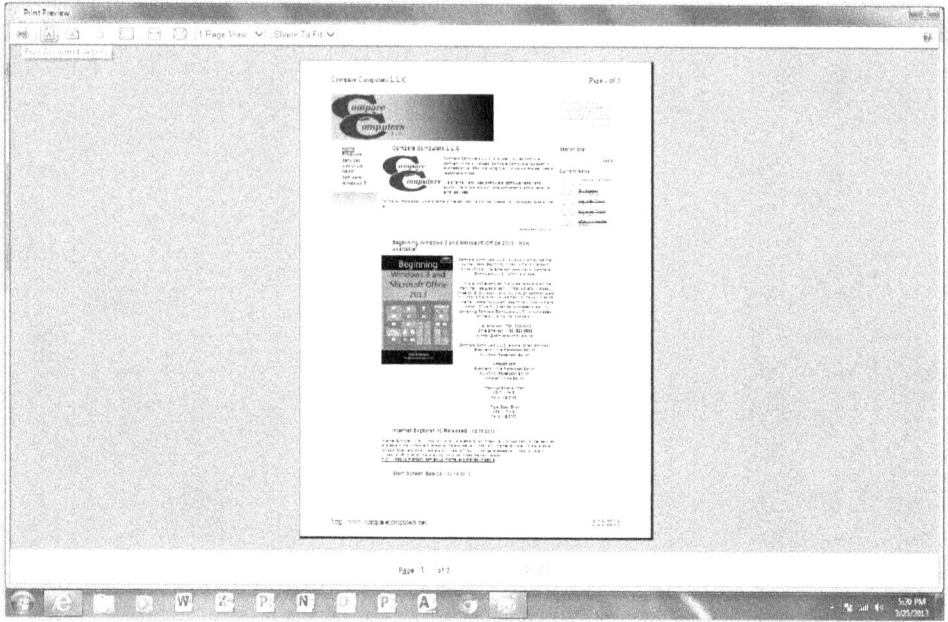

Figure 5.18: Print Preview

When you click the Print button you will see the options for choosing your desired printer, along with the options for the number of copies and pages to print.

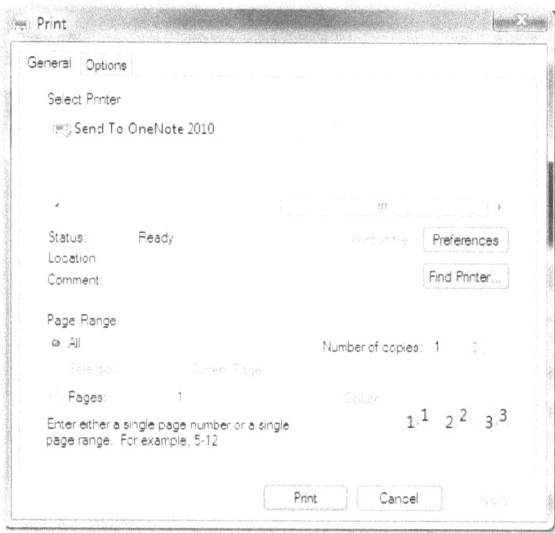

Figure 5.19: Printer Selection Window

In the next two sections we will look at Mozilla Firefox and Google Chrome-two other widely used web browsers in Windows 7.

Mozilla Firefox

Mozilla Firefox® is another widely used web browser designed for web standards compliance. It supports an active developer community that creates a variety of add-ons that increase the functionality of the browser.

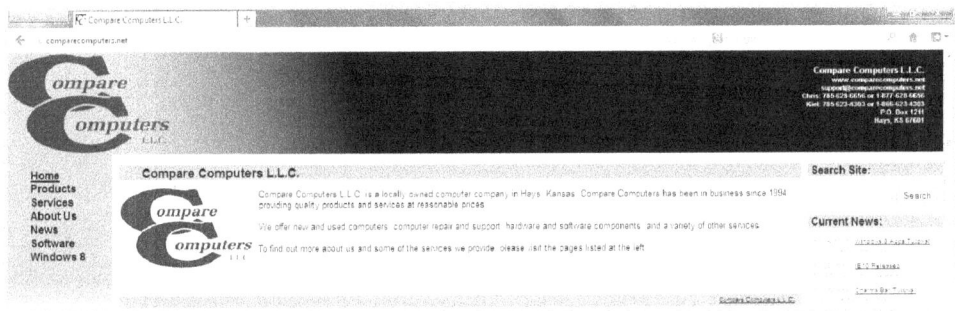

Figure 5.20: Mozilla Firefox Start Page

The Firefox button in the upper-left corner provides access to settings for displaying the web page, printing, using add-ons, and accessing bookmarks.

Figure 5.21: Firefox Menu Button

To the side of the Firefox button are tabs for the open browsing sessions. You can choose to use just a single tab, or use multiple ones by clicking the "+" tab to open a new tab.

Figure 5.22: New Tab Button and Grid

Below those sections, you will find the back navigation button, Address Bar, and search box. Just like Internet Explorer, you can enter a web site address or a search term into the Address Bar. The search box will utilize the listed search engine for results typed into the search box. To the right of the search box you will see the home button and the bookmarks button. Clicking on the bookmarks button will expand out your bookmarks. At the top of the bookmarks menu you can find the Add to Bookmarks link. You can also click the star icon in the Address Bar to add the current page to your bookmarks.

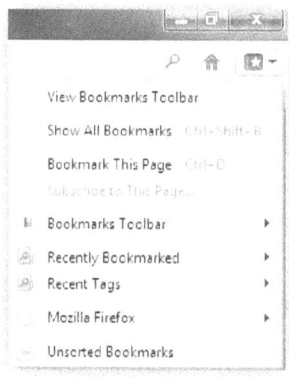

Figure 5.23: Bookmarks Menu

Figure 5.24: Bookmark Page Icon

Next we will look at how to use the Google Chrome web browser and examine some of its features.

Google Chrome

Google Chrome is another popular web browser. It features fast performance and JavaScript rendering, and excellent security. Tabs are located at the top of the window, with the navigation buttons, Address Bar/Search Bar, and settings button below the tabs.

Figure 5.25: Google Chrome

Google and the Google logo are registered trademarks of Google Inc., used with permission.

The settings button on the far right of the Address Bar can be used to print, change settings, and access bookmarks.

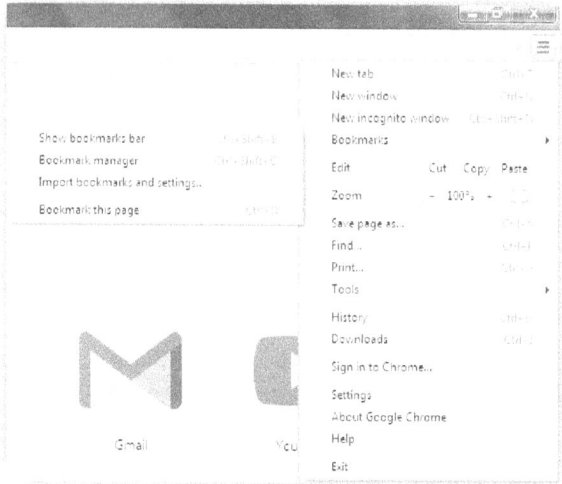

Figure 5.26: Settings Button

Google and the Google logo are registered trademarks of Google Inc., used with permission.

When you download a file or program in Chrome, a download progress tile will appear in the bottom left corner of your screen. When the download completes, you can click to open the item, or click on the arrow to expand out available options.

Figure 5.27: Chrome Downloads

Google and the Google logo are registered trademarks of Google Inc., used with permission.

In Chapter 6 I will explain how to access and change a number of settings in the control panel and how to connect your PC to a network.

Chapter Review Questions:

1. Describe how to access favorites/bookmarks in Internet Explorer 10, Firefox, and Google Chrome. How do you add a website to your favorites/bookmarks list?
2. Describe how to manage add-ons and extensions for each of the three browsers discussed in this book.
3. Describe the process for saving an executable file from a website to your PC.

Chapter 6 - Networking, Security, and Control Panel Settings

When you open the Control Panel link on the Start Menu, you will see a window similar to the one in Figure 6.1. The Control Panel is the primary hub for adjusting numerous system-wide settings.

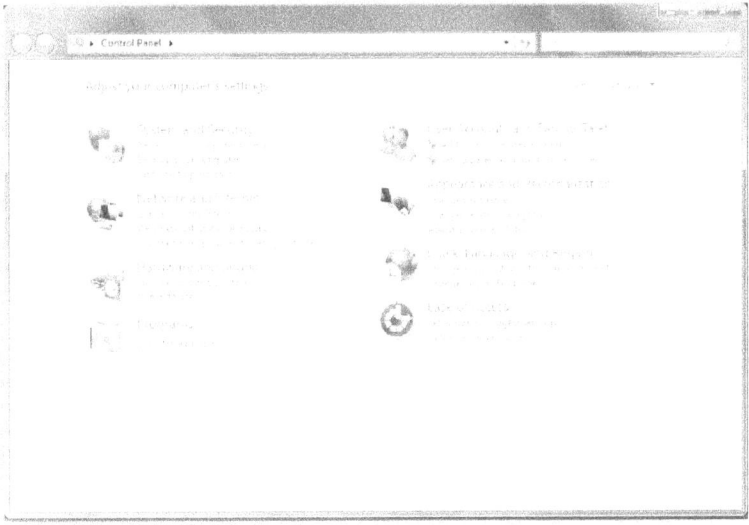

Figure 6.1: Control Panel

The System and Security category provides access to security-related tasks like Windows Update and the Windows Firewall. Other system tasks can be accessed through this category as well. Here you will find system power settings and backup options.

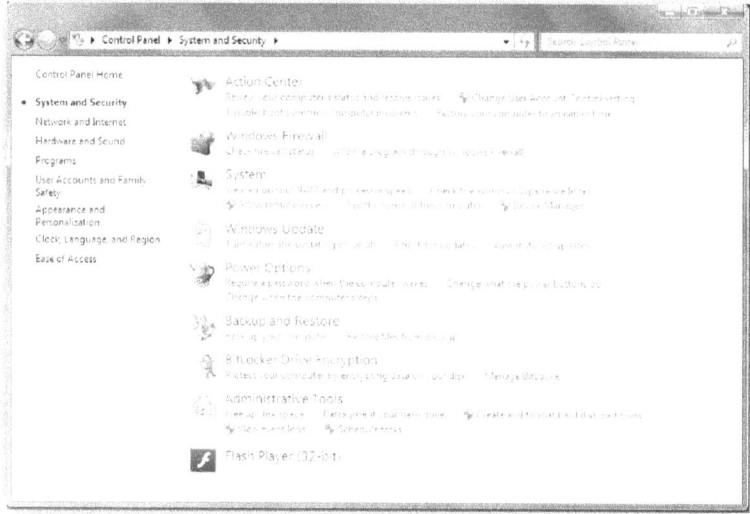

Figure 6.2: System and Security

The Network and Internet category is used to access the Network and Sharing Center and HomeGroup settings. Internet Explorer Options can also be accessed through this Control Panel category.

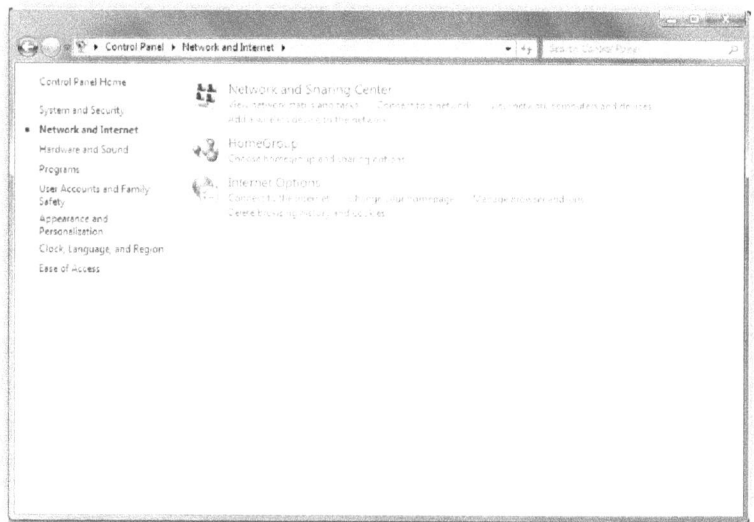

Figure 6.3: Network and Internet

The Hardware and Sound category contains links to the Devices and Printers configuration as well as Sound, Display, and Power Options.

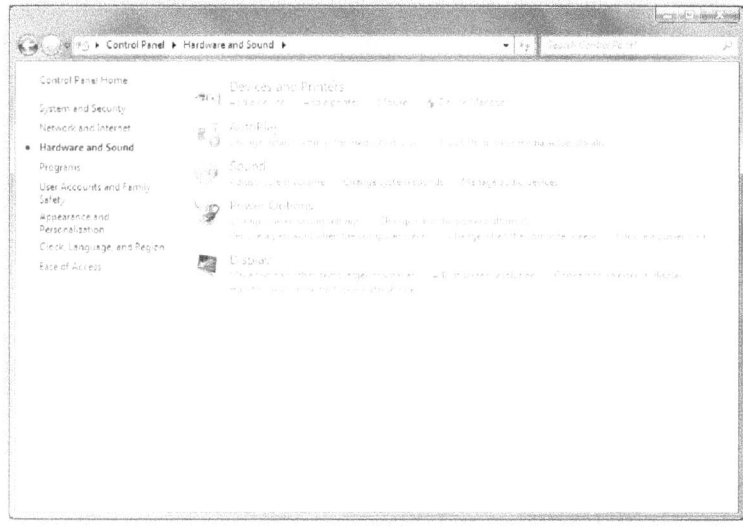

Figure 6.4: Hardware and Sound

The Programs control panel category allows you to uninstall programs and manage the default programs on the PC. You can also add and manage Desktop Gadgets.

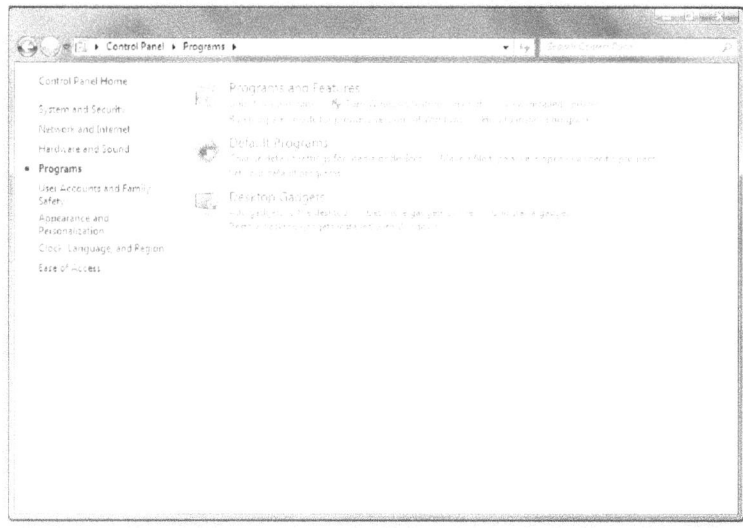

Figure 6.5: Programs

The User Accounts and Family Safety category can be used to manage user accounts on the PC and configure parental controls. Information Cards and Windows credentials can also be managed through this category.

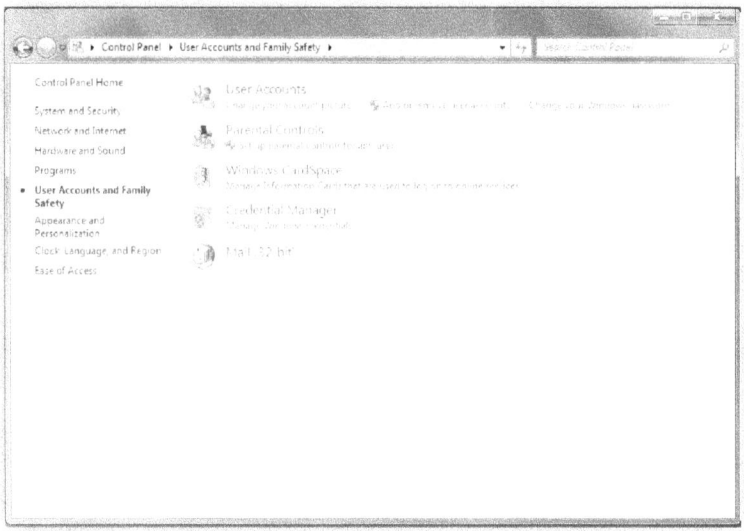

Figure 6.6: User Accounts and Family Safety

The Appearance and Personalization category can adjust personalization and display options. Start Menu and Taskbar settings, folder options, and fonts can be adjusted through this category as well. The Ease of Access Center is used to manage accessibility options for those with disabilities.

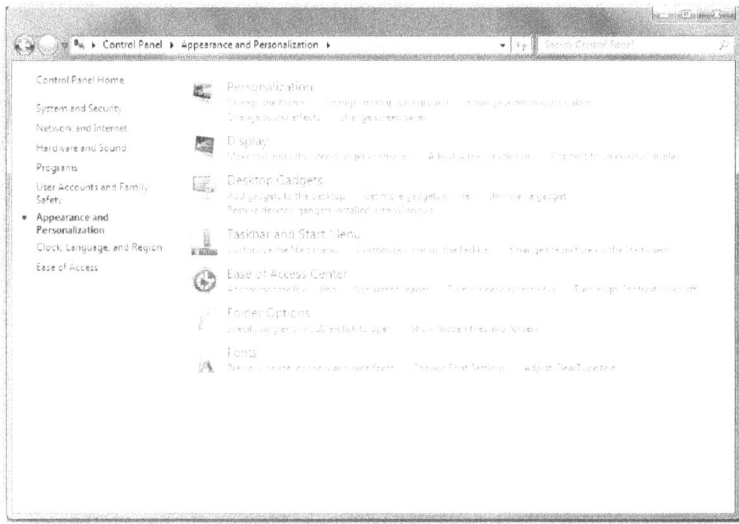

Figure 6.7: Appearance and Personalization

The Clock, Language, and Region category is used to adjust date, time, and language settings.

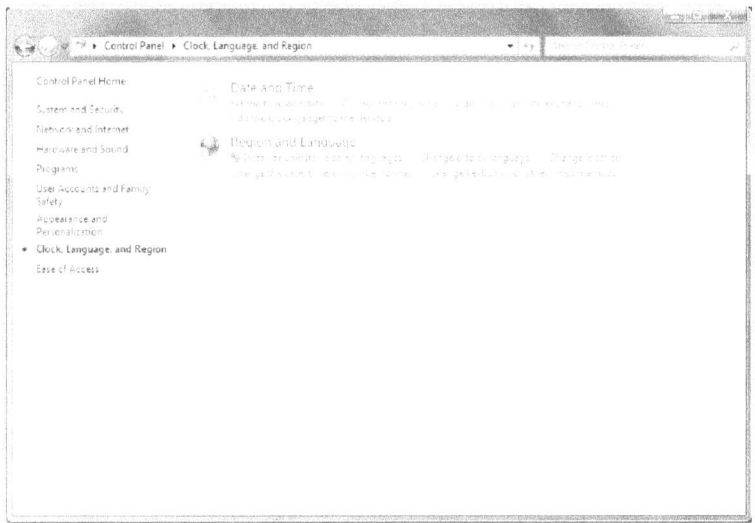

Figure 6.8: Clock, Language, and Region

The Ease of Access category can be used to adjust options for those with disabilities. From here you can increase readability for the vision impaired, adjust settings for the hearing impaired, and set up speech recognition.

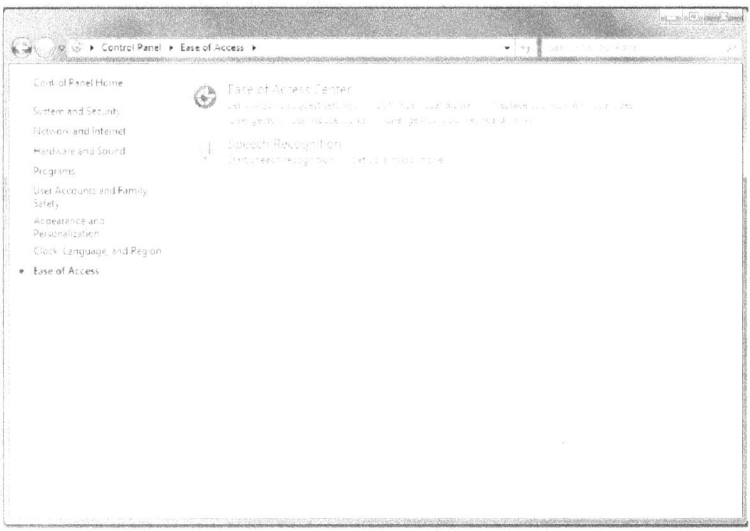

Figure 6.9: Ease of Access

System Information is available through the System and Security category. With the System window open you can view information about the PC and manufacturer. You can also access the Device Manager to update and manage hardware on the PC.

51

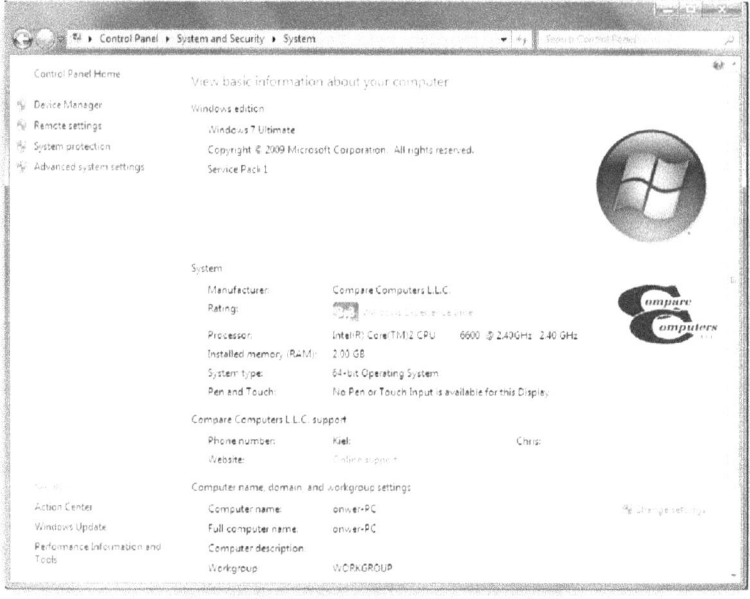

Figure 6.10: System Information

Hardware categories in the Device Manager can be expanded to expose specific hardware components on the computer. Right-clicking on an item opens a context menu, which allows you to update drivers, remove/disable the device, and view properties for the component. You can also scan for hardware changes to install drivers for unknown devices.

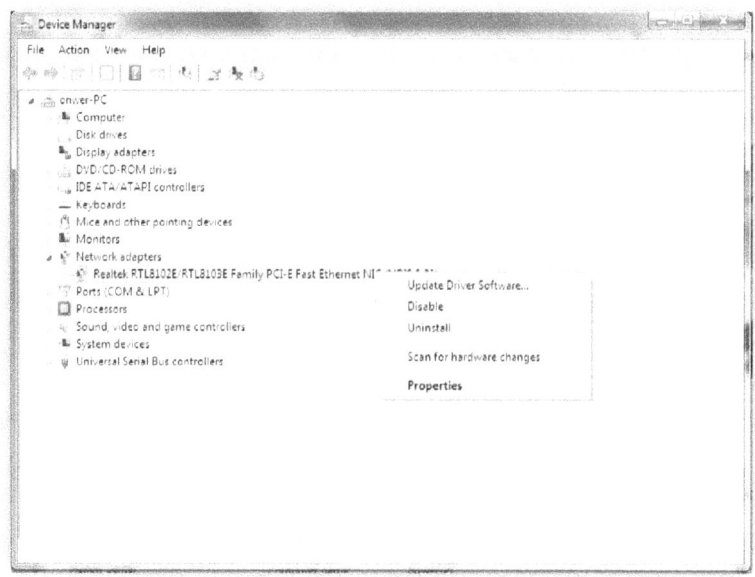

Figure 6.11: Device Manager

The Power Options settings under the System and Security category can manage the various power saving options for the PC. You can select a preconfigured plan, or manually adjust settings by clicking on the Change Plan Settings link.

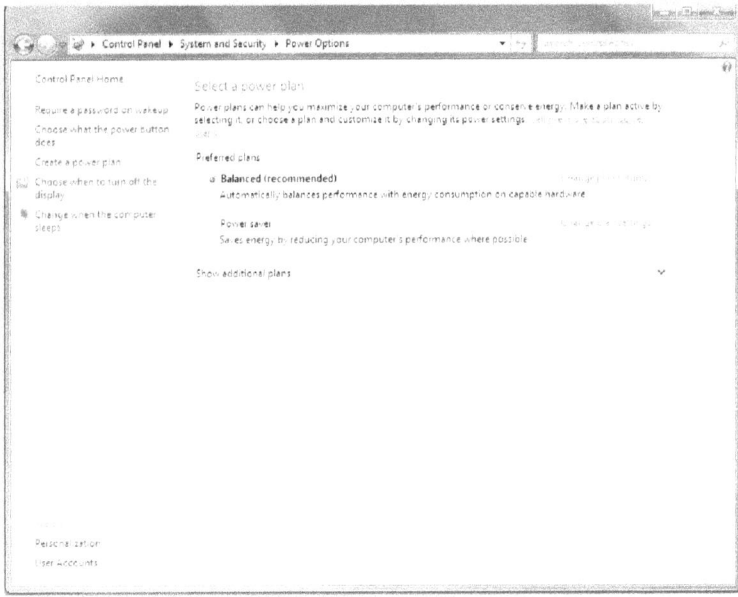

Figure 6.12: Power Options

From the Edit Plan Settings window you can select power options from the drop-down list or click the Change Advanced Power Settings link to manage many other available options.

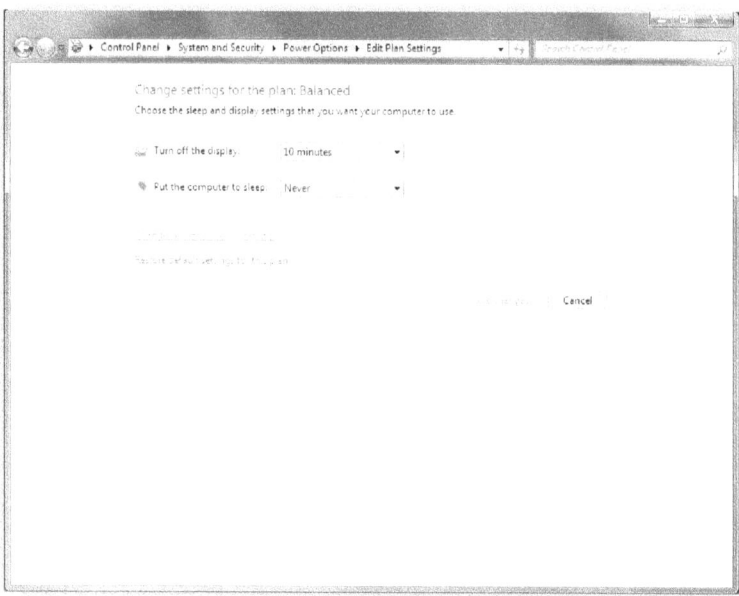

Figure 6.13: Edit Plan Settings

The Advanced Power Options Settings window provides options for sleep and hibernation, as well as settings for powering off the monitor and hard disk drive. Entering in a value of "0" will set the option to the value of "never".

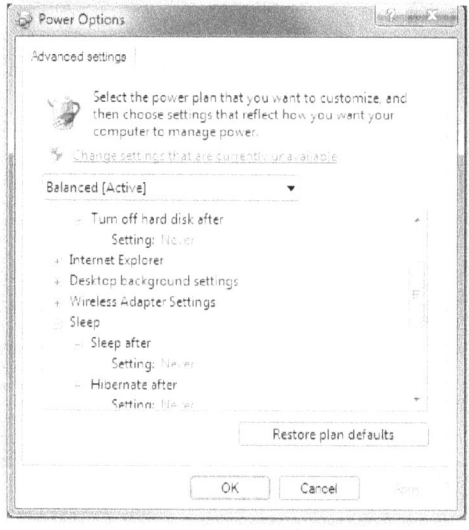

Figure 6.14: Advanced Power Options

Now that we have examined the Control Panel categories, we will review managing and connecting to networks.

Connecting to a Wired Network

To connect to a wired local area network, simply connect the Ethernet cable to your PC's network interface card. Depending on your network configuration you may need to set up a manual IP address, or enter in a PPPOE username & password. For most home networks though, the router and PC will automatically configure your system to connect to the network and internet.

Connecting to a Wireless Network

To connect to a wireless network, be sure you have both a wireless card installed in your PC, and a wireless router or access point to connect to.

Figure 6.15: Wireless Connection Setup Process

In the right corner of the Windows taskbar you will see an icon with signal bars and a star. When you hover over this icon it will show that wireless network connections are available. A list of available networks will appear when you click this icon.

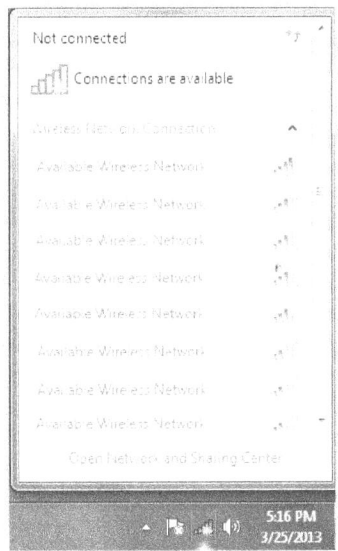

Figure 6.16: Available Wireless Networks

Select the network in the list that you wish to join and click the Connect button. An orange shield will appear above the signal bars if the network is unsecured.

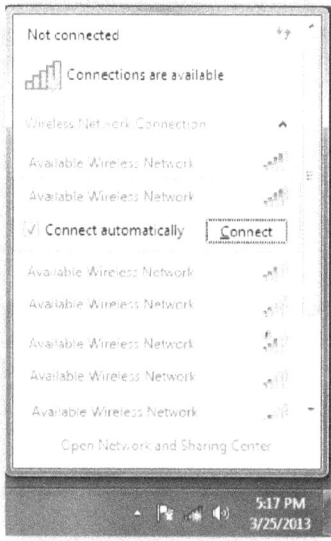

Figure 6.17: Connect to Wireless Network

You may see a warning about an unsecured connection if the access point is unsecured. If your access point requires a security key or passphrase to connect, type it in the window requesting the key. If you don't know what the key or passphrase is, check your router's documentation or check with your internet service provider or computer technician for assistance.

Figure 6.18: Enter Network Security Key

⚠️ Be sure your wireless router is configured to use WPA2 or higher security. Use caution when connecting to public hotspots.

If the key was entered correctly and the network configuration is correct, you will see the wireless signal bars turn white. If internet access is available, the text "Internet Access" will be listed in a small box while hovering over the network icon in the taskbar.

Figure 6.19: Internet Access

To troubleshoot network problems or access the Network and Sharing Center, right click on the network icon in the taskbar.

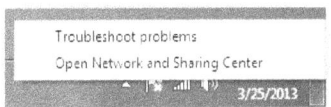

Figure 6.20: Network Context Menu

When connecting to a public access point, keep in mind that information sent over the connection may be accessible to others without your knowledge. For your privacy and security I recommend that you limit sensitive tasks when connected to public access points. I also recommend that you use an up-to-date antivirus program and firewall.

Network and Sharing Center

The Network and Sharing Center is a central location for performing network related tasks on the PC. From this Control Panel component you can manage network and internet connections, configure network sharing options, and troubleshoot issues with the network.

To open the Network and Sharing Center, right-click on the network icon in the taskbar or select the Network and Sharing Center link from the Control Panel.

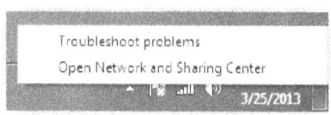

Figure 6.21: Network Context Menu

In the Network and Sharing Center main window you can view the status of your network and internet connection in the center pane. You can also set up new network connections and troubleshoot problems by clicking the links in the center pane. In the left pane you can change settings for network adapters on the PC, manage saved wireless networks, and configure sharing options. You can also open the Internet Options window, configure the Windows Firewall, and manage HomeGroup settings through links in the lower left pane.

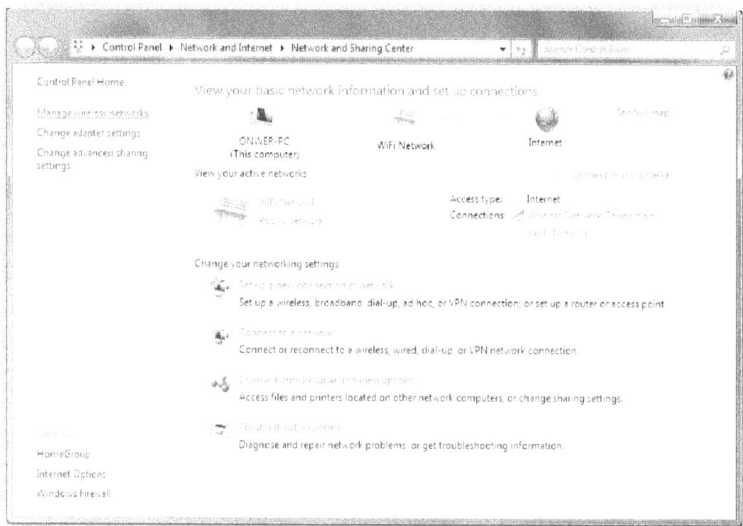

Figure 6.22: Network and Sharing Center

To view saved wireless networks that you have connected to, click the Manage Wireless Networks link in the left pane. To remove a saved network from the list you can highlight the network name and click the Remove button.

Figure 6.23: Manage Wireless Networks

We will now look at managing a HomeGroup and configuring network sharing options.

HomeGroup

HomeGroup is a feature introduced in Windows 7 that allows for easy networking of home computers and devices. You can easily configure sharing access to printers, documents, and media, so that other computers can access those resources.

To set up a HomeGroup, open the desktop control panel and navigate to the Network and Sharing Center. In the lower-left corner of the window, you will find a link for HomeGroup.

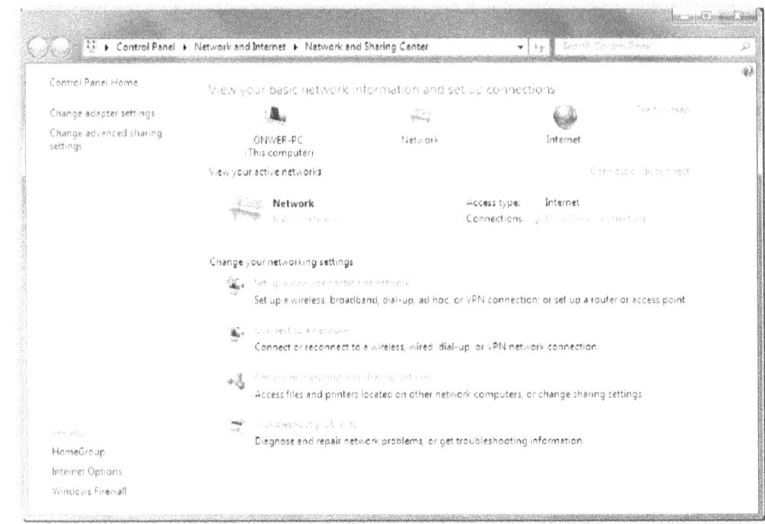

Figure 6.24: Network and Sharing Center

Click on the HomeGroup link, and the window will open (Figure 6.25). Click the Create a HomeGroup button to begin.

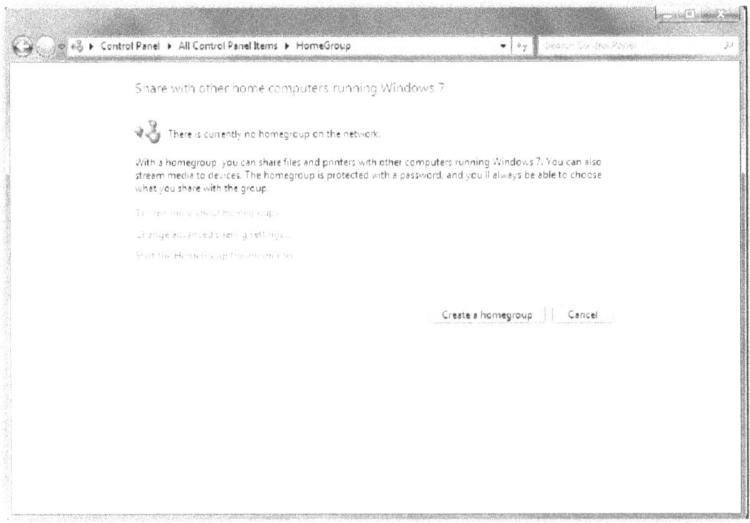

Figure 6.25: HomeGroup Control Panel Options

You will be presented with a short wizard that will walk you through the HomeGroup setup process. The wizard lets you choose what libraries and devices you will be sharing with other computers over the network. Click the checkbox to change sharing options for each item.

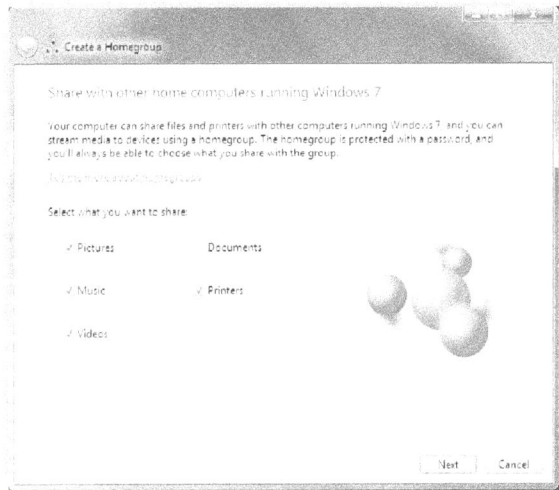

Figure 6.26: Choose Sharing Options

⚠ Use caution when enabling sharing options. Others with access to the computer or HomeGroup may be able to access or delete files that are shared.

The final screen of the wizard will provide you with a case-sensitive password that will be needed for any computer to connect to the HomeGroup. Be sure to write this password down and store it in a safe place.

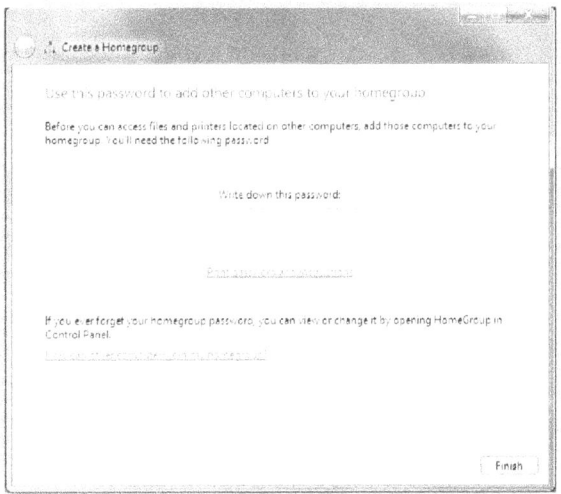

Figure 6.27: Record HomeGroup Password

Sharing options for the HomeGroup can be modified at any time by opening the HomeGroup link in the Network and Sharing Center.

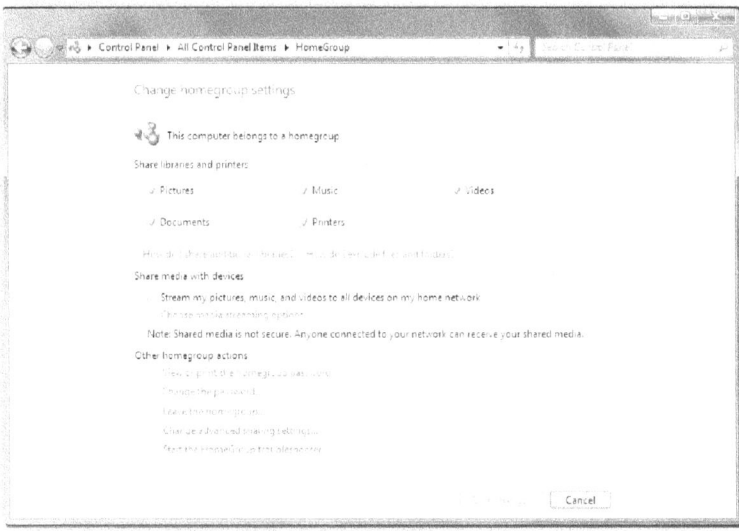

Figure 6.28: HomeGroup Sharing Options

You will now be able to see content on other computers connected to your HomeGroup. Click on the HomeGroup folder on the left panel in Windows Explorer to access the shared HomeGroup resources. Shared printers will show as available devices when you choose to print.

In the next section we will look at setting up and managing user accounts on the PC.

User Accounts and Family Safety

In the Control Panel, the User Accounts and Family Safety section allows you to add, manage, and remove user accounts from the PC. You can also set up family safety controls to set time limits for use, allowed times for using the PC, and for setting up content restrictions for family members.

Managing User Accounts

We will need to open the control panel to begin managing user accounts on the PC. Select the Control Panel link on the Start Menu, then choose User Accounts and Family Safety.

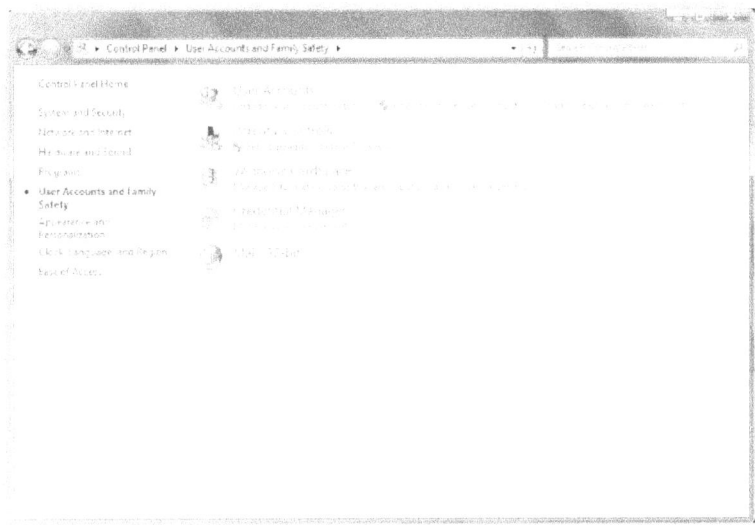

Figure 6.29: User Accounts and Family Safety

To make changes to your user account or to modify other accounts, click the User Accounts link. In the displayed window you can change the name and password for the current account and also set the user as either a standard user or a system administrator.

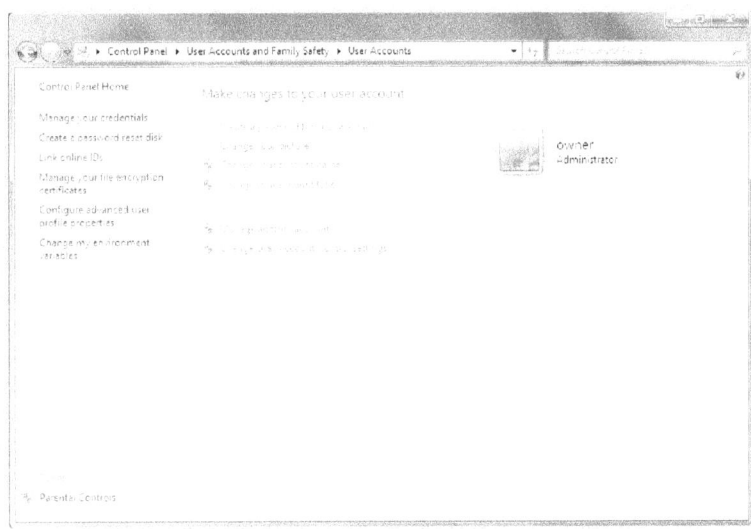

Figure 6.30: User Account Settings

To create a password for the current account, click the Create a Password for Your Account link. To modify another account on the PC you can select the Manage Another Account link. You can then choose the account that you wish to change.

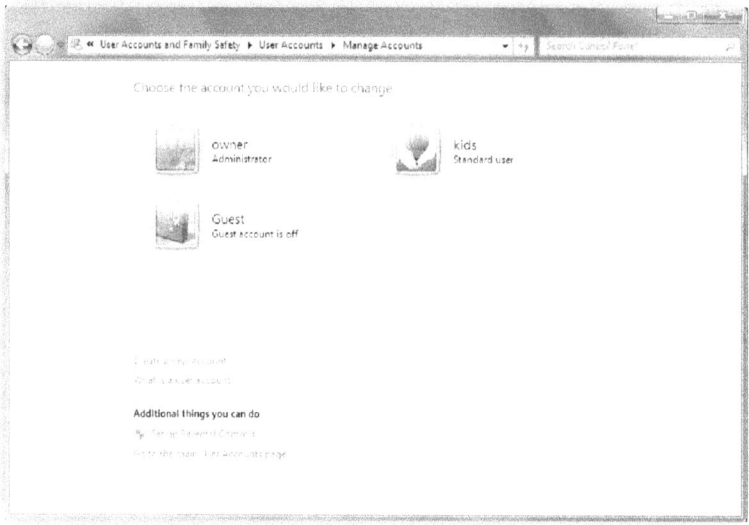

Figure 6.31: Choose User Account to Change

From here you can modify a number of settings for the selected user. Click the Create a Password link and fill in the required information to create a password for the user.

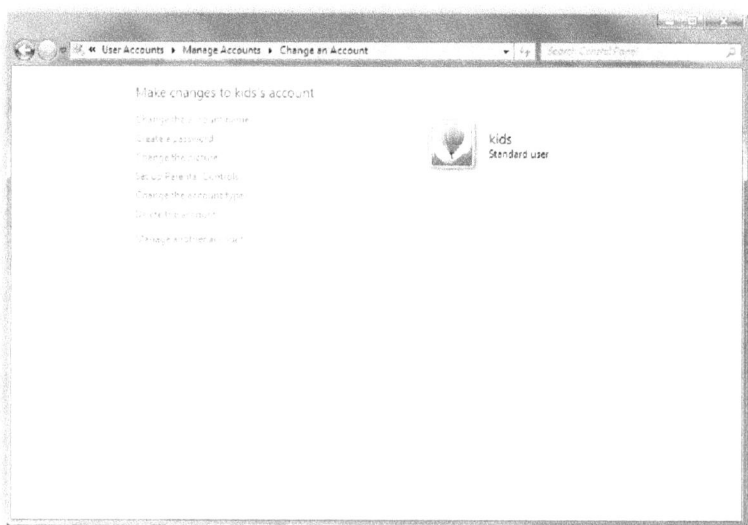

Figure 6.32: Change the Selected Account

Next we will look at setting up Family Safety settings for user accounts on the PC. These settings will restrict the type of content the specified user will be allowed to access and can be used to restrict the times of use.

Family Safety Management

Family safety settings can be configured by clicking the Family Safety link in the User Accounts and Family Safety Control Panel section.

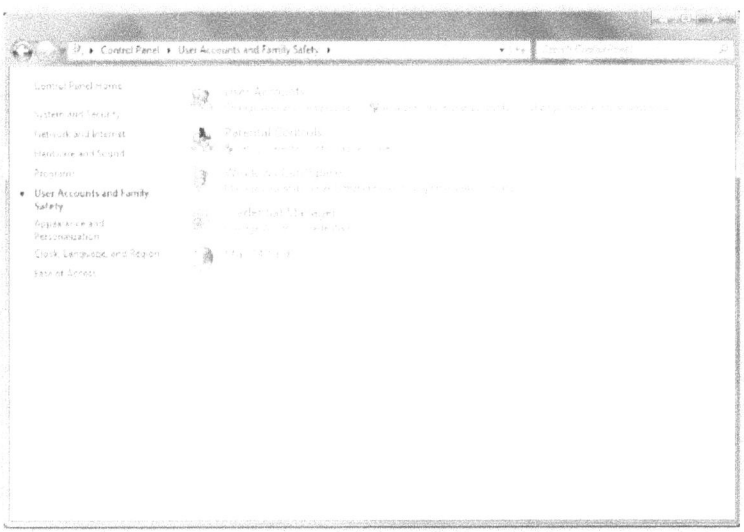

Figure 6.33: Family Safety Link

To set up Family Safety, you will need a password-enabled Administrator account and a Standard User account. Select the user account you wish to restrict and choose the desired account settings.

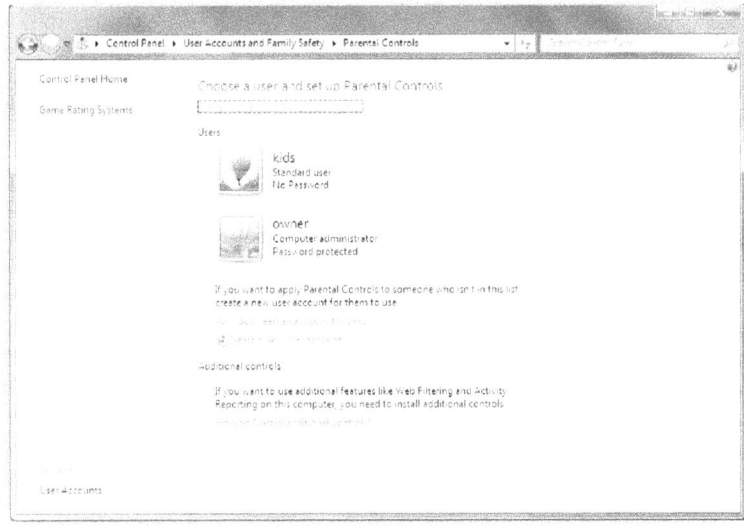

Figure 6.34: Family Safety Options

65

In the User Settings window, you can turn on or off the Family Safety feature for that user account. From this screen you can also enable or disable activity reports for the administrator to view. The links for Time Limits, Games, and Allow or Block Specific Programs will allow you to manage restrictions for the selected user account.

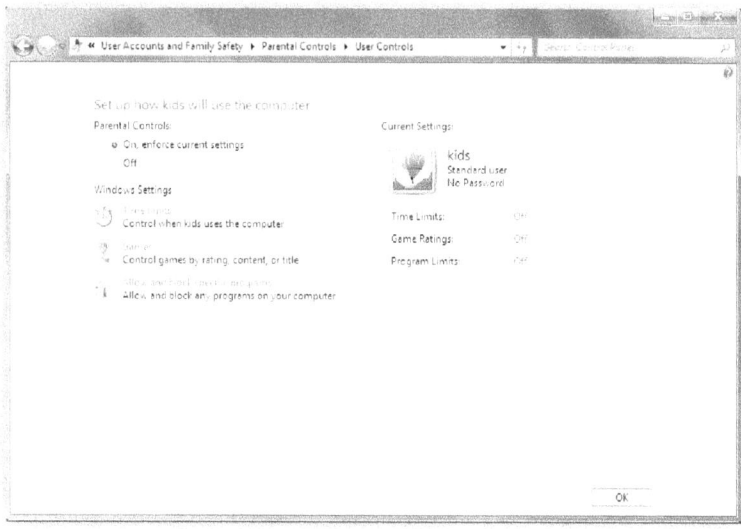

Figure 6.35: Family Safety User Settings

Under the Time Restrictions option you can control allowed weekdays and times that the PC can be used. Simply click and drag to highlight allowed times during each weekday.

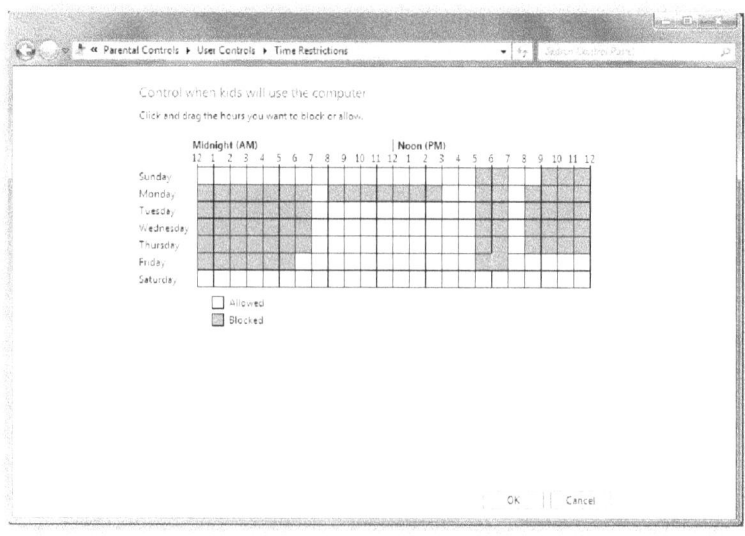

Figure 6.36: Set Curfew

Clicking the Games link in the Family Safety User Settings window lets you choose the game ratings and games that will be playable on the PC. From this window you can set a maximum allowable game rating and also allow or block specific games.

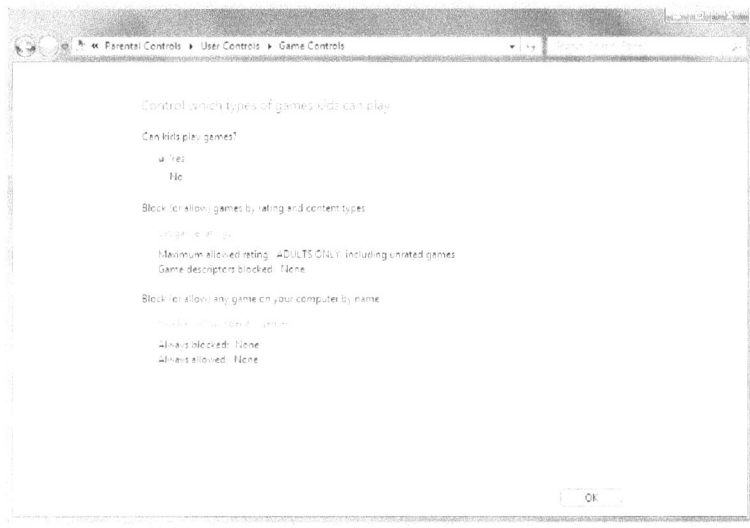

Figure 6.37: Game Safety Settings

When you click on the Set Game Ratings link you will see a screen with blocking options for the game rating as well as for specific types of content. Select the desired maximum game rating and any content that you would like to block.

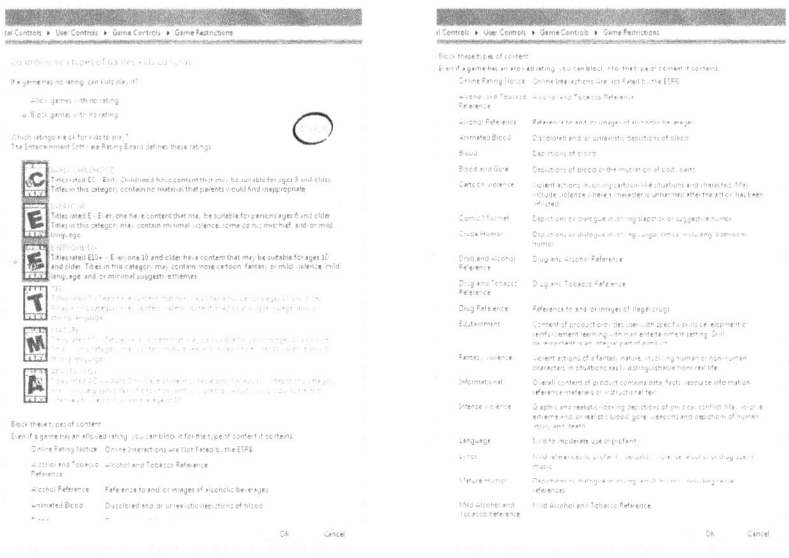

Figure 6.38: Allowed Game Ratings

Clicking the Allow or Block Specific Games link in the main Game Controls window will allow you to manage restrictions for specific games on the PC.

Figure 6.39: Game Restrictions

The Application Restrictions link in the Family Safety User Settings window is used to manually allow or block specific programs on the PC. You can limit access to only a specific program such as Microsoft Word, or allow any other listed program to be run.

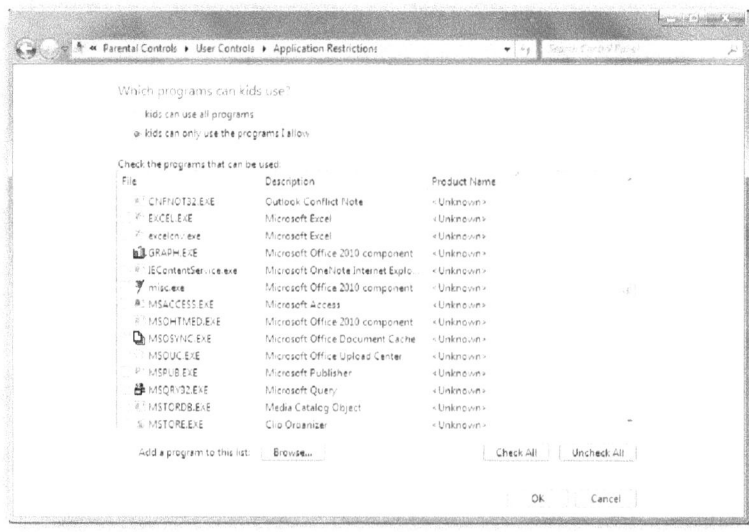

Figure 6.40: App Restrictions

Next we will look at the User Account Control feature and how it can help protect the system from unwanted changes.

User Account Control

The User Account Control (UAC) feature helps to protect the PC by requiring administrator approval before application installation and setting changes are made that affect other users on the PC. The UAC will darken the screen and prompt you for an action before changes are made to the PC. I recommend leaving UAC at its default settings or higher, and not lowering the security level unless absolutely necessary.

When you see a User Account Control alert prompting you to allow or deny a program to make changes to the computer, be sure you know the program and the action it is performing before you allow the process to continue.

User Account Control options can be accessed through the System and Security Control Panel options. Under Action Center, click the Change User Account Control Settings link.

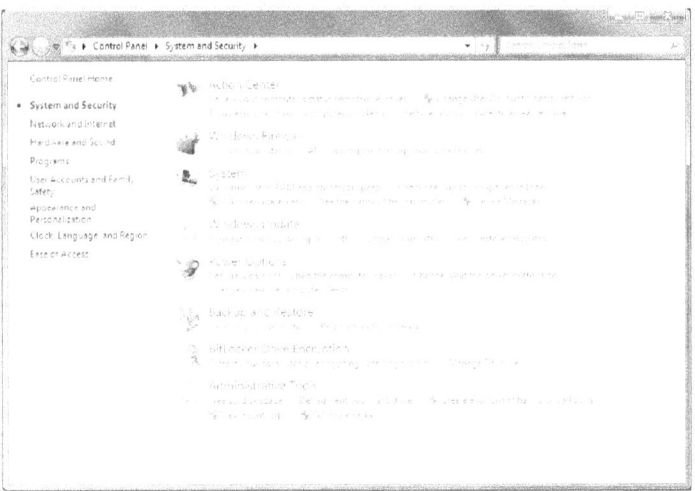

Figure 6.41: System and Security Control Panel Options

Adjust the slide bar to your desired settings, but be aware that lowering the UAC setting may put your PC at risk of malware and other security threats.

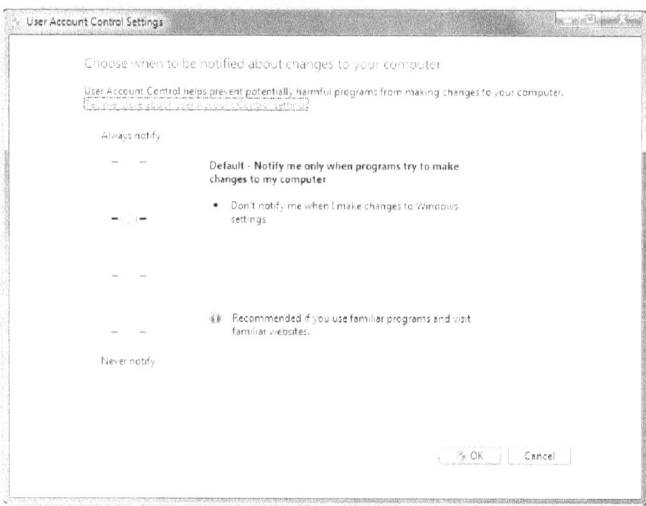

Figure 6.42: User Account Control Settings

Next we will look at the built-in antispyware protection in Windows 7.

Windows Defender

In Windows 7, Microsoft has included the Windows Defender antispyware program as a built-in component to the operating system. It runs silently in the background unless an issue needs to be addressed.

On the Home tab you can view the status of the program, and start a quick or full system scan.

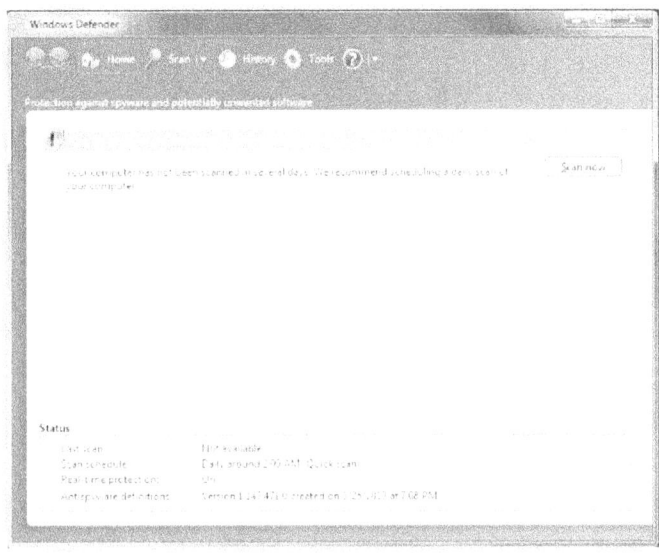

Figure 6.43: Windows Defender

To manage settings in Windows Defender, click the Tools button at the top of the window. Click the Options link on this window to manage Windows Defender settings.

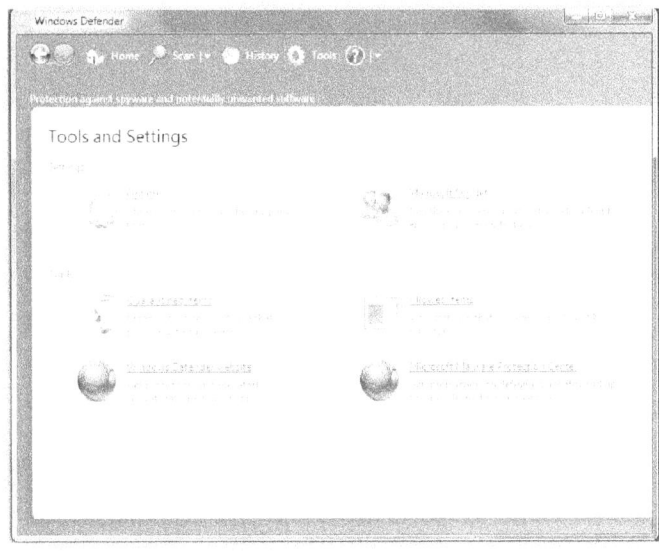

Figure 6.44: Windows Defender Tools

71

On the Options page you can configure scan settings, real-time protection, and what action to take when malware is detected.

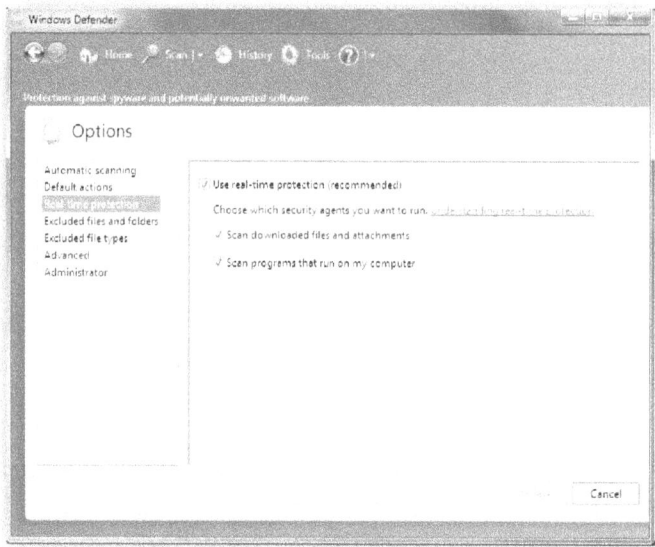

Figure 6.45: Windows Defender Options

I recommend running a full scan at least once a month, along with installing any Microsoft critical security updates and patches for other programs installed on the PC.

In addition to an active, up-to-date, real-time antispyware and antivirus program, another critical component is a firewall to protect against network attacks. In the next section we will explore the Windows Firewall.

Windows Firewall

The Windows Firewall in Windows 7 provides a two-way layer of protection for your computer by protecting against both inbound and outbound security threats. To view the firewall settings, open the System and Security Control Panel option and select the Windows Firewall link.

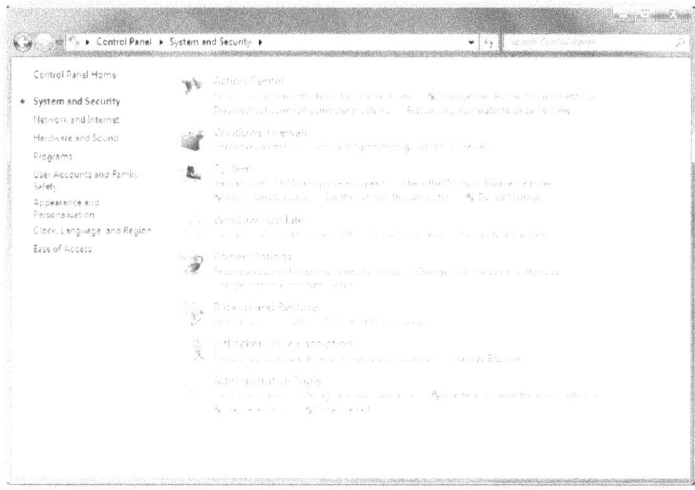

Figure 6.46: System and Security Control Panel Category

From the main Windows Firewall window you can configure numerous settings for the firewall. It can be enabled and disabled for certain network types. You can also customize access for specific programs and network ports.

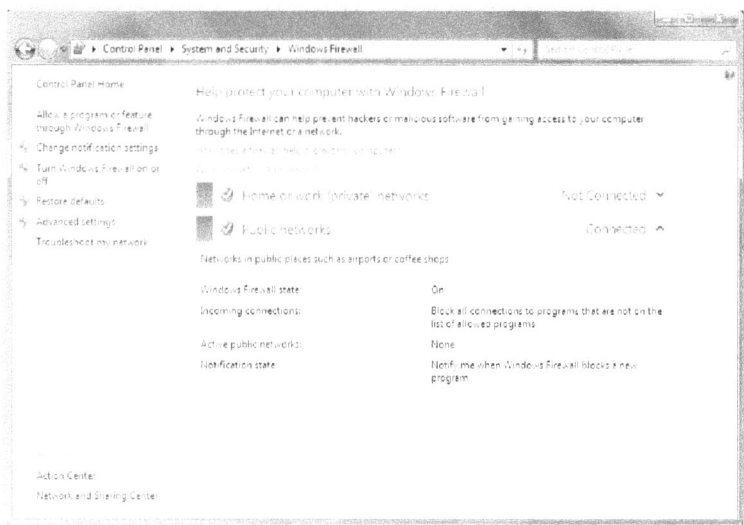

Figure 6.47: Windows Firewall Main Window

Selecting the Turn Windows Firewall On or Off option on the left pane will display the screen in Figure 6.48. From here you can turn the firewall on or off for private or for public networks. I recommend leaving both settings enabled unless you are experiencing a specific issue that requires the firewall to be disabled.

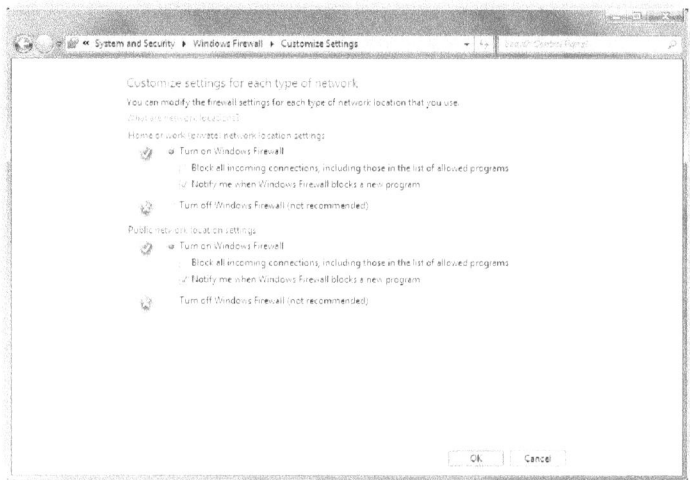

Figure 6.48: Turn On or Off the Firewall for Specific Network Type

⚠ Leave the Windows Firewall settings in their default configuration unless you experience a specific issue with the default settings.

Selecting the Allow a Program or Feature Through the Windows Firewall link on the main window will take you to the customization page (Figure 6.49). Here you can allow specific applications to pass through the firewall on public or private networks by checking the checkbox next to the application name.

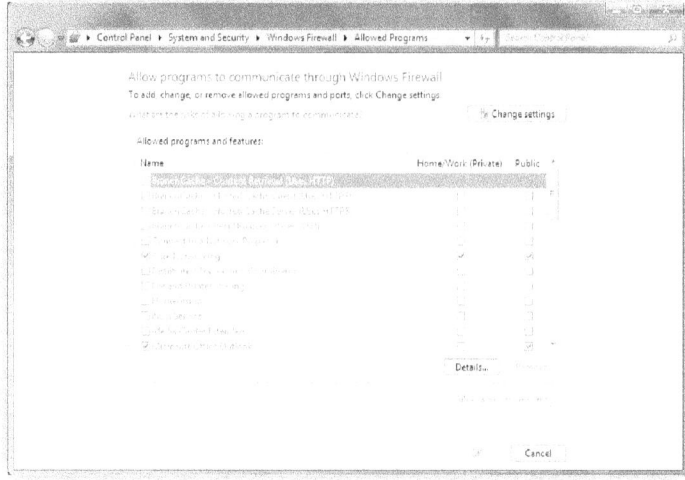

Figure 6.49: Program Allow List

Under the advanced settings for the Windows Firewall, you can create rules, allow specific port access, and many other in-depth settings. I recommend leaving this section unchanged unless you experience a specific issue that requires changing these advanced settings.

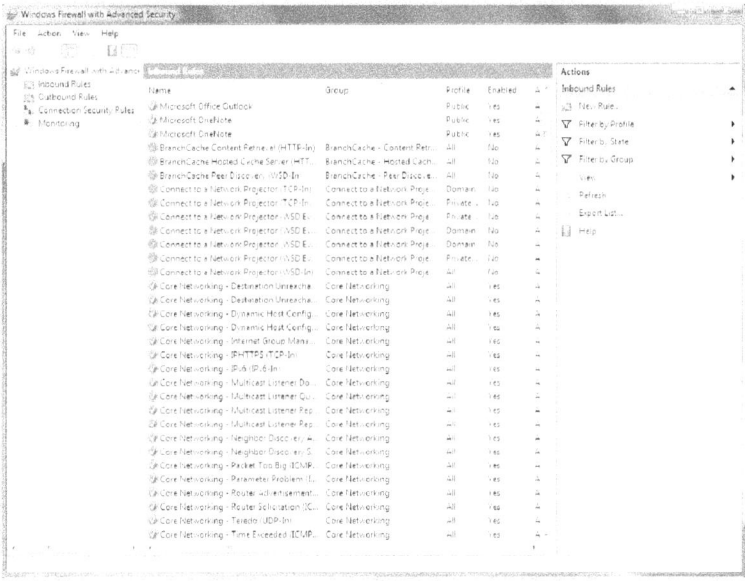

Figure 6.50: Advanced Firewall Settings

Not only is it important to use an antivirus software and firewall program, but it is also very important to keep Windows and other installed programs patched and up-to-date. Windows Update is the application that keeps Microsoft applications updated and patched for security.

Windows Update

Windows Update is used to install critical security updates and new features for Microsoft software on your PC. Your computer will check for updates and install most patches on its own with the default settings. Occasionally, some updates may require a restart of your PC to finish installing. Some updates, such as new programs not currently on your PC, may not install unless you manually select those items to install in the Windows Update program.

To open the Windows Update program, open the Control Panel and navigate to the System and Security category. Click Windows Update from the listed links to open the program.

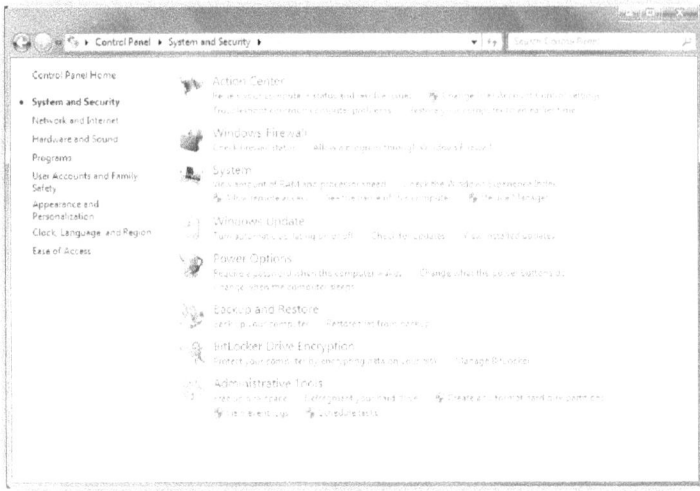

Figure 6.51: System and Security Control Panel Category

Press the Check for Updates link in the left pane to check for the newest updates. To manually select the updates you wish to install, you can choose the link for important updates or for optional components.

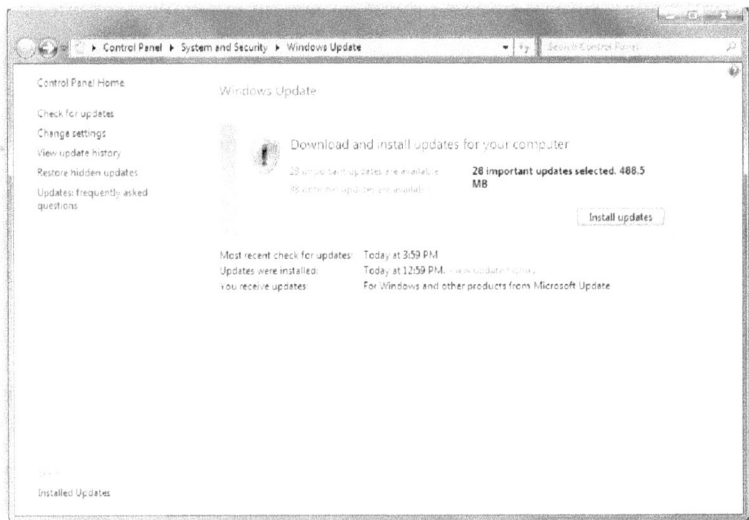

Figure 6.52: Windows Update Main Window

After clicking the link for important or optional updates, you can view both the important and optional updates by clicking on the category in the left pane. In the middle pane you will see a list of updates that are available for installation. Check items you wish to install from both sections. Click the OK button to begin when your selection is complete.

Depending on the size and number of updates selected and the speed of your internet connection, the updates may take some time to download and install. When finished, you may be prompted to restart your computer to complete the installation.

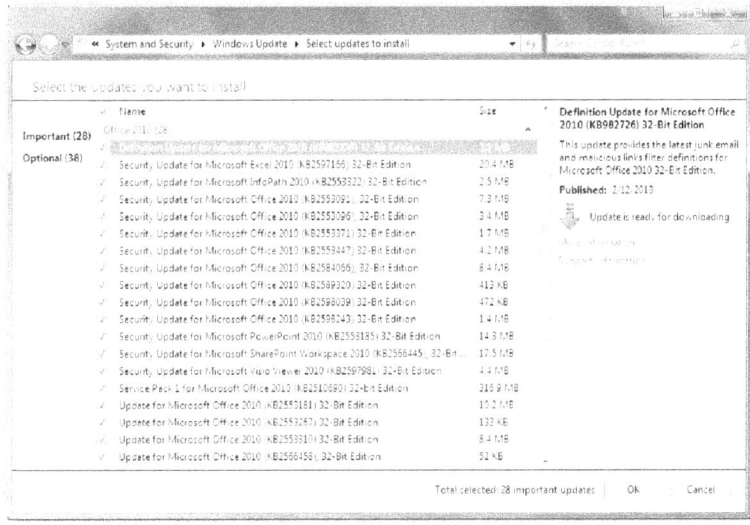

Figure 6.53: Select Updates to Install

To modify Windows Update settings you can click the Change Settings link in the left pane of the main Windows Update window. From here you can choose to automatically download or install updates and select the type of updates that will be installed.

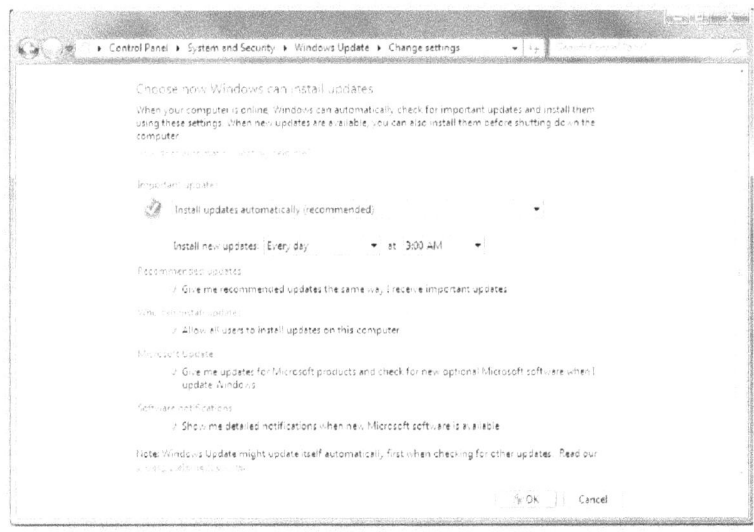

Figure 6.54: Windows Update Settings

> **Tip** Allowing Windows to automatically download and install updates will help to keep your PC patched and up-to-date against security vulnerabilities.

To see a list of updates that have previously been installed, click the View Update History link in the left pane of the Windows Update window. This history of updates will list the patch name, date, type of update, and whether the update was installed successfully. If you encounter issues after installing updates, you may want to check what updates were recently installed and evaluate uninstalling them if they caused the system to become unstable.

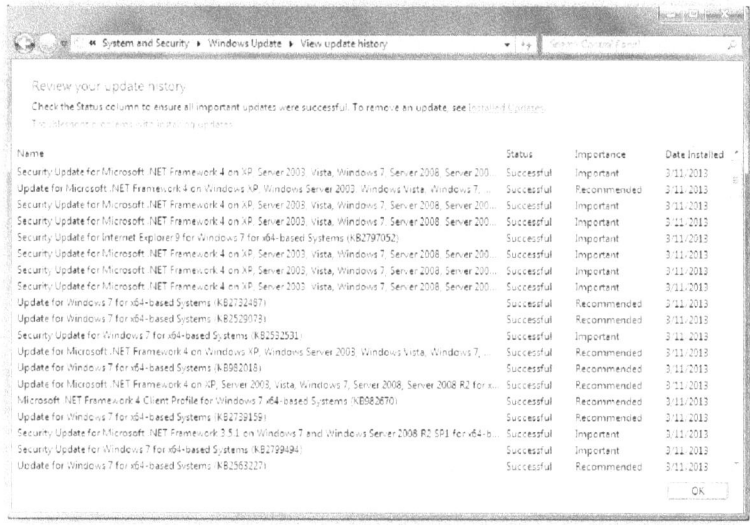

Figure 6.55: Windows Update History

Next we will take a look at viruses, malware, and how to protect your PC from many common threats.

Viruses, Malware, Phishing, and Securing your PC

What Are Viruses and Spyware?
Viruses and spyware are programs on your computer that may spread between computers, cause errors, collect information, self-replicate, change system settings, interfere with regular computer use, and/or delete or corrupt files on your computer.

How do Viruses and Spyware Infect My Computer?
There are many ways that virus and spyware threats can infect a computer. The list below provides several examples of ways these threats can infect your PC:

- E-mail Attachments or Embedded Code in E-mail Messages or Instant Messages.
- Visiting websites with malicious code present or malicious advertisement code.
- Downloading infected files from the web or P2P downloading programs.
- Installing free games or programs online that contain malicious code.
- Downloading or installing pirated software, music, or other files that are infected.
- Not installing Service Packs, updates, and patches for your operating system, and also for all 3rd party software currently installed on the PC.
- Not using a real-time, up to date Antivirus and Antispyware program on a regular basis.

Symptoms of a Potential Infection:
- The computer runs slower than normal or locks up frequently.
- The computer restarts on its own or crashes.
- The computer displays pop-ups, error messages, or alerts you are not familiar with.
- Your e-mail address may send out unwanted e-mails to people in your contact list.
- You receive excessive amounts of spam e-mail.
- Programs on the computer do not work normally.
- Your Antivirus is unable to download updates, run scans, or provide real-time protection.
- Security settings or firewall settings are changed on your computer.
- Shortcuts or links appear on your computer to questionable websites or programs.
- Programs, toolbars, or files you did not install may appear on the computer.
- There may not be symptoms of an infection, but threats may silently collect information.

How to protect yourself from infection:
- Install all Service Packs, Updates, and Patches for Microsoft software on the PC.
- Install all Service Packs, Updates, and Patches for all 3rd Party Software on the PC.
- Install the latest Antivirus definitions for your real-time Antivirus software and run regular full system scans.
- Install the latest Antispyware definitions for your real-time Antivirus software and run regular full system scans.
- Do not open questionable e-mails, attachments, or websites. Do not install, run, or download questionable files or programs from websites or P2P file sharing applications.
- Check the file extension before opening files or attachments, and check that the file does not contain a hidden double file extension.
- Read all security prompts carefully and do not run programs unless you are certain of their authenticity and safety.
- Scan removable storage devices to minimize the risk of re-infection.
- Use a Standard User account and password for Windows, instead of an Administrator account, to help minimize security risks and limit system wide changes.
- Use extreme caution when responding to e-mails requesting confidential information, even when the e-mails appear to be from a known sender. Phishing e-mails can be spoofed so they appear to come from a particular sender. Confirm the request for information by another means before responding directly in the e-mail. Be certain you trust websites prompting for personal or financial information, and be sure the page is secure.

• Use the Phishing Filter in Internet Explorer.

• Do not click on links in e-mails that direct you to another website, as the link's address can be spoofed. Type the address into a browser window and manually navigate to the site instead.

• Be cautious opening e-mails, even from known contacts. Just because an e-mail came from someone you know, it does not mean the e-mail, attachments, or links are safe. A Trojan may be bundled with a video or other file that someone wants to share, and they may not be aware of the hidden components of the file. Compromised e-mail accounts are commonplace, and often hijacked accounts send e-mails to all contacts using similar means to gain access to those accounts as well.

• Only install add-ons from websites that you trust. Web browser add-ons can install useful software for your PC, but also may install malicious software. Make sure you trust the site and add-on before installing any software if prompted.

Now we will look at how to install new hardware and device drivers on the PC.

Installing New Hardware and Devices

When you first connect a new piece of hardware to your computer, Windows will need to locate and install drivers to communicate with the new device. Windows may connect to Windows Update during this process to download device drivers for the hardware. You may be prompted to insert an installation disc that came with the hardware if no drivers are found. You may also be prompted to download the drivers from the manufacturer's website. Not all hardware will be compatible with Windows 7, but Microsoft has worked hard to include a large number of drivers with the OS and make future drivers available online.

Figure 6.56: Detecting New Hardware

While drivers are being downloaded and installed you may see a screen similar to the image in Figure 6.57 showing the progress of the installation. You can also click on the Installing Device Driver Software balloon to see the installation progress.

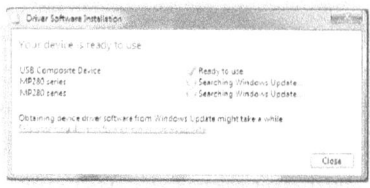 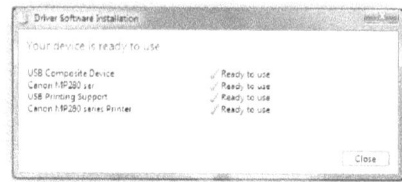

Figure 6.57: Printer Installation Progress

Click on the Devices and Printers link on the right side of the Start Menu to view installed hardware peripherals. Some of the items listed here are virtual hardware components, like the Microsoft XPS Document Writer and the Send To OneNote items in Figure 6.58, while others are physical hardware devices connected to the computer. You can select devices listed and view properties and settings for each device.

To set the printer shown in Figure 6.58 as the default printer for the PC, simply right-click on the printer and select the Set as Default Printer option.

Figure 6.58: Devices and Printers

Right-click the printer and select the Printer Properties option from the list to view properties for the printer. To print a test page, click the Print Test Page button from the Printer Properties window.

Figure 6.59: Printer Properties Window

Now that our hardware is installed, we may need to remove a piece of hardware with removable storage, like a USB flash drive or hard drive. In the next section we will look at how to safely remove the hardware from the PC.

Safely Removing Hardware

When you connect a removable storage device or other hardware, it is recommended that you use the Safely Remove Hardware feature prior to removing the component from the PC. This feature ensures the device is no longer in use and at risk of data loss, and disables the device for safe removal.

When you first connect a removable device, such as a USB flash drive, you will see a brief prompt that allows you to choose AutoPlay options for that type of device. With a USB flash drive, you can use Windows ReadyBoost to speed up the PC, set up the drive to be used as a backup drive, view files and folders, or you can take no action at all.

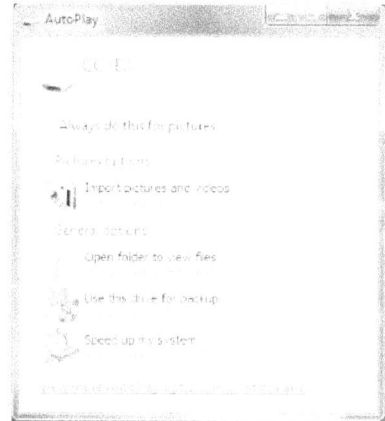

Figure 6.60: Flash Drive AutoPlay Options

When you are done working with your removable device you will need to use the Safely Remove Hardware feature. This link is sometimes hidden in the taskbar. You may need to click the small arrow icon to show hidden icons.

Figure 6.61: Show Hidden Icons Arrow and Safely Remove Hardware Icon

Single left-click on the Safely Remove Hardware USB plug icon, then left-click on the device listed in the menu that you wish to remove.

Figure 6.62: Safely Remove Hardware Menu

If Windows was able to verify the drive is no longer in use and also able to disable the drive, then you will see the message bubble that it is now safe to unplug the device. If you receive a message that the device cannot be stopped, check to make sure no programs or files are open that may be accessing the device.

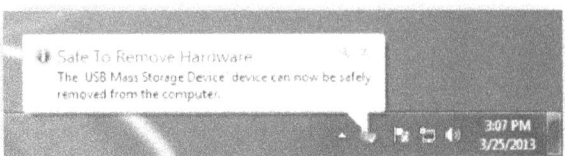

Figure 6.63: Safe To Remove Hardware Balloon

Now that we know how to safely remove hardware we will look at how to remove installed software applications from the computer.

Uninstall Desktop Applications

Typically when a desktop application has been installed on a PC it can be uninstalled through the control panel. To uninstall a desktop program, open the control panel and click on the Uninstall a Program link.

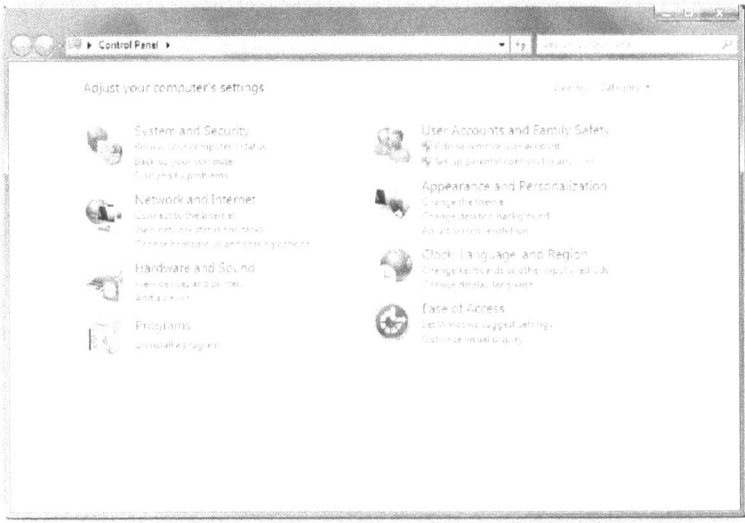

Figure 6.64: Control Panel Window

After the list of installed programs loads you can select the program you wish to remove and click the Uninstall button located at the top of the list. Follow the prompts while the program is removed. The program should be removed from the list when the uninstall is complete.

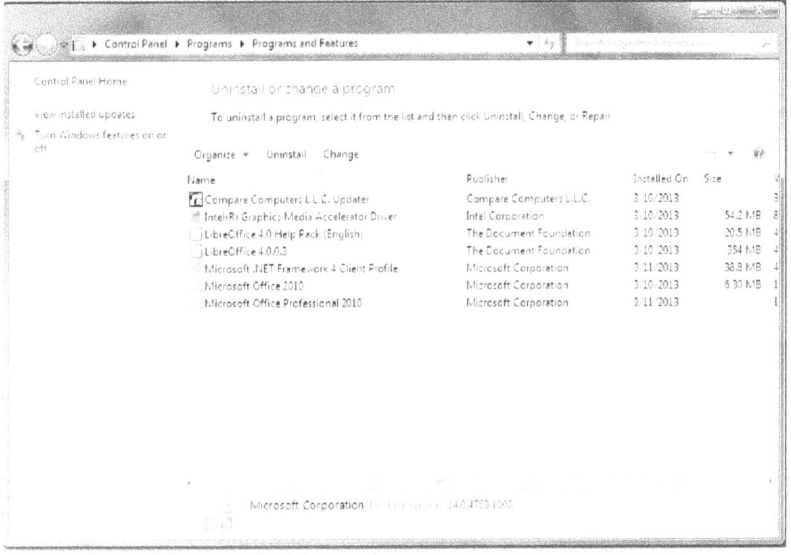

Figure 6.65: Uninstall Programs and Features

⚠ Use caution when uninstalling programs from the PC so that required software and utilities are not accidently removed.

In the next section we will look at using the Task Manager utility to manage actively running applications and services.

Using Task Manager

Task Manager can be used to manage programs running on the system, applications and services that load with Windows, and for viewing performance information about the PC. To open the Task Manager you can press the ALT + CTRL + DEL keys on your keyboard at the same time and select the Start Task Manager option.

From the Applications tab in the Task Manager, an unresponsive program can be selected then forced to close by clicking the End Task button. You can manually start a new program by clicking the New Task button and locating the program you wish to run.

Figure 6.66: Task Manager Applications Tab

Under the Processes tab you can view active programs, background processes, and Windows processes; and also view the system requirements of the application in real-time.

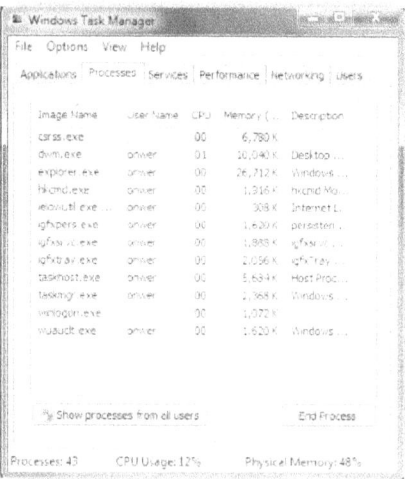

Figure 6.67: Task Manger Processes Tab

Under the Services tab you can quickly view services and their status, as well as start and stop individual processes.

Figure 6.68: Task Manager Services

Under the Performance tab, CPU, RAM, and hard disk performance is plotted in a real-time graph for use in monitoring performance to troubleshoot problems with the system. Clicking on the Resource Monitor button will launch the Resource Monitor application. This program provides an in-depth analysis of system performance.

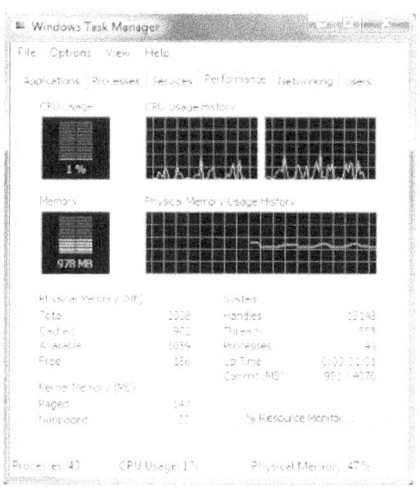

Figure 6.69: Task Manager Performance Tab

The Networking tab provides data on the network utilization and state of the connection.

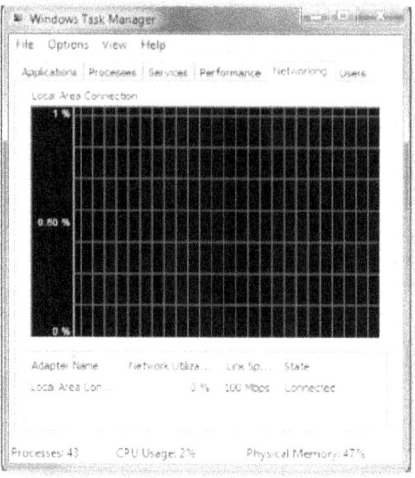

Figure 6.70: Task Manager Networking Tab

Users logged into the system can be viewed by clicking on the Users tab in the Task Manager. The Disconnect and Logoff buttons can be used to sign out a user from the PC.

Figure 6.71: Task Manager Users Tab

In the next few sections I will go over the process of personalizing your PC by adjusting the themes, configuring the display options, and managing user settings.

Desktop Personalization Options

To set the display options like screen resolution, multiple monitor configuration, and refresh rate, right-click on a blank area of the desktop and select Screen Resolution from the menu.

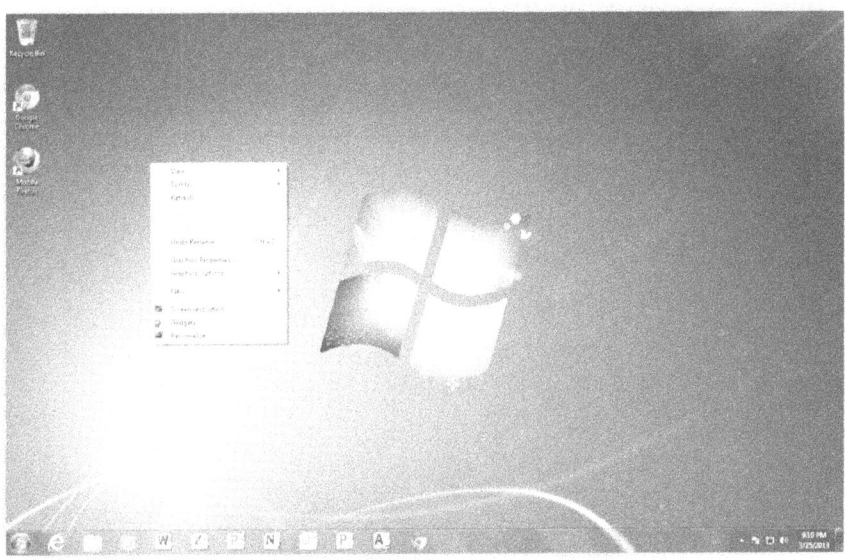

Figure 6.72: Desktop Context Menu

From the screen resolution screen you can add multiple displays, change the resolution via the dropdown menu, and change the screen orientation. Clicking the advance settings link gives other options like the refresh rate for the monitor.

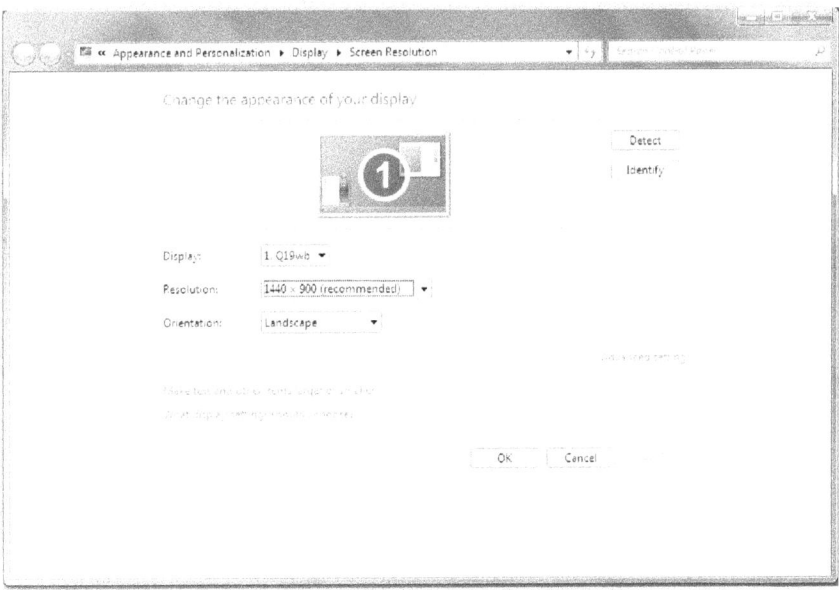

Figure 6.73: Screen Resolution Configuration

The Make Text and Other Items Larger or Smaller link will enable you to set the size of all items, or just that of the text for specific items.

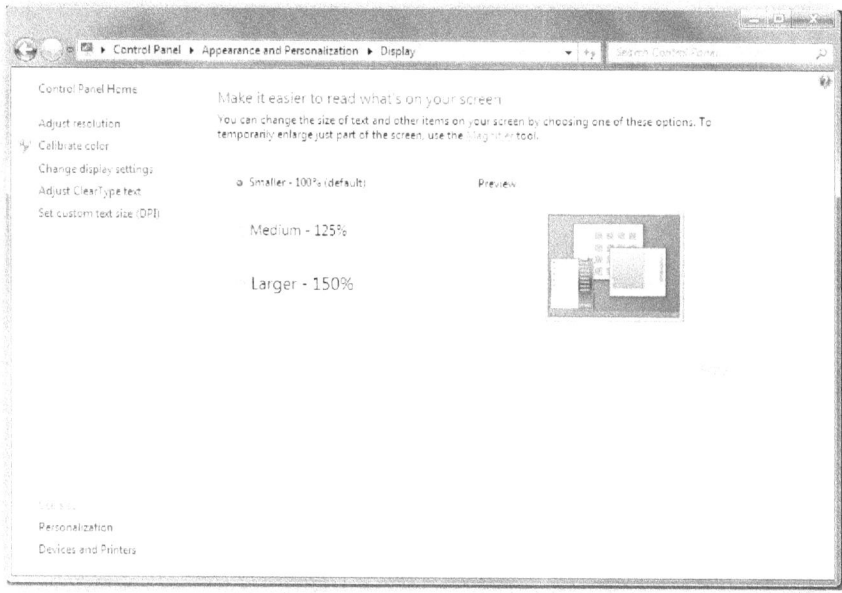

Figure 6.74: Change Size of Items and Text

To change the desktop wallpaper, theme, sound effects, and screen saver, simply right-click on a blank area of the desktop and choose the option Personalize from the list.

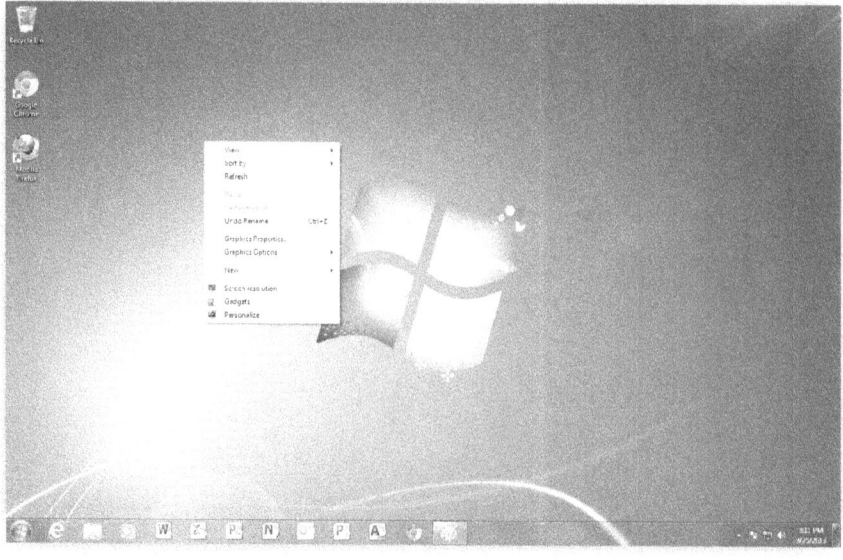

Figure 6.75: Desktop Context Menu

You can choose a preconfigured theme from the list or click on one of the links at the bottom of the window to change just the wallpaper, color, sounds, or screen saver.

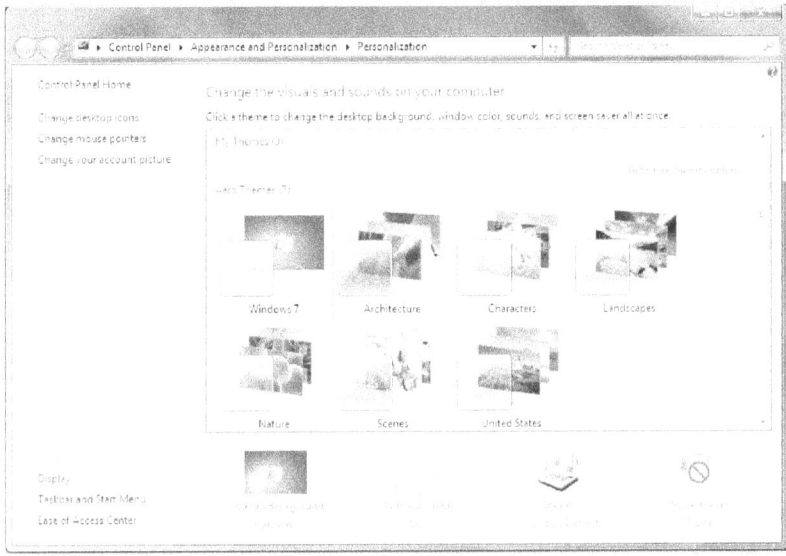

Figure 6.76: Personalization Menu

The desktop wallpaper screen lets you choose a type of wallpaper or background color from the dropdown list. Multiple backgrounds can be selected and cycled at a specified time interval. You can also choose the fill options for the picture to fit your screen.

Figure 6.77: Set Desktop Background

91

> **Tip** To select multiple wallpapers that change after a given interval, hold the CTRL key while left-clicking wallpapers in the list. Choose the desired time interval from the list.

To change the color of the taskbar, Title Bars, and other controls, choose the Color option at the bottom of the main Personalization screen. From this window you can choose the color you prefer.

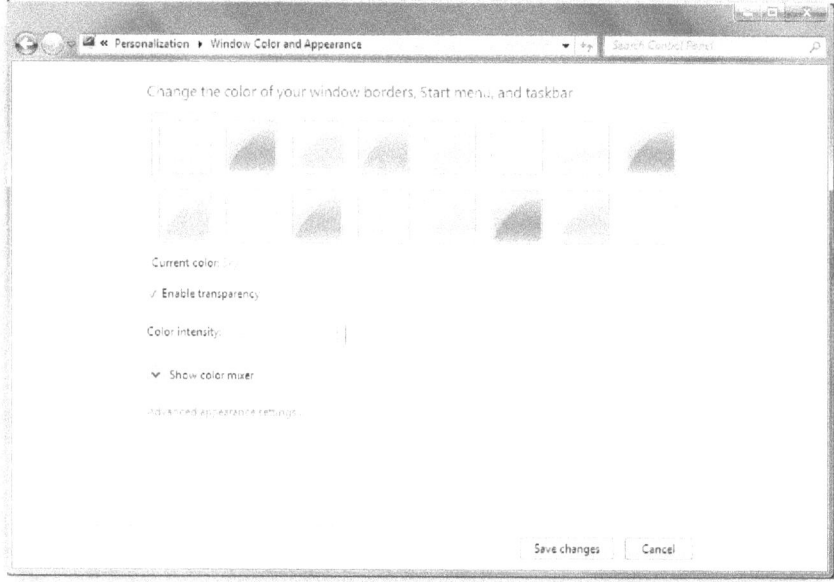

Figure 6.78: Color and Appearance Selection

In Chapter 7 we will review how to perform many common tasks, like importing pictures and burning CD's.

Chapter Review Questions:

1. Which Control Panel category can be used to manage users and configure parental controls?
2. Describe the steps for connecting to a wireless router with WPA2 security.
3. Why do you need to be cautious of shared files and permissions on a HomeGroup?
4. What are three programs discussed in this chapter that limit the risk of virus and malware infections?
5. Describe the process for setting the wallpaper to randomly change backgrounds every 5 minutes.

Chapter 7 - Common Computer Tasks

Importing Photos From A Digital Camera Memory Card

The process of importing pictures from a memory card will vary depending on the program used to import pictures. We will explore manually copying pictures and using the built-in picture and video transfer option.

When you first connect your camera's memory card to your PC's card reader, or when you plug in your camera's USB connection to the PC, you will likely see the AutoPlay options for memory cards when the card is first connected. If you choose the Open Folder to View Files option you will be able to browse the files and folders on the card and manually copy files to your hard drive.

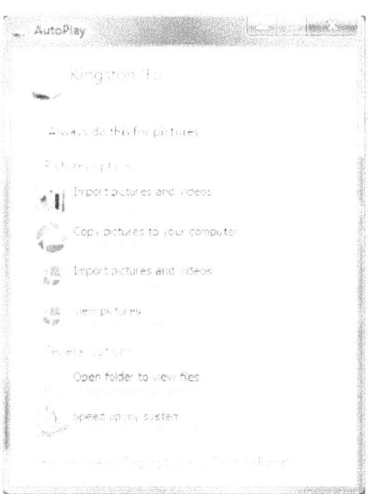

Figure 7.1: Memory Card AutoPlay Options

The folder structure of your camera memory card will vary. Select the pictures you wish to transfer to the hard drive, click the Organize button, and select Copy. Open your Pictures Library folder and create a new folder if you desire. Inside the newly created folder, click the Organize button, then choose Paste. This will copy the selected pictures from the camera memory card into the new folder that you just created. The pictures on the card will remain on the card, unless you choose the Cut option instead of Copy.

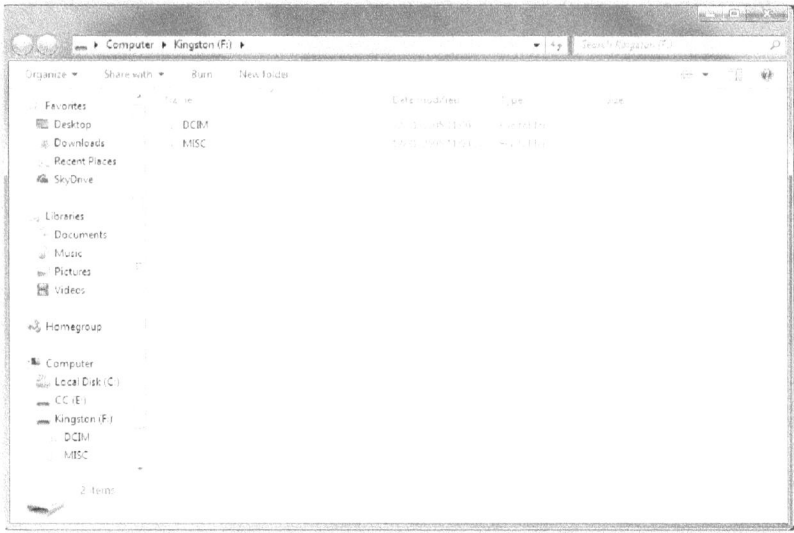

Figure 7.2: Memory Card Folder

To automatically import new pictures on the camera memory card into a new folder in your Pictures folder, you can use the built-in import option in Windows 7. If you choose the Import Pictures and Videos option in the AutoPlay window you will be able to import selected photos to your PC quickly and easily.

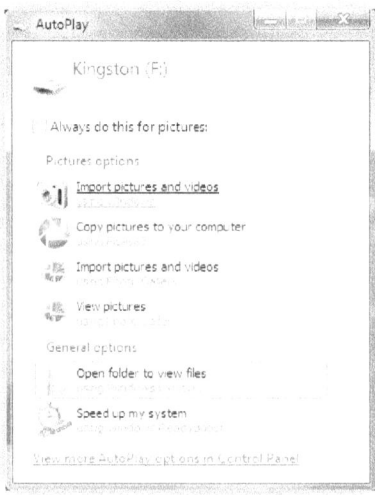

Figure 7.3: Camera Memory Card AutoPlay Prompt

Windows will detect pictures on the memory card that have not yet been imported to the Pictures Library folder. You will be prompted to click the Import button to transfer these files after optionally tagging the pictures with a description. Click the Import button to begin the process.

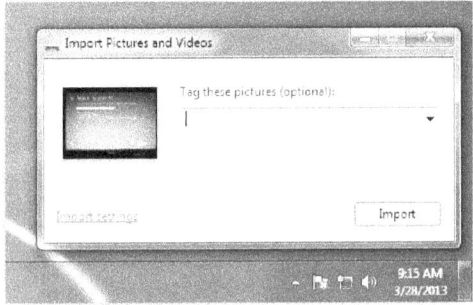

Figure 7.4: Import Pictures Prompt

To change the default settings for importing pictures you can click the Import Settings link in the previous example. From the settings screen you can opt to delete pictures on the card that have been transferred, choose the location and folder name for imported pictures, and set options for rotating imported pictures.

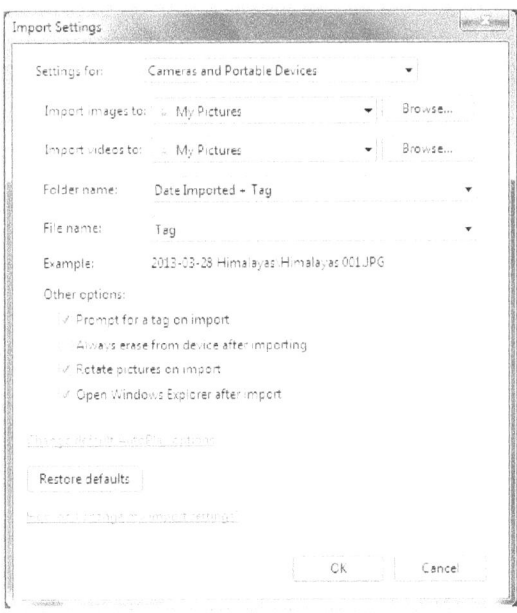

Figure 7.5: Import Settings

The import process will show a progress bar during the import process. This step may take some time depending on the number of pictures being transferred.

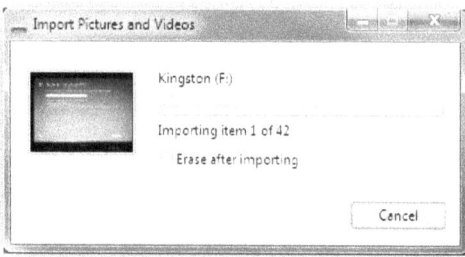

Figure 7.6: Import Progress

When the import is complete you can view the imported files on your hard drive.

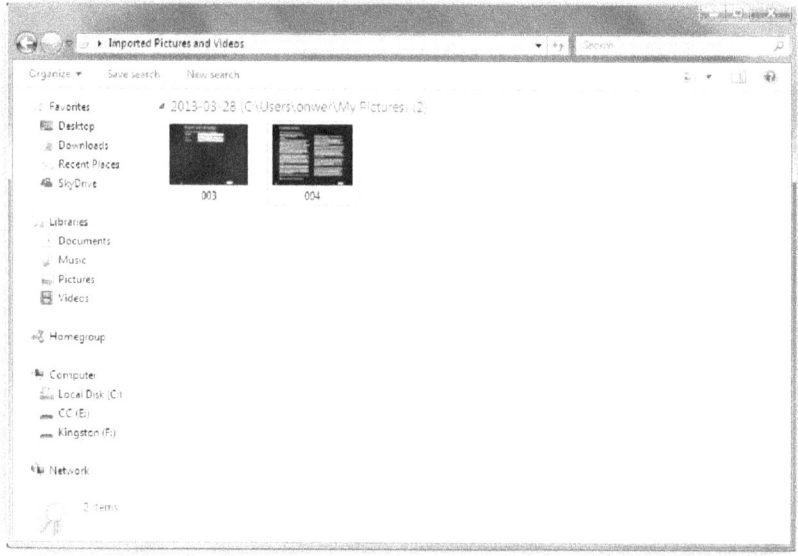

Figure 7.7: Imported Pictures

Now that we have learned how to add digital pictures to the PC we will move on to converting physical pictures into digital pictures and importing them to the computer.

Scanning a Document or Picture to a File

You may need to convert a physical photo or document into a digital file on your PC. To do this you can use a scanner or all-in-one printer. Insert the document face down on the scanner bed. The document needs to be in the corner of the scanner bed where there will usually be an arrow or mark.

Next we will use the WIA scanning feature to scan the document. Not all scanners support this feature. If you scanner doesn't have this feature, consult your scanner's documentation on how to scan using the manufacturer's software instead.

Click on the Devices and Printers link on the right side of the Start Menu. Right-click on the printer or scanner from the list that has your document or photo on its bed. Select the Start Scan option from the context menu as seen in Figure 7.8.

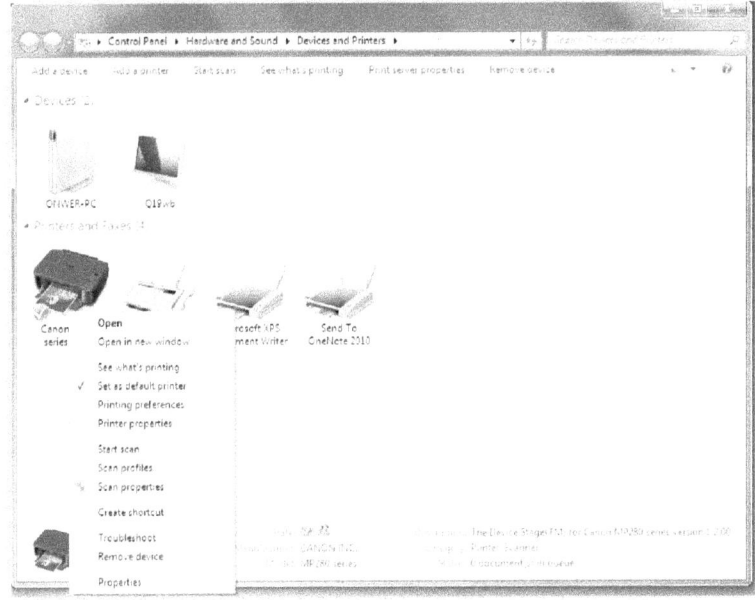

Figure 7.8: Context Menu Scan Option

From the New Scan window you can preview the scan and adjust the settings for the scanned image. If you are scanning a document instead of a photo, you can select a different profile from the Profile drop-down box. When you are ready to scan in the image to a file, click the Scan button. This process will take a short time, during which you will see a progress bar on the screen.

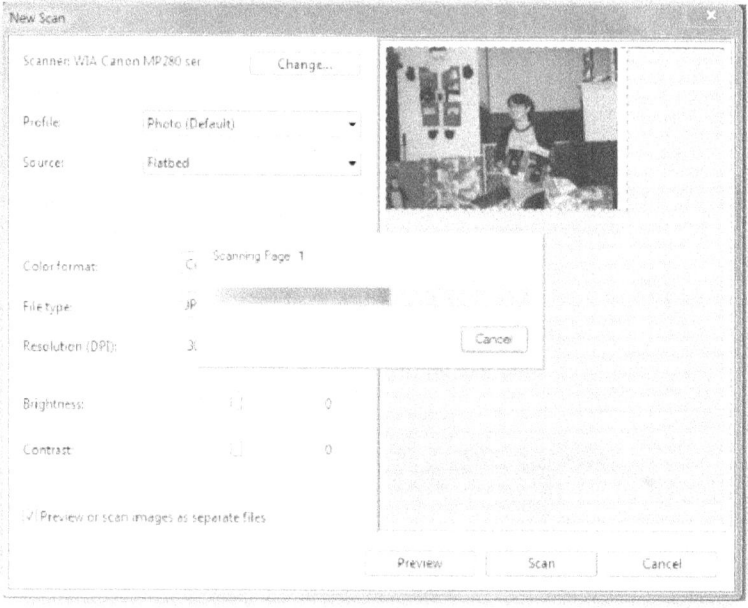

Figure 7.9: Scan Progress

After the scan is complete you will be prompted to optionally tag pictures that were scanned. Click the Import button to import the image into your Pictures library.

Figure 7.10: Import and Tag Images

Next we will work with various type of optical media and external storage, and learn how to make backups of our important pictures, documents, and files.

Optical Media and Data Backups

Working with audio CD's, DVD/Blu-Ray movies, CD-R's, DVD+/-R's, and flash drives are a common task. You can watch DVD movies using the DVD-ROM or Blu-ray drive in your PC, rip an audio CD to transfer to an mp3 player, and create backups using CD's, DVD's, and flash drives. In the following sections we will walk through the process of performing these steps.

Rip Audio From an Audio CD With Windows Media Player

To rip audio tracks from an audio CD into individual audio files on your hard drive, insert the disc in your drive and wait for the AutoPlay prompt. Select Play Audio CD Using Windows Media Player. If you do not see the AutoPlay prompt or if Windows Media Player does not automatically open, open Windows Media Player from the Start Menu.

Figure 7.11: Audio CD AutoPlay Prompt

In Windows Media Player, select the audio CD in the left pane and click the Start Rip button. You can see the progress of the rip for each individual track. By default the tracks are ripped as the ".wma" format, but you can change this setting in the Windows Media Player options section. When the rip is complete you can transfer the audio tracks to your mp3 player or listen to them through the library on your PC.

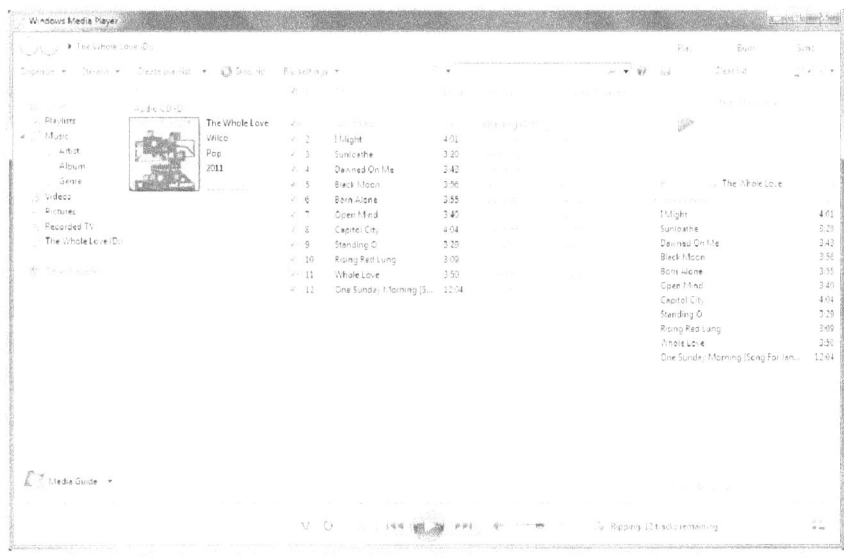

Figure 7.12: Windows Media Player Rip Progress

Burning an Audio CD With Windows Media Player

To burn an audio CD of music tracks stored on your hard drive, open Windows Media Player or click the Burn an Audio CD Using Windows Media Player link in the AutoPlay prompt.

Figure 7.13: Blank CD AutoPlay Prompt

Click on the Burn tab in the upper-right corner of Windows Media Player. Drag files you wish to add to the CD into the burn list (right pane).

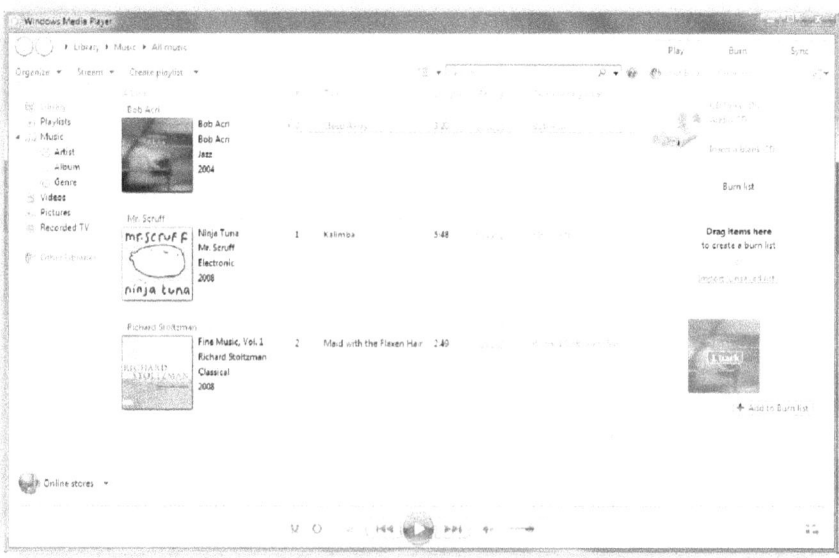

Figure 7.14: Windows Media Player Burn Tab

When you are ready to burn the disc, click the Start Burn button and wait for the process to finish. You can then eject the disc and listen to it on a CD player.

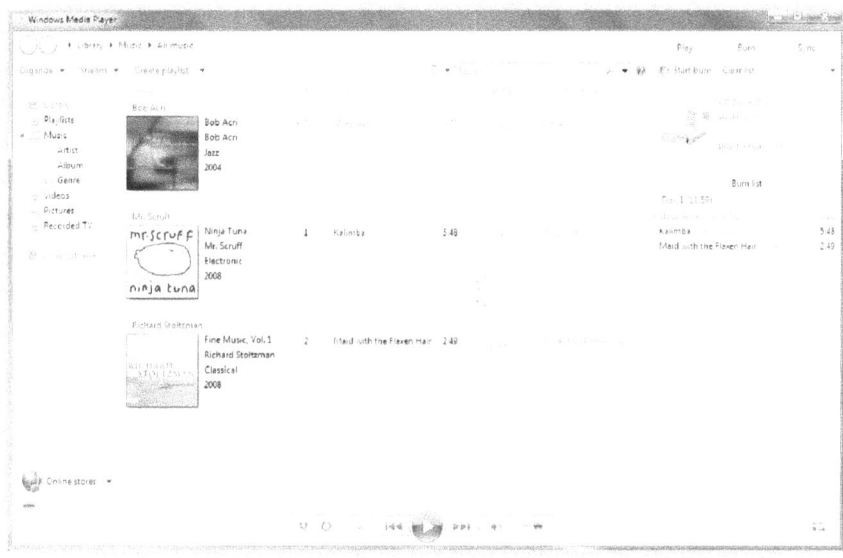

Figure 7.15: Start Burn Process

Burning Data to CD-R

When you insert a blank CD-R in your drive you will see the blank CD AutoPlay prompt. We will use the File Explorer option to burn data files to the blank CD. Select that option to continue.

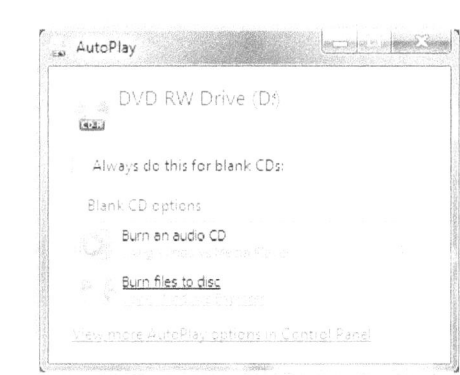

Figure 7.16: Blank CD AutoPlay Options

You may find an option like the one in Figure 7.17 regarding the format of the disc. In most cases I recommend that you choose the option "With a CD/DVD Player" instead of the "Like a USB Flash Drive" option. Choose the option you prefer to continue.

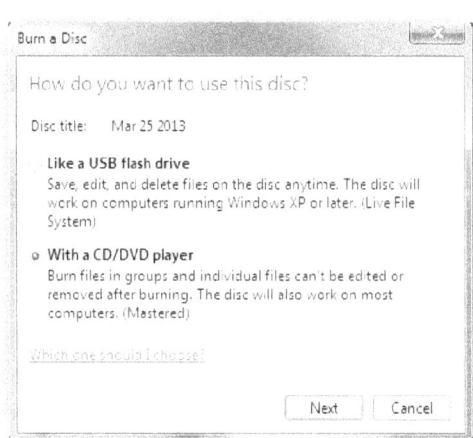

Figure 7.17: CD-R File System Formatting Options

A Windows Explorer window will open showing the contents of the blank CD. Files you wish to add to the CD can be selected and dragged to the CD-R window. You can also select the items and from the right-click context menu, select Send To, then choose the DVD RW Drive option. Files shown in the Windows Explorer window for the drive are pending to be burned and are not yet on the disc.

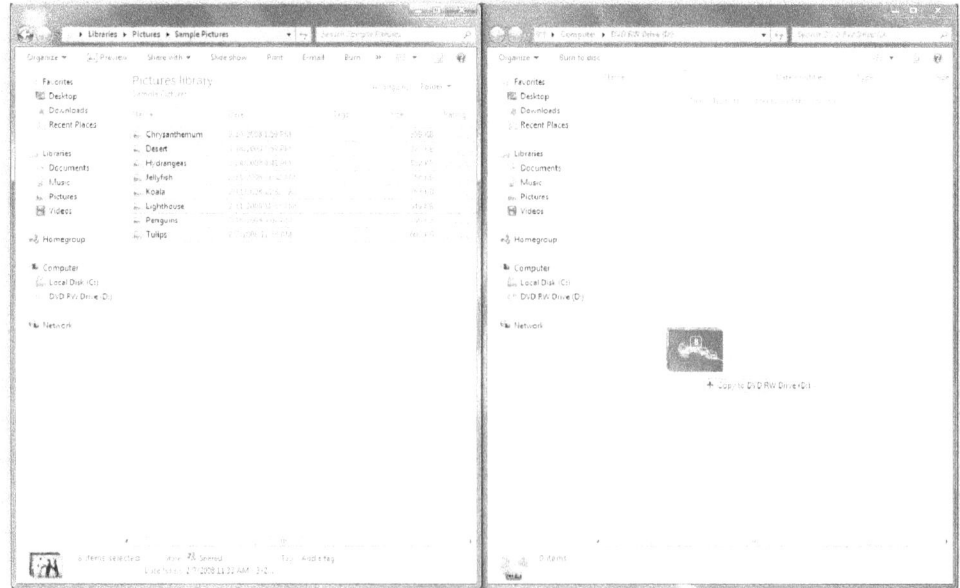

Figure 7.18: Drag and Drop Files to the Disc

Click the Burn to Disc button when you are ready to burn and finalize the disc. This will open the disc burning wizard to write the data to the CD. Enter a name for the disc in the wizard and optionally select a burning speed. I recommend leaving the burning speed set at the default speed, unless you encounter an issue burning at that speed or if your media requires a different setting. Click the next button to start the burning process.

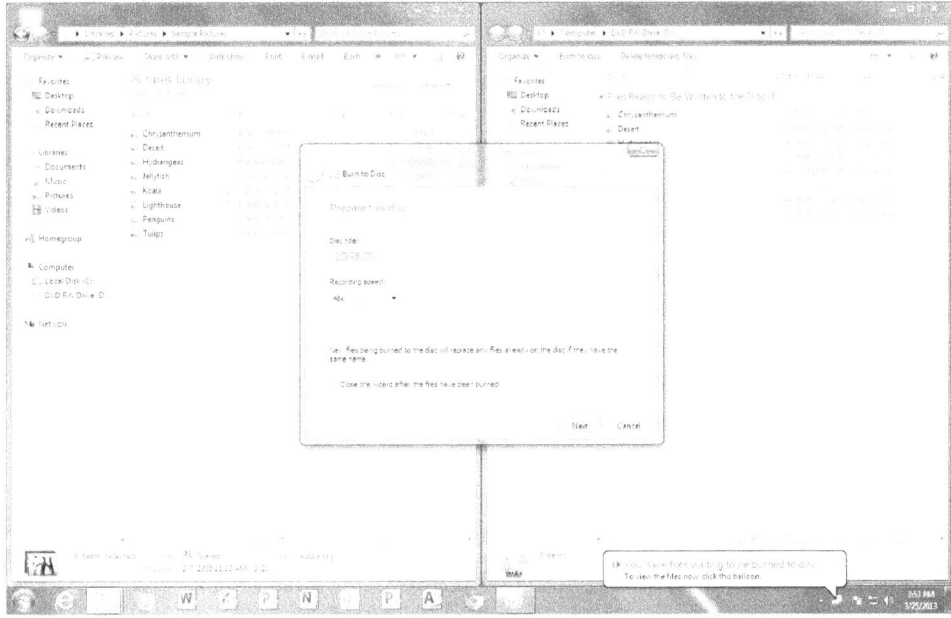

Figure 7.19: Burn to Disc Wizard

Burning Data to a DVD+R

When you insert a blank DVD in your drive you will see the blank DVD AutoPlay prompt. Use the File Explorer option to burn data files to the blank DVD. Select that option to continue.

Figure 7.20: Blank DVD AutoPlay Options

If you see a window asking how you want to use the disc, I recommend that you choose the option "With a CD/DVD Player" instead of the "Like a USB Flash Drive" option. Choose the option you prefer to continue.

Figure 7.21: Blank DVD Formatting Options

A Windows Explorer window will open showing the contents of the blank DVD. From here you can drag and drop files you wish to backup to DVD. When you are ready to finalize the disc and burn the data to the DVD, click the Burn to Disc option under the Manage tab. You can then name the DVD and finish the burning wizard.

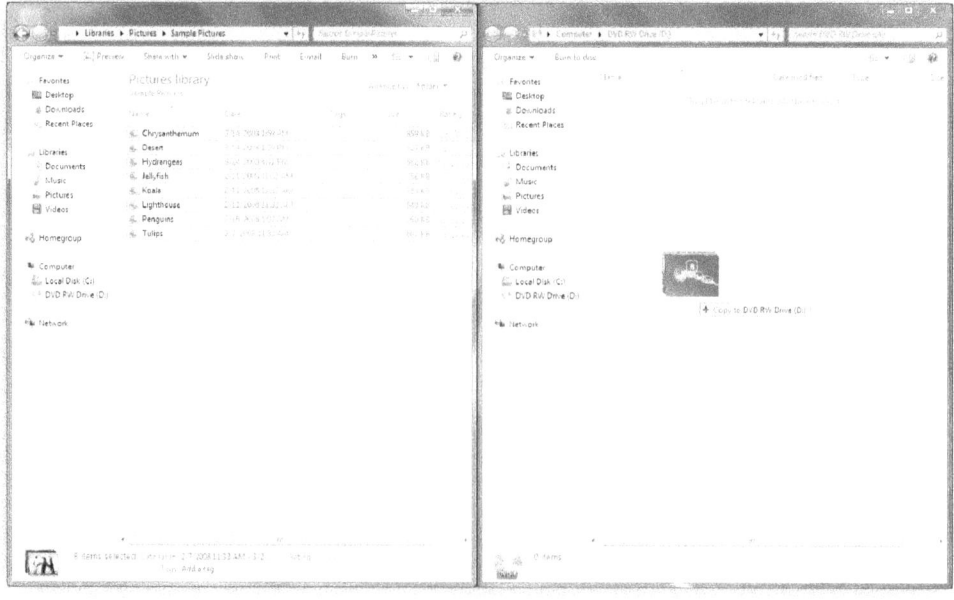

Figure 7.22: Files To Be Burned to DVD

DVD Playback in Windows 7

In order to play back DVD movies in Windows 7 you can either use Windows Media Player, Windows Media Center, or you can install a desktop program with DVD playback capabilities. VLC media player is a free media player that can be used for DVD playback in place of Windows Media Player. Once installed, VLC Player will be available via the AutoPlay options when a DVD movie is inserted in the PC.

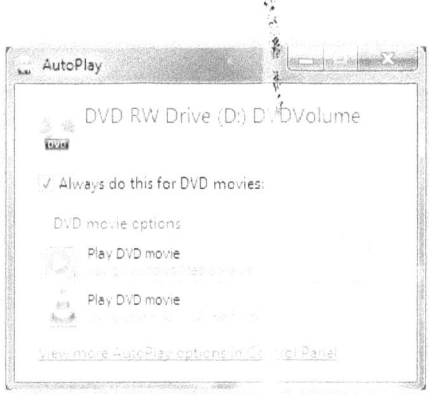

Figure 7.23: DVD Movie AutoPlay Options

Choosing the option to playback the DVD with VLC player will open the VLC player main window. Playback options are located at the bottom of the window. There are a variety of other desktop media players with similar capabilities.

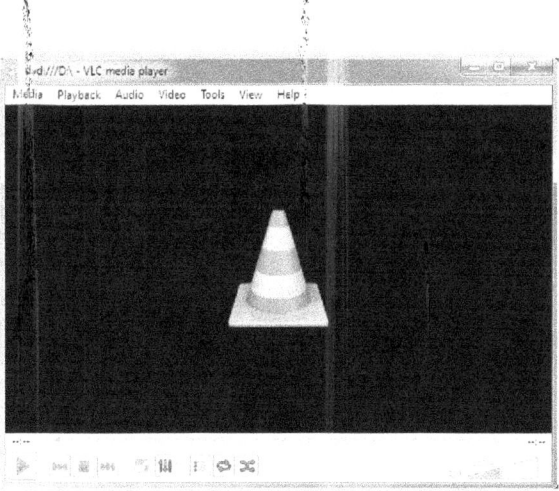

Figure 7.24: VLC Media Player Main Window

When you use Windows Media Player for watching a DVD, you will see a video window similar to Figure 7.25. The controls for DVD playback are located on the menu at the bottom of the screen.

Figure 7.25: Windows Media Player

Stop, Previous, Pause/Resume, and Next buttons control movie playback. The volume slider will adjust the movie volume. The Full Screen/Restore button is located in the lower-right corner of the window.

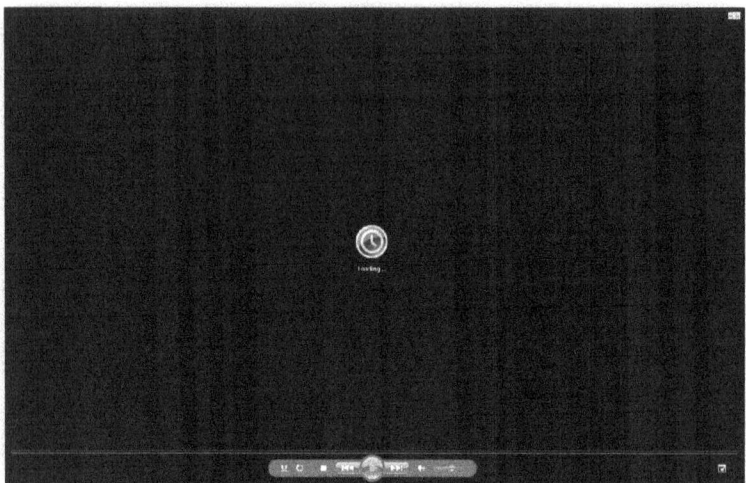

Figure 7.26: Full Screen Windows Media Player

Next we will look at backing up our data to external storage devices.

Backing Up Data to an External Drive

To back up files to an external hard drive you can either drag-and-drop files to the drive in the same way that you did with a CD-R, or you can use the Windows Backup utility to save backup copies of your files to an external drive. The Windows Backup utility can also create a system image of your hard drive that can be used to restore your entire hard drive.

⚠️**Tip** Be sure to back up your data to an external storage device to minimize the risk of data loss. Verify data on the backup is valid and up-to-date.

When you first connect an external storage device you will see the AutoPlay window prompting you to select an option for accessing the device. Select the Use This Drive for Backup option to open the Windows Backup utility.

Figure 7.27: Removable Storage AutoPlay Options

When you first start the backup configuration process you will see a progress bar while the program is loading.

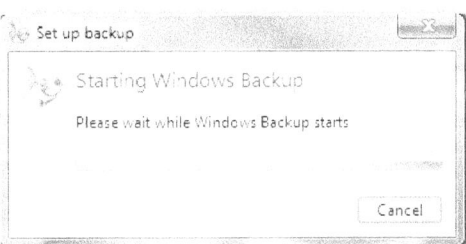

Figure 7.28: Windows Backup Loading Progress

Next you will be given the option to let Windows choose what to back up or choose for yourself. If you have folders or files stored on other partitions or drives, you may want to select the Let Me Choose option.

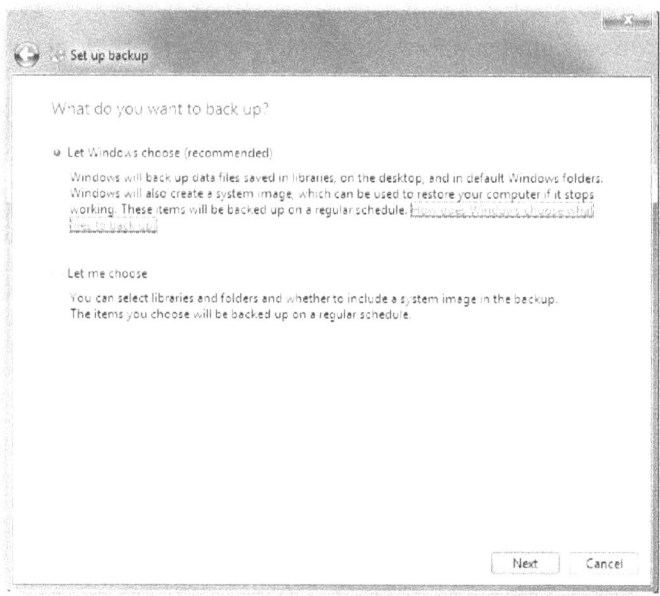

Figure 7.29: Windows Backup Choose Backup Options

If you chose the automatic option you will be able to review the locations and settings for the backup in the following screen. From this screen you can also adjust the backup schedule for future backups.

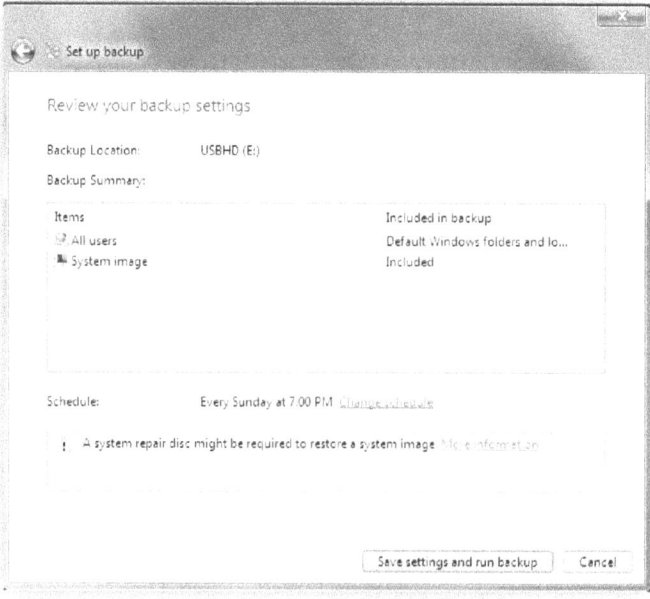

Figure 7.30: Review Backup Options

If you selected the Let Me Choose option, you will be presented with a screen allowing you to select the specific locations to be included in the backup. You can select the system image option to create an image of the hard drive that can be used to restore the entire PC. Click the next button to review settings and adjust the automatic backup schedule if desired. If all settings look correct, begin the backup process.

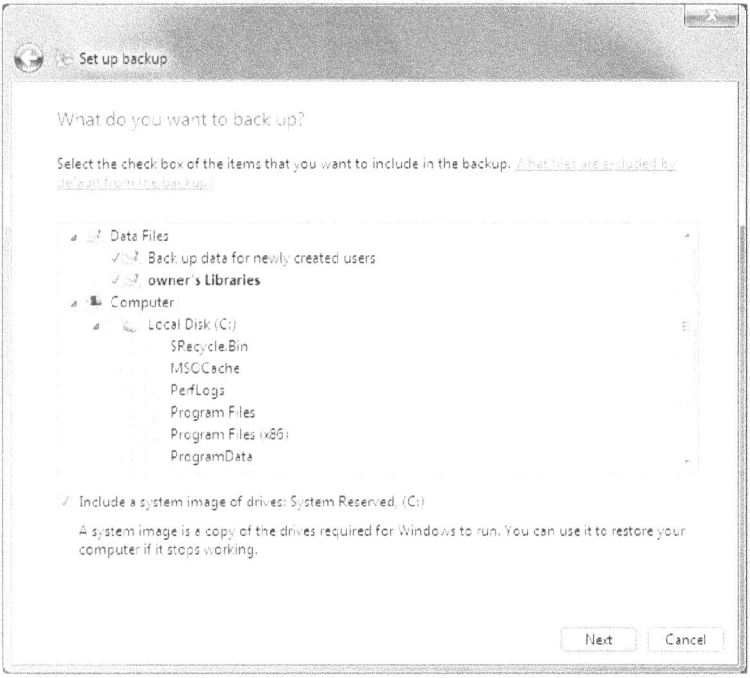

Figure 7.31: Let Me Choose Backup Option

Once the backup is started, you can view the progress in the Backup and Restore Control Panel option.

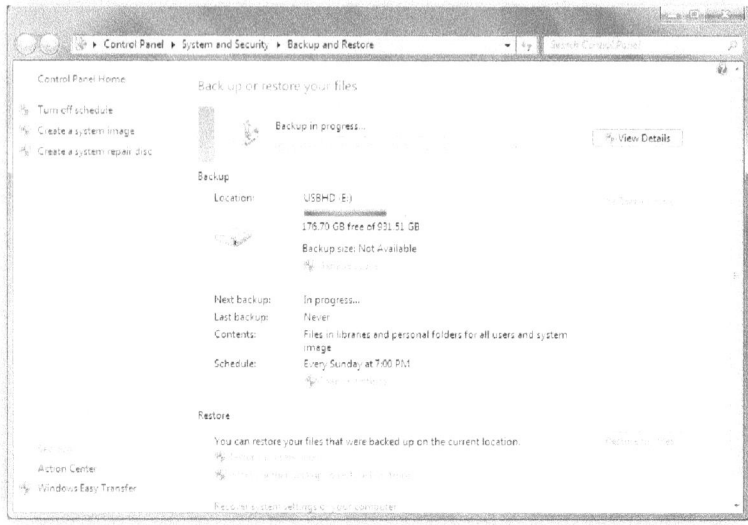

Figure 7.32: Backup In Progress

If you did not choose the Windows Backup AutoPlay option when connecting the external storage device, open the Control Panel to launch the Windows Backup utility. Select the System and Security link and then the Backup and Restore link. Click the Set Up Backup link if your backup drive is connected and Windows Backup has not yet been configured.

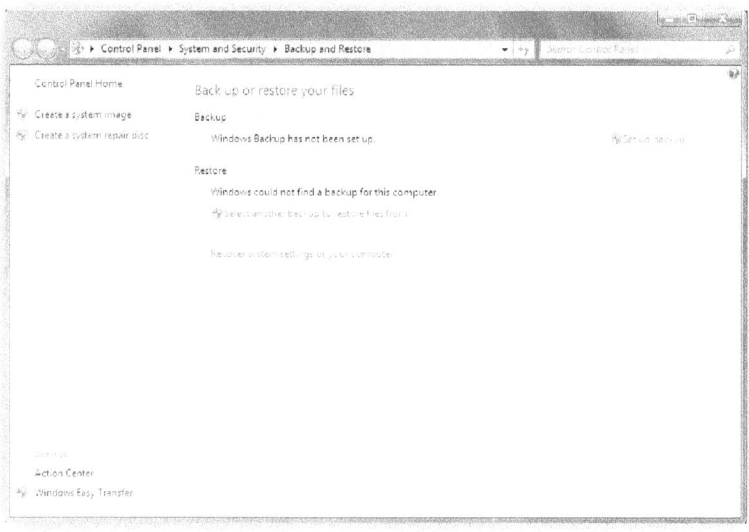

Figure 7.33: Backup and Restore

You will be prompted to select the drive that will be used to store the backup. Select the desired external storage device and click the Next button to continue.

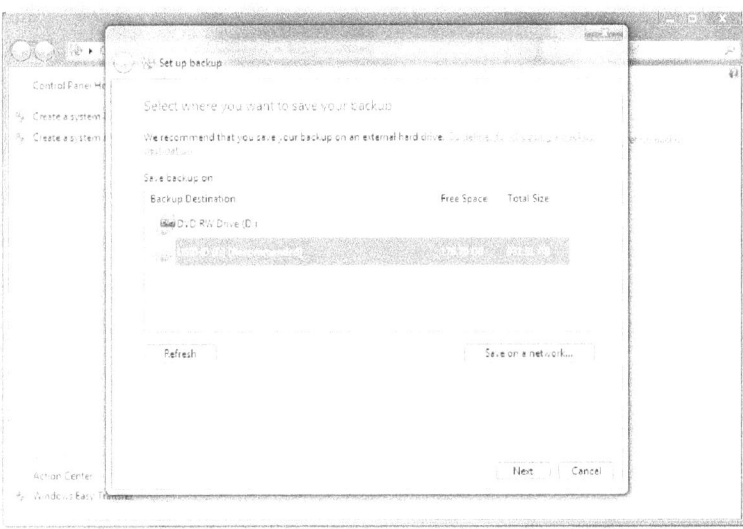

Figure 7.34: Select Drive for Storing Backups

To manage the settings for the backup, click the Manage Space link in the Backup and Restore Control Panel window. From this window you can view detailed information about the backups and the space used by various types of backups on the drive.

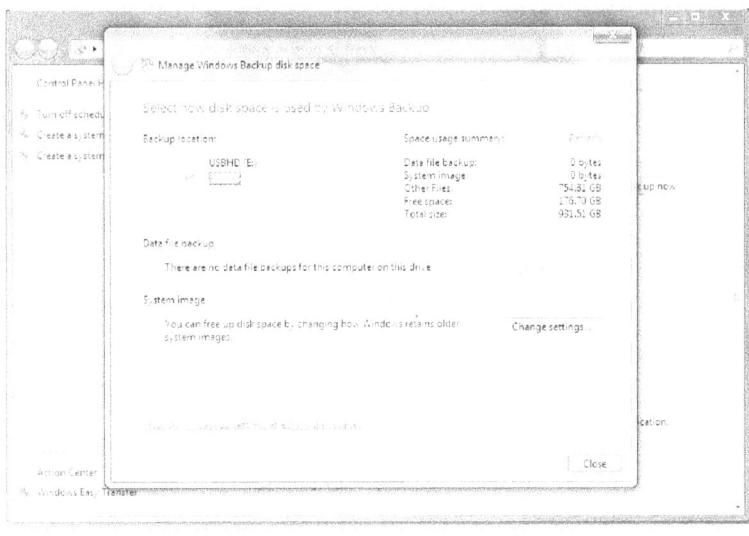

Figure 7.35: Manage Backup Space

Clicking the Change Settings button under the System Image section will allow you to modify the number of past system image backups stored on the drive. You can choose to let Windows automatically handle the space used for backup history, or you can keep only the most recent image. We recommend letting Windows manage the backup history space, as keeping only the most recent backup image may limit options for recovering the system prior to the most recent backup.

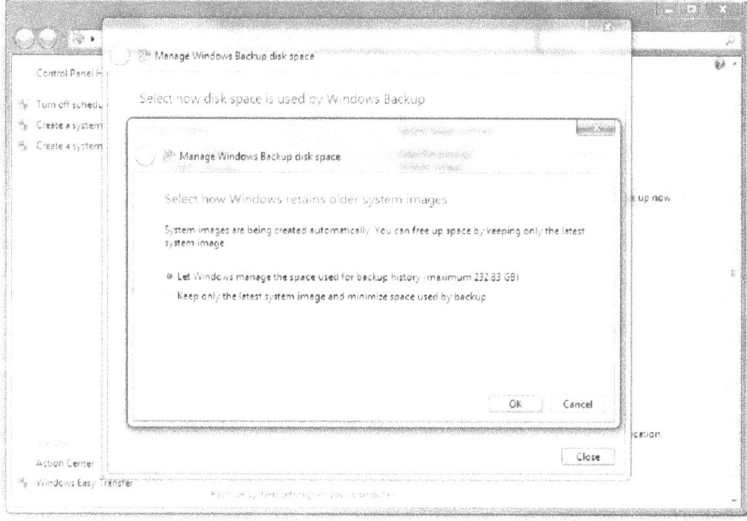

Figure 7.36: Change Backup Space Settings

If you choose to manually copy files to the external storage you will notice a file copy progress window showing the progress of the transfer, the source and destination, and options to pause or cancel the transfer.

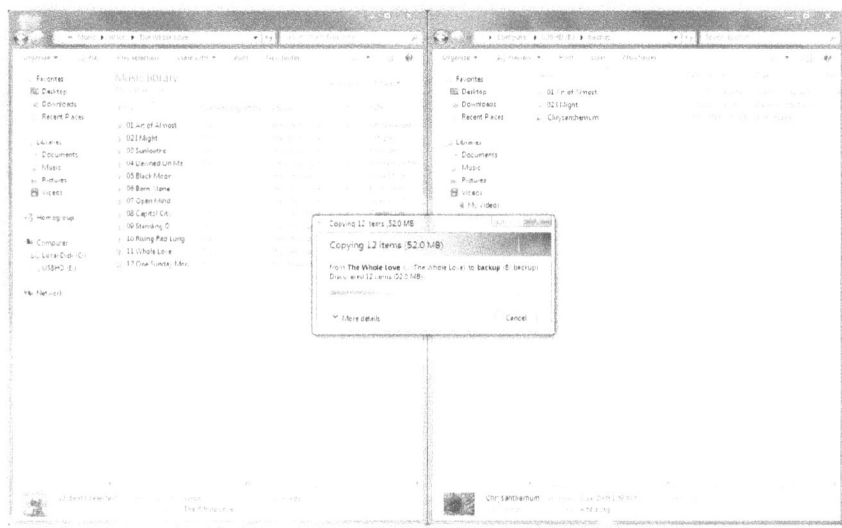

Figure 7.37: File Copy Progress Window

Clicking the More Details link expands the window to show more detailed information. Expanded details include the remaining transfer time and current file details.

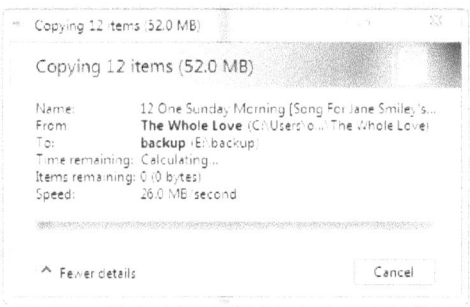

Figure 7.38: Detailed File Copy Progress Window

If the destination already contains a file with the same filename, you will see a window asking if you would like to replace the file in the destination folder with the file from the source folder, or to keep both files by renaming the copied file.

Figure 7.39: Replace Files Prompt

In the next section, we will look at several commonly used programs that are compatible with Windows 7.

Chapter Review Questions:

1. Using a Live File System when burning a CD-R limits compatibility with versions of Windows older than what release?
2. How do you manually limit the number of Windows Backups kept on an external storage device?
3. Copying your documents to a Backup folder on your C: drive is a good method for backing up files – True or False. Why?
4. Name three programs that can be used to play DVD movies in Windows 7.

Chapter 8 - Commonly Used Programs

Apple iTunes

Apple iTunes is a widely used program to manage music, movies, and other content on your PC. The program is also used to purchase content through the iTunes Store. You can use iTunes to transfer music and movies from your PC to your iPod, iPhone, and iPad.

Playback controls are located in the upper left corner of the window, your libraries are available via the dropdown menu on the left side, your playlists are located in the center, and the iTunes Store link is located on the right.

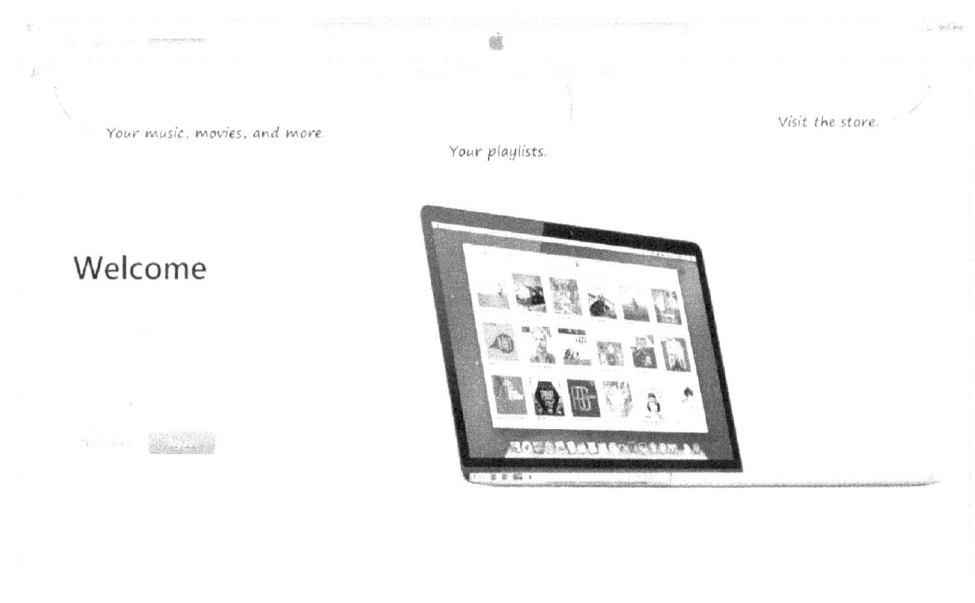

Figure 8.1 : iTunes Main Window

Figure 8.2: iTunes Application

You can purchase individual songs, albums, movies, and TV shows in the iTunes Store. Click the dropdown next to each category to select a genre to browse.

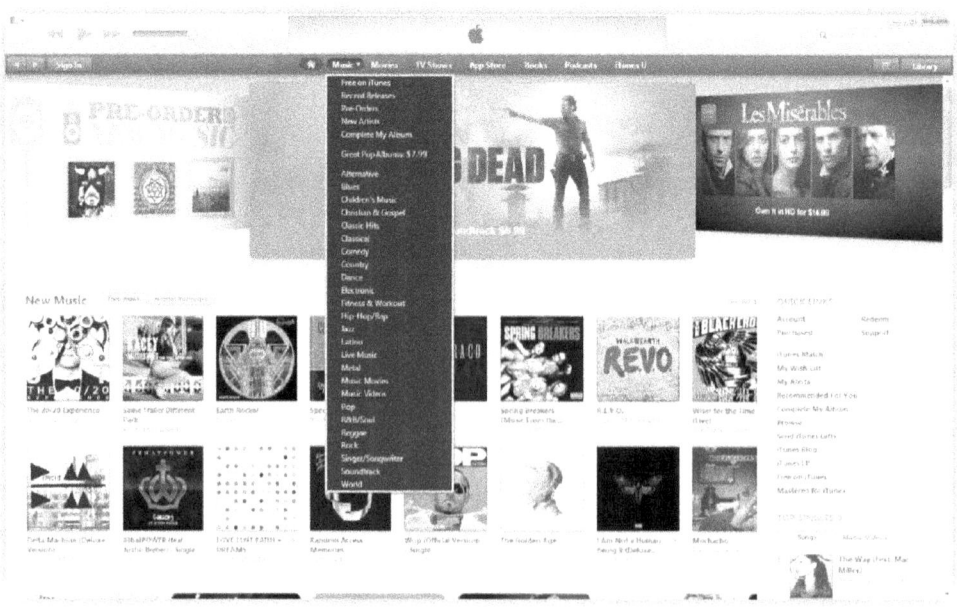

Figure 8.3: iTunes Store

To play music or movies from your library, choose the desired library from the left dropdown menu and select the tracks you wish to listen to. From here you can create playlists and select tracks to sync to your mp3 player.

Figure 8.4: iTunes Music Library

Google Picasa – Basic Photo Editor

For basic photo editing tasks like cropping, red eye removal, and applying filters, the Google Picasa application is a free program that supports many common tasks.

Figure 8.5: Picasa Application Window

Google and the Google logo are registered trademarks of Google Inc., used with permission.

117

The photo selected for editing will appear in the right pane. A variety of editing options are available in the left pane. From the left pane options you can remove red eye, crop the photo, add text, and make automatic corrections to the image. From the other menu tabs you can adjust the color and contrast of the image, and select from many different preset filters.

In the bottom window pane you can choose sharing options, print, and e-mail the image. You can also view people, places, and tags for the image. The photo can be uploaded to a Web Album for sharing with others.

Features in Picasa are somewhat limited, but for basic photo editing this free program provides several useful tools for enhancing and editing photos.

Windows Live Mail

Windows Live Mail is one of the most commonly used free e-mail clients in Windows 7. Previous version of Windows included a built-in e-mail client, but in Windows 7 the e-mail client is part of the free Windows Live Essentials 2012 program and is not part of a clean Windows 7 installation. Some manufacturer's may include the Windows Live Essentials package with their new PC's, however. To download Windows Live Essentials 2012, visit download.live.com.

Windows Live Mail has a layout somewhat similar to its predecessors. The Ribbon UI along the top of the screen will contain common tasks under each tab heading. The left-pane contains storage folders for accounts configured in the program, as well as links to the Mail, Calendar, Contacts, Newsfeeds, and Newsgroups portions of the program. The middle-pane lists e-mail messages that are in the selected e-mail account folder. To the right of the e-mail list, you will see the e-mail Preview Pane. This section will display a preview of the selected e-mail message. The far right-pane will display a calendar and appointment reminders.

Figure 8.6: Windows Live Mail

To set up your e-mail account in Windows Live Mail, click on the blue menu button in the upper-left corner. Choose Options from the drop-down list and select E-mail Accounts.

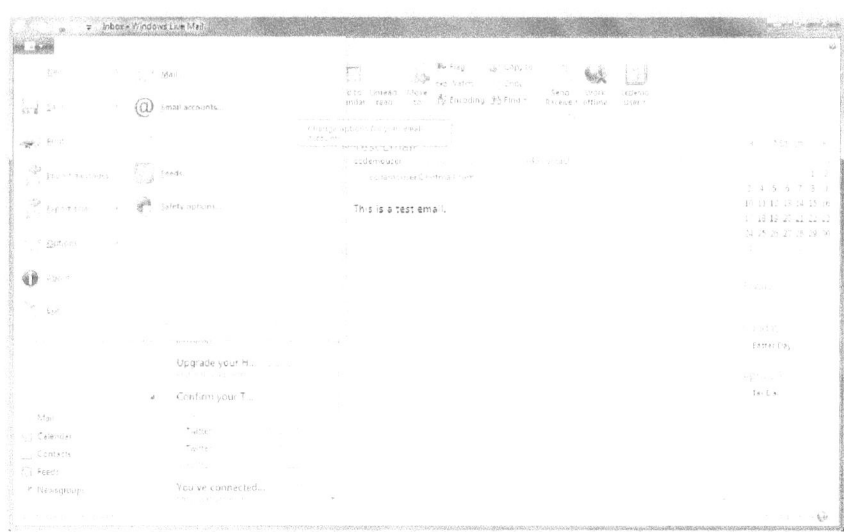

Figure 8.7: E-mail Accounts Options

Click the Add button in the Accounts window to configure settings for accessing the e-mail account.

Figure 8.8: Accounts

Select E-mail Account from the Account Type box followed by the Next button.

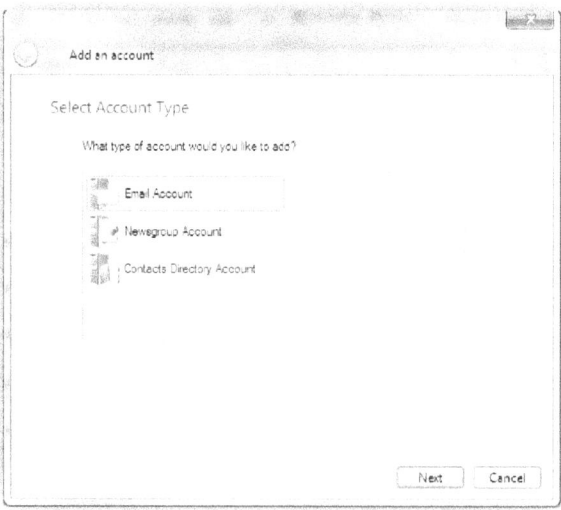

Figure 8.9: Add an Account

In the Add Your E-mail Accounts window, enter the e-mail address, password, display name, and manual mail server settings if needed.

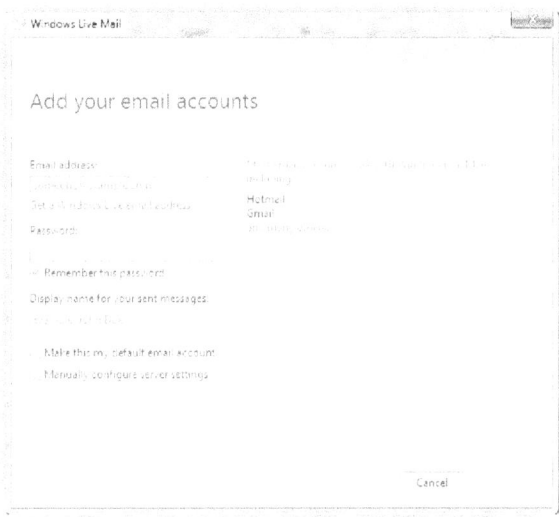

Figure 8.10: Add E-mail Account

If you are unsure of your e-mail server settings, contact your e-mail service provider to obtain the correct settings for your service. Enter the settings in the manual server configuration window, and click the Next button to finish the wizard. After completing the wizard, Windows Live Mail will attempt to download e-mails for the account. If you receive any errors, verify your account and mail server settings are correct.

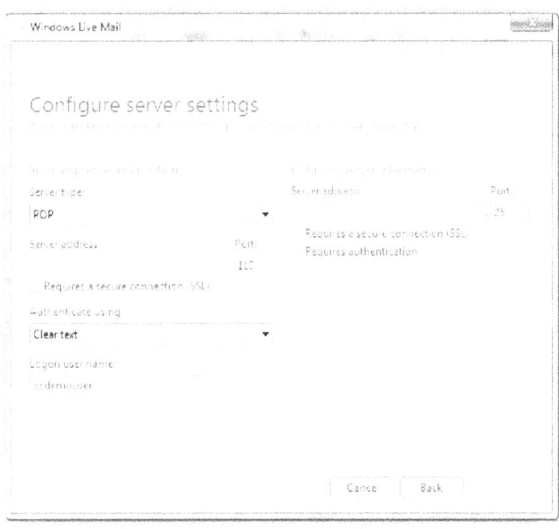

Figure 8.11: Manually Configure Server Settings

The Home tab contains many of the common elements used for most tasks. The E-mail Message link is used to create a new, blank e-mail message. Photo E-mail will create a new e-mail message with attached pictures. The Items link can be used to create new calendars, tasks, and other items. To delete a selected message or mark the message as junk, simply click the Delete or Junk buttons on the Home tab. To respond to a selected e-mail, click the Reply, Reply All, or Forward buttons on the Home tab. Items in the Actions group on the Home tab can be used to mark or flag messages, and to locate or copy text. The Send/Receive button is used to check for any new e-mails and send any pending e-mails. The button on the right side of the Home tab is the Windows Live sign-in button. Certain features in Windows Live Mail may prompt you to sign in with your Windows Live account or Microsoft Account. These credentials may be different than your e-mail address and password used in Windows Live Mail. If you don't have a Windows Live account or Microsoft Account, you can create one for free online.

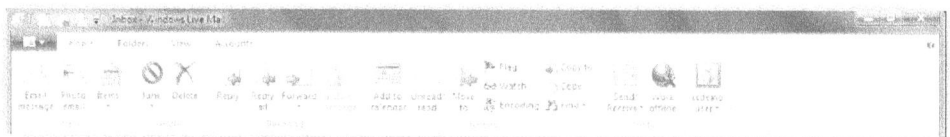

Figure 8.12: Home Tab

The Folders tab contains options for creating new storage folders, as well as managing and navigating messages in folders.

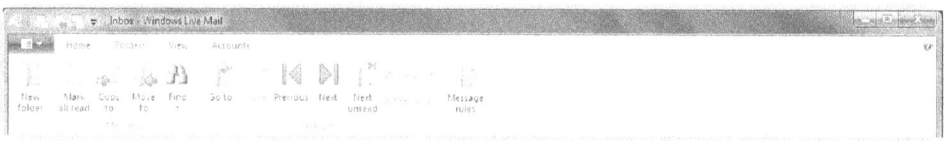

Figure 8.13: Folders Tab

The View tab contains options for managing the views and layout of the program. Grouped conversation mode can be turned on or off from this tab as well.

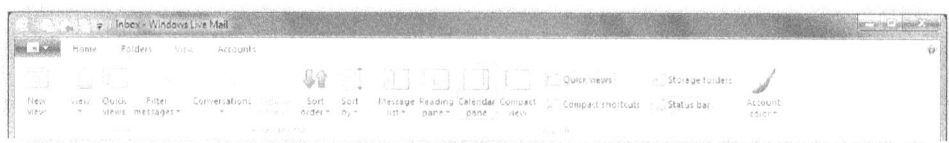

Figure 8.14: View Tab

The Accounts tab can create new e-mail and newsgroup accounts and display the properties for existing accounts.

Figure 8.15: Accounts Tab

To create a new e-mail message, click the E-mail Message link on the Home tab. A new window will open with a blank e-mail message.

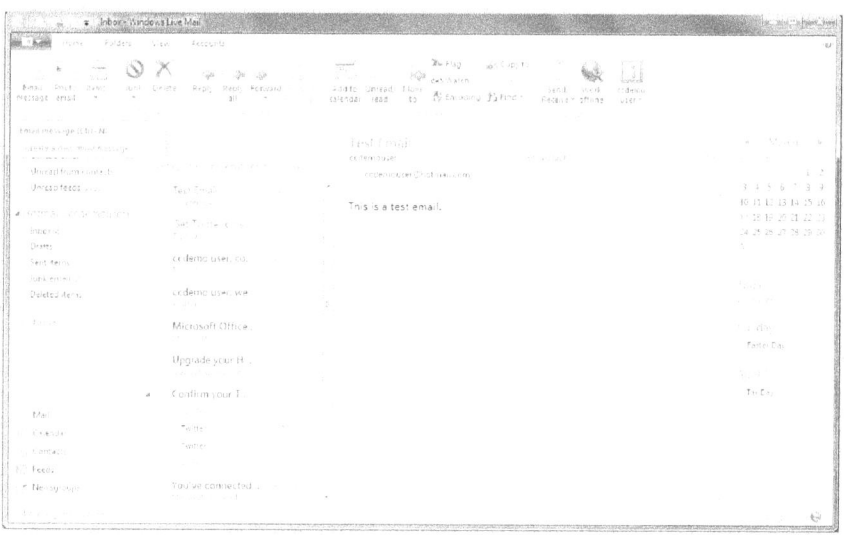

Figure 8.16: Email Message Button

If you have saved contacts in your Contacts list, they will appear in a list as you type their name or e-mail address in the "To…" field. You can also click the "To…" button to select contacts from your Contacts list. Enter an e-mail subject in the Subject field and your e-mail text in the area below the Subject line. You can adjust the font options in the e-mail text through settings in the Message tab. To attach a file, such as a document, picture, or other file, click the Attach File link. To check spelling in your e-mail message, click the Check Spelling button on the right side of the Message tab.

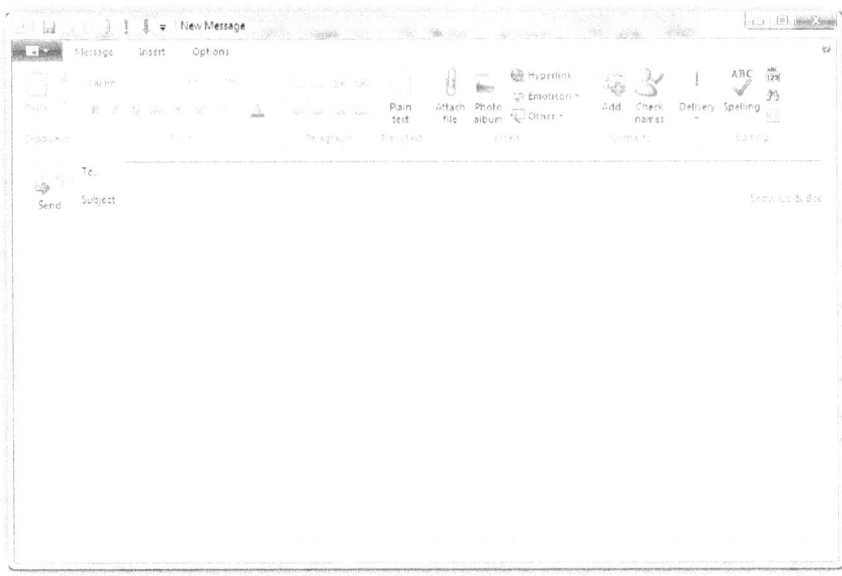

Figure 8.17: New Message Window

Clicking the Photo Album button allows you to add multiple pictures into a photo album. This feature requires a Windows Live account. Enter your Windows Live or Microsoft Account login information, or create an account for free if you do not already have one.

Figure 8.18: Sign In to a Windows Live Account

On the Insert tab, you can include a file attachment (document, picture, PDF), business card, or signature. You can also insert a divider line in the document text. Photos can be added as a regular attachment, or as a single photo or photo album. As a reminder, some photo features require a free Windows Live or Microsoft Account. Hyperlinks and emoticons can be added to the document text through the Insert tab as well.

Figure 8.19: New Message Insert Tab

The Options tab provides methods for encrypting, signing, and encoding your message, as well as the option to send the e-mail later. Encrypting the e-mail will help to ensure the contents of the message are more secure against eavesdropping.

Figure 8.20: New Message Options Tab

When you receive an attachment in an e-mail, you will see the file's icon at the top of the message window (Figure 8.21). Right click the attached file for options to open or save the attachment. Clicking the Open option will open the file with the default program. If no installed program can open that file type, you may be prompted to locate a program that can open the file. The Save As option will allow you to save the selected file with a specified name and location. The Save All option can be used to save all attached files in the current e-mail message to a location on your computer.

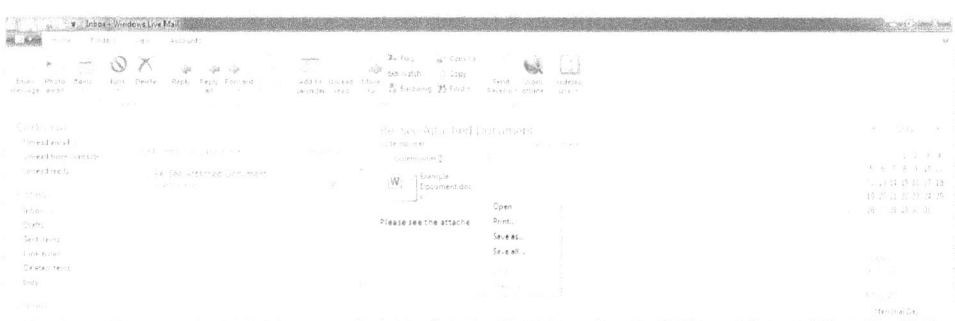

Figure 8.21: Saving Attachments

Now that we have explored setting up and accessing your e-mail, and sending new e-mail messages, we will look at the calendar portion of Windows Live Mail.

To access the calendar in Windows Live Mail, click on the Calendar link in the lower-left corner of the main program window. In the left pane you will see a small calendar and options for the types of calendar displayed. In the middle pane you will see the daily, weekly, or monthly view. To create a new event on the calendar, click the Event button on the Home tab.

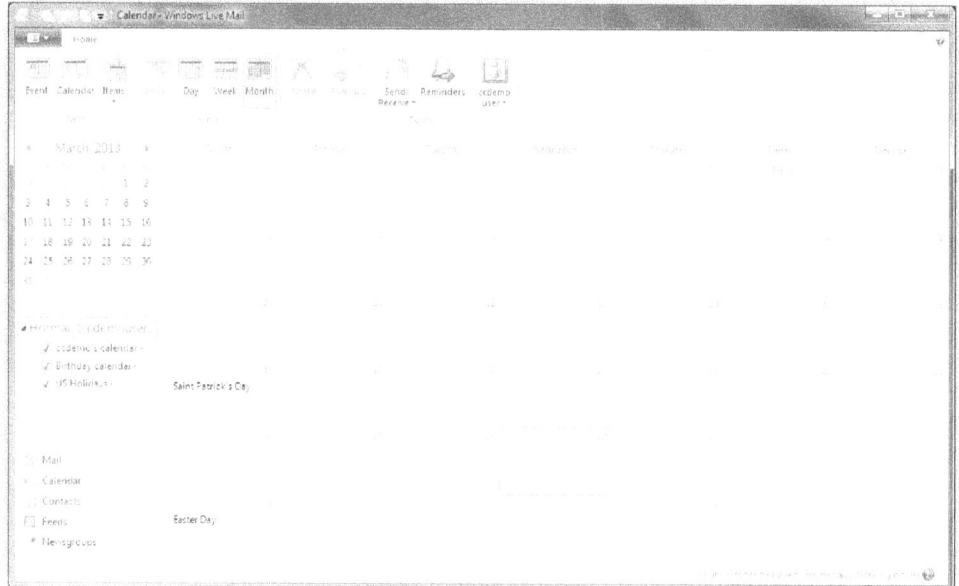

Figure 8.22: Calendar

In the New Event window you can create a subject name and location for the event. The date and time can be set by selecting from the drop-down menus on the screen. From the Event tab, you can save the event and forward it to recipients. You can also set reminders and choose the calendar name to save the event to.

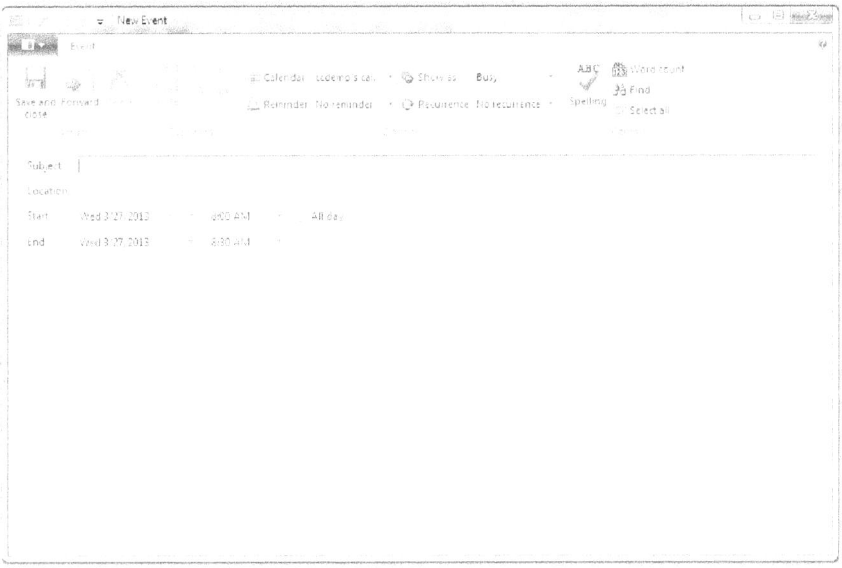

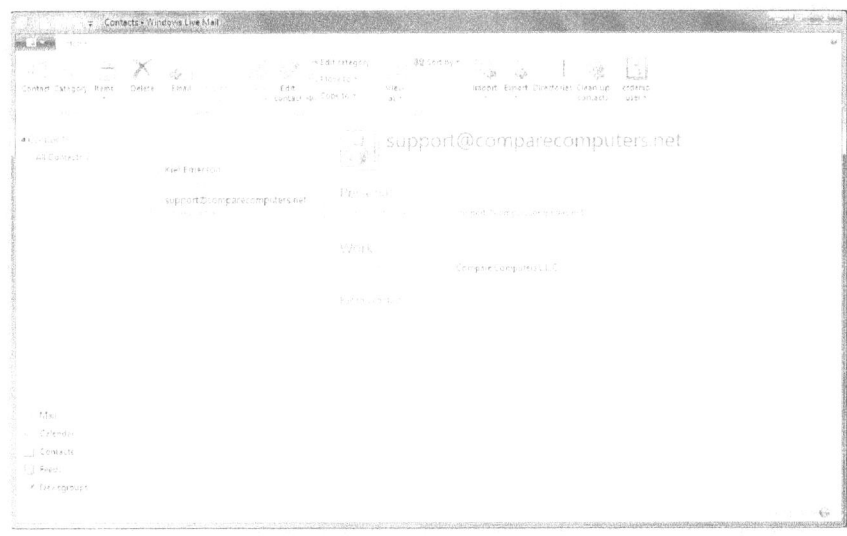

Figure 8.23: New Event Window

Clicking on the Contacts link in the lower-left corner will take you to the Contacts List in Windows Live Mail. The Home tab in the Contacts List can be used to add contacts and create categories for contacts. You can edit contact information by selecting the contact from the list and clicking the Edit Contact button. Your contact list can be exported into another format for use in another program or as a backup. Contacts can also be imported into your Contact List through the option on the Home tab.

Figure 8.24: Contacts

127

Clicking the Feeds link in the lower-left corner of the screen will load the Feeds window in Windows Live Mail. This feature displays RSS news feeds from websites that you have subscribed to. Many websites and news providers have RSS feeds on their website that you can subscribe to. RSS feeds are generally basic headlines and text that can provide information quickly and easily to an RSS reader like Windows Live Mail.

News feeds can be added via the Feed button on the Home tab. You can delete, forward, and manage feeds that you receive through the buttons on the Home tab. Clicking on a feed article will display the contents in the right-hand Preview Pane.

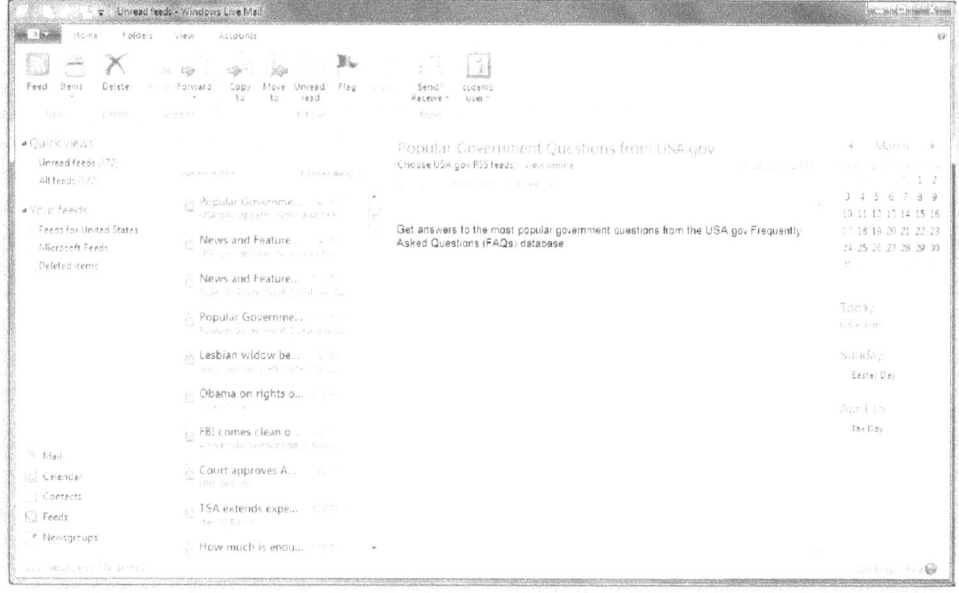

Figure 8.25: News Feeds

The Newsgroups link in the lower-left corner of the window will open the Newsgroup feature of Windows Live Mail. Newsgroups are similar to discussion forums on websites. You can read and reply to posted content on the newsgroup server. Since newsgroups are not commonly used by most users, we won't go into detail on this portion of Windows Live Mail.

Figure 8.26: Newsgroups

Now that we have explored the Windows Live Mail application we will move onto another program that is part of the Windows Live Essentials 2012 package – Microsoft SkyDrive.

Microsoft SkyDrive

SkyDrive is Microsoft's cloud storage platform for storing pictures, documents, and other files in the cloud. By signing into your Microsoft Account you can access your SkyDrive from any supported PC, tablet, and phone. You can also configure sharing and access to others, so that you can easily share pictures with family without sharing other personal files.

When you first launch SkyDrive, you will see a quick wizard that will step you through the process of syncing your files to the cloud. During this process you will be prompted to sign in with your Microsoft Account. If you don't have a Microsoft Account you can sign up for free by using the link in the same window.

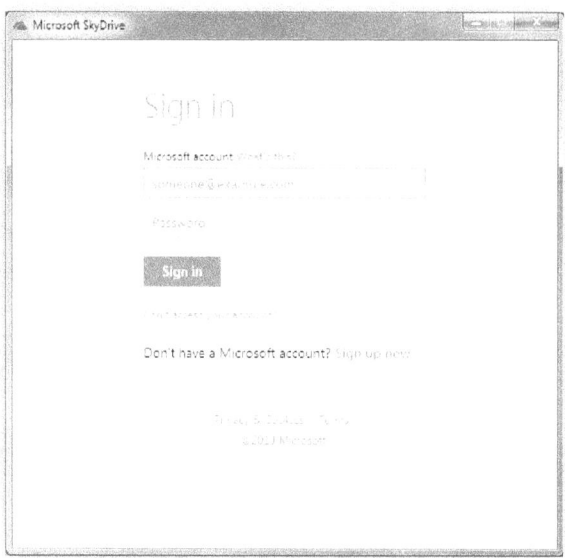

Figure 8.27: Microsoft SkyDrive Sign-in

After signing in to your Microsoft Account you will be able to choose the location for your local SkyDrive folder and select the folders in your SkyDrive that you want to sync to this PC.

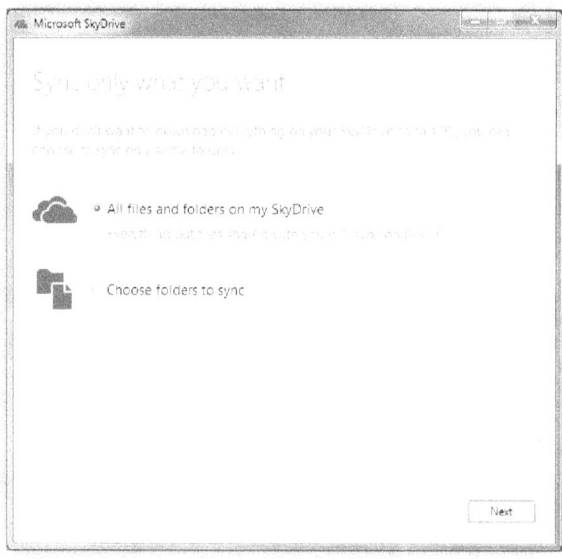

Figure 8.28: SkyDrive Sync Options

The Fetch feature can be used to access files on this PC that are not in your SkyDrive folder from other devices. Check the checkbox at the bottom of the window to use this feature.

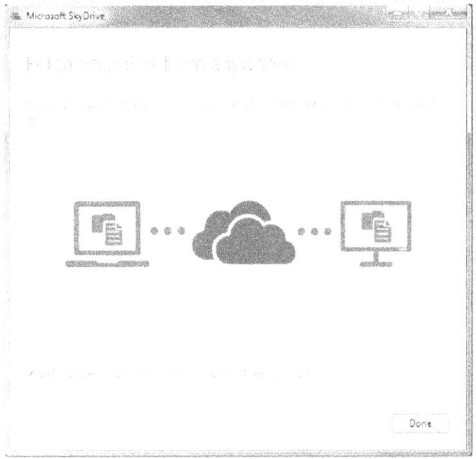

Figure 8.29: Enable Fetch Feature

After clicking the Done button, your local SkyDrive folder will open in Windows Explorer. Inside the SkyDrive folder you will see a Documents, Pictures, and Public folder. SkyDrive can be configured to allow or restrict access to files and folders in your drive. To adjust these sharing options, right-click the SkyDrive cloud icon in the Taskbar's notification area and choose the Go To SkyDrive.com option.

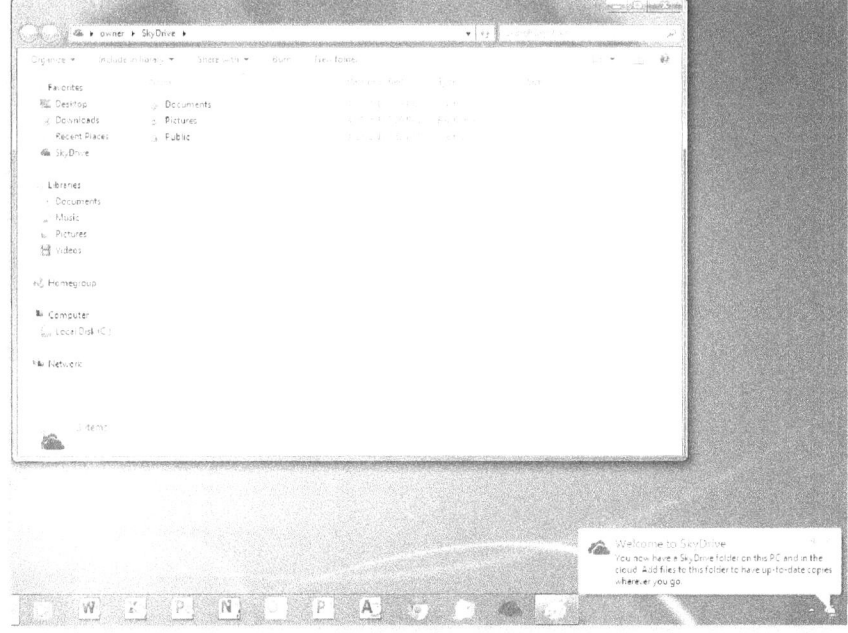

Figure 8.30: SkyDrive Folder

To adjust settings for the SkyDrive application, right-click the SkyDrive cloud icon in the Taskbar notification area. Choose the Settings option to change program settings, such as the folders you wish to sync and improve performance by using batch uploads.

Figure 8.31: SkyDrive Settings Context Menu

SkyDrive has made it easy to access files from anywhere on the internet. To access friends and family from anywhere online, you can use the Skype program for instant messaging and video chats.

Skype

Skype^{TM} is an instant messaging program that can also be used for voice and video calls to other computers and devices. The service can be used to make calls to an actual phone number for a charge. To use Skype, install the program on your PC if it isn't already installed and sign in with a Skype Account, Microsoft Account, or Facebook Account. All three accounts can be created for free if you don't already have one.

Figure 8.32: Skype Sign-in Window

After signing in you will see the Skype main window. The left-pane will list your Skype contacts and show their status. Contact will be sorted by their online status and name. Clicking on a contact's name will display their information in the right-pane. In the right-pane you can choose to call or video call the contact by clicking on one of the green Call buttons. The Video Call button will be displayed if you or your contact have a supported webcam available. To instant message your contact, you can simply type a message in the chat box at the bottom of the Skype window.

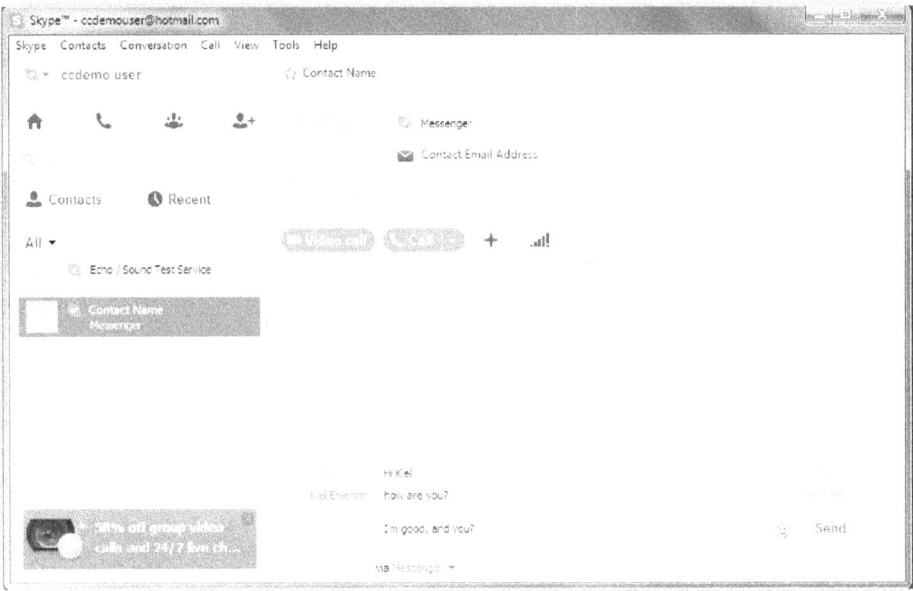

Figure 8.33: Skype Window

To call a phone number (charges apply) you can click on the phone icon to the right of the Home button. The right-pane will then display a dial pad for entering in the number you wish to call.

Figure 8.34: Dial Screen

To the right of the Phone button is the Group button. This feature allows you to drag contacts into the group area in the right-pane so that you can have a group chat or voice/video conference. Messages and calls made here will be available for all group members.

Figure 8.35: Group Conference Screen

The Add Contacts button is located to the right of the Group button. Enter the name, e-mail, number or Skype Name to search for and add a contact. The selected person will be visible in your contacts list once you have added them.

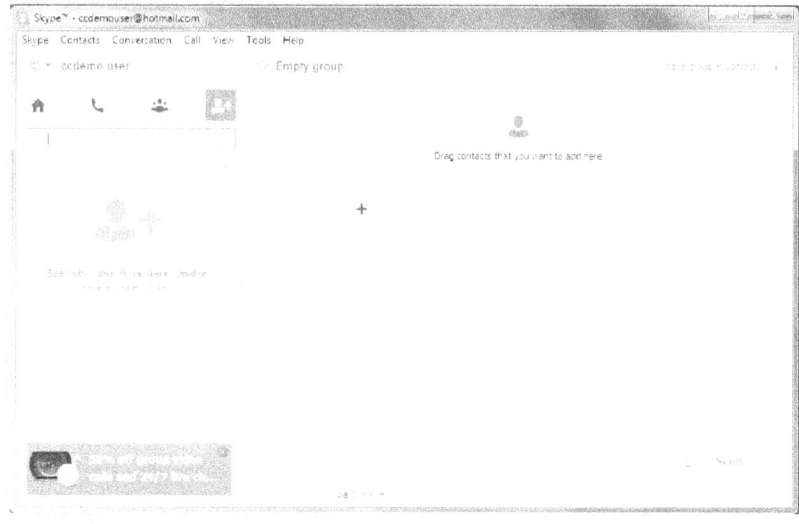

Figure 8.36: Add Contacts Screen

135

When you click the Video Call button, you will see a screen similar to Figure 8.37. The menu at the bottom of the screen can be used to turn on or off the webcam, microphone, and to end the call. The left side of the menu has options for showing your contacts and instant messaging window. You can view the call quality status and adjust the full-screen options on the right side of the menu.

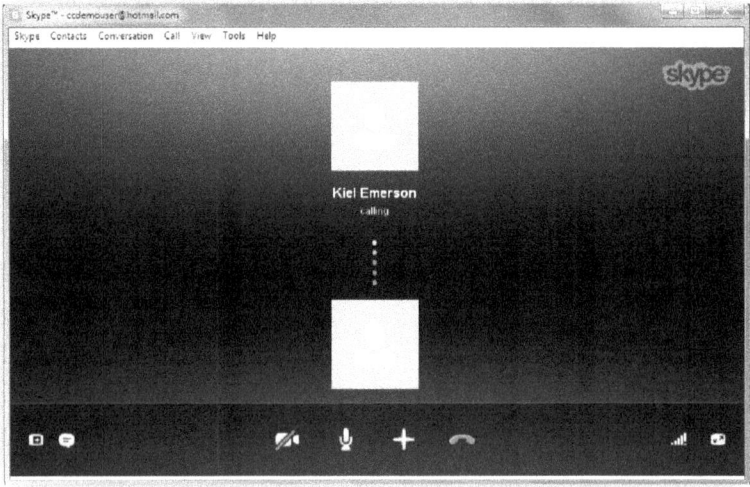

Figure 8.37: Calling a Contact

Clicking the plus icon in the middle of the video call menu bar gives you options for taking a picture, sending files, and sharing screens and contacts.

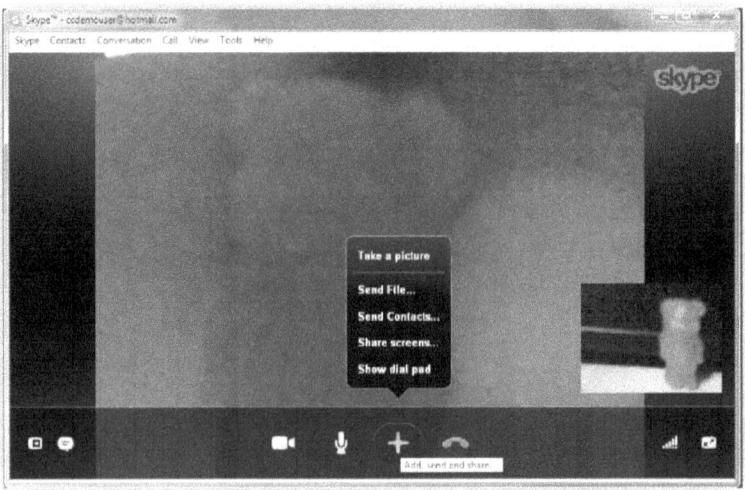

Figure 8.38: Call Menu Options

Once the contact answers the video call, you will be able to see their webcam and also a small thumbnail image of your webcam picture in the corner of the screen.

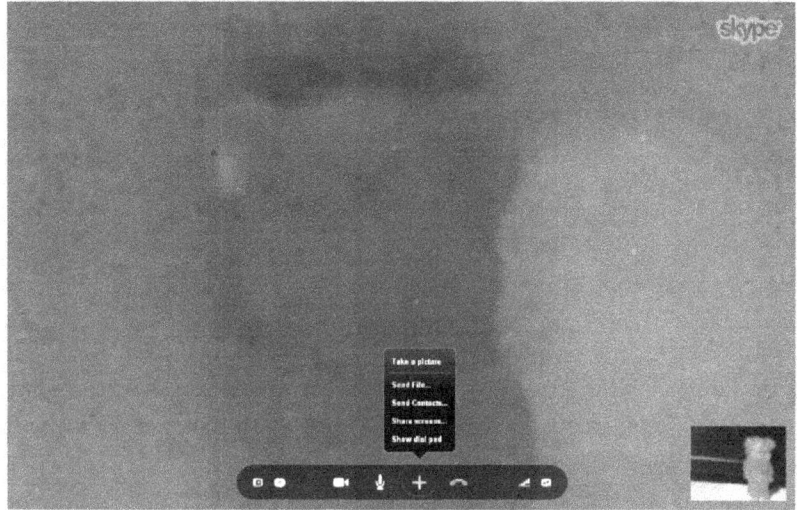

Figure 8.39: Video Call Window

If Skype is minimized during the video call you can still see a small video call window on the desktop.

Figure 8.40: Webcam Thumbnail Image

When someone sends you a video call request, you will see a popup similar to Figure 8.41. You can choose to answer the call, answer the call with video, or to decline the call.

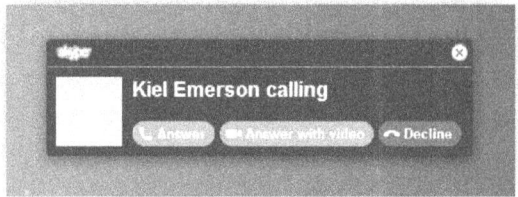

Figure 8.41: Incoming Call Prompt

To quit the Skype application, right-click on the Skype icon in your Taskbar notification area. Select Quit from the list and accept any confirmation messages about quitting the program you may receive.

Figure 8.42: Quit Skype Program

The next program we will explore is the Windows Photo Gallery application. This program can be used to view, import, and edit photos on the PC. Windows Photo Gallery is part of the Windows Live Essential 2012 package of programs.

Windows Photo Gallery

Windows Photo Gallery is a tool for easily sorting, editing, and sharing photos with others. When you first launch the program, photo and video folder locations are listed in the left pane, and photos and videos are grouped in the right pane.

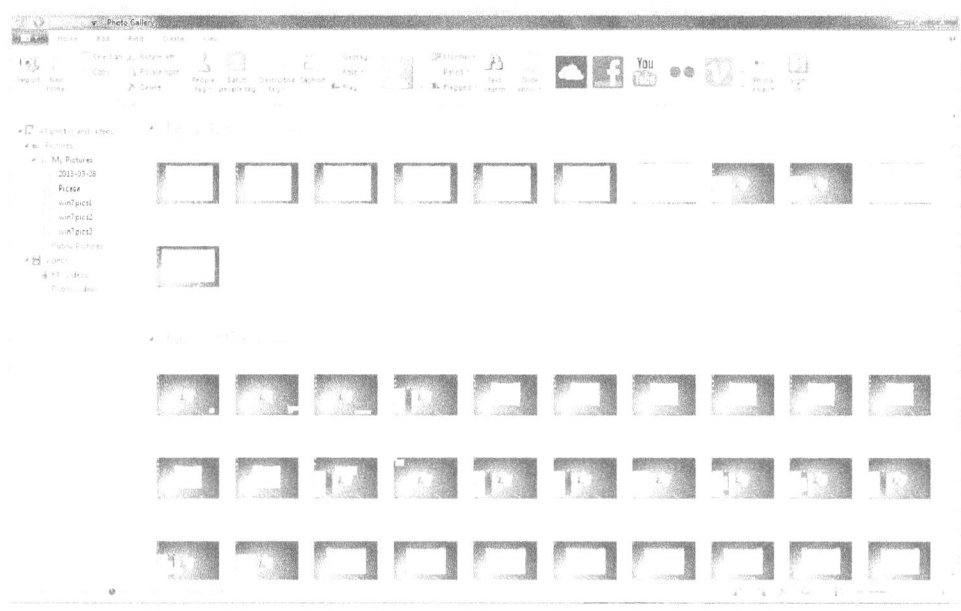

Figure 8.43: Windows Photo Gallery

The Home tab can be used to import images from a device. You can manipulate images with the Manage section options, and organize photos through tagging. Pictures and video can be shared through the listed social-media links in the Share section. You can use the Photo e-mail button to add selected photos to an e-mail in your default mail program.

Figure 8.44: Home Tab

The Edit tab can be used to make adjustments to pictures and apply filters to the image.

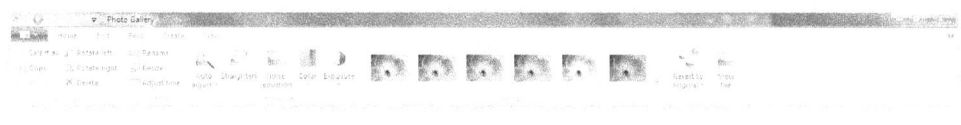

Figure 8.45: Edit Tab

The Find tab can locate pictures by date, tagged individuals, and by rating.

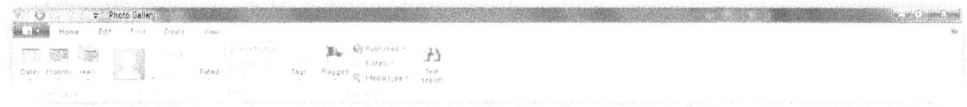

Figure 8.46: Find Tab

The Create tab is used to create images based on selected options. You can create a panorama from selected images or automatically create a collage. Pictures and video can be shared through the social-media sites listed, and also by e-mail and blog.

Figure 8.47: Create Tab

You can arrange photos through the View tab and also view photo details.

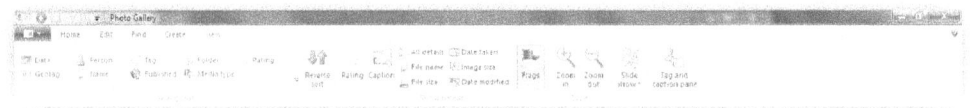

Figure 8.48: View Tab

To import pictures from your camera or other device, you can use the Import button on the Home tab. We will look at using the Import feature to import a picture from our all-in-one printer's scanner.

Figure 8.49: Import Button

After clicking the Import button, we will see a list of supported devices. I will select the MP280 all-in-one and click the Import button.

Figure 8.50: Import Photos and Videos Window

From the New Scan window you can preview the scan and adjust the settings for the scanned image. When you are ready to scan in the image to a file, click the Scan button. This process will take a short time, during which you will see a progress bar on the screen.

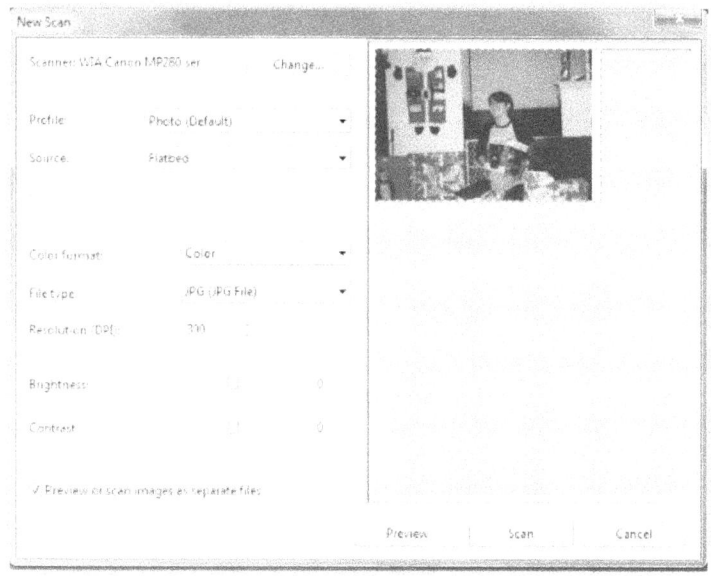

Figure 8.51: New Scan Window

After the file is saved to the PC you will be able to edit the image by double-clicking the photo in Windows Photo Gallery. At the top of the screen you will see options for editing the photo and applying filters. To crop the image click the Crop button. Use your mouse to select the desired area of the picture to crop.

Figure 8.52: Edit Image – Crop Photo

To remove red eye from a photo you can click the Red Eye button. Drag a box around the eye that needs to be modified.

Figure 8.53: Remove Red Eye

To e-mail a photo in Windows Photo Gallery, click the Photo E-mail drop-down button. You can either send a photo e-mail or send the photos as an attachment in an e-mail.

Figure 8.54: Photo E-Mail Options

Sending the photos as a photo e-mail will upload the pictures to SkyDrive for a limited time. This will reduce the size of the e-mail being sent since the pictures are not being added on to the e-mail itself. This feature requires a free Microsoft Account to use.

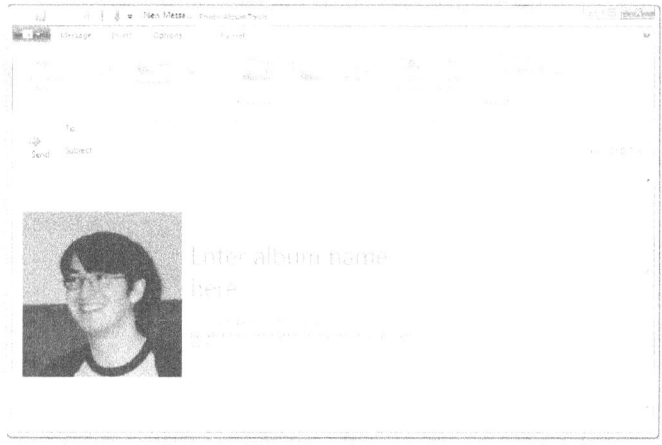

Figure 8.55: Photo E-mail

The second option, Send Photos as Attachments, will attach the selected photos to an e-mail using your default mail program. Depending on the size and number of photos attached, this may greatly increase the size of the e-mail being sent. This is the traditional way that many pictures are sent via e-mail.

Figure 8.56: Send Photos as Attachments

While using specific features of the Windows Photo Gallery or Windows Live Mail programs, you may be prompted to sign in with your e-mail address or Microsoft Account. You may see a screen similar to Figure 8.57. If you don't have a Microsoft Account, click the Sign Up link in the window to create a free account to utilize those features of the program.

Figure 8.57: Windows Live Sign-in

Now that we have covered working with Windows 7 and using programs in the new OS, in Chapter 9 we will turn our focus towards exploring one of the most commonly used programs today, Microsoft Office. In this chapter we will look at Microsoft Office 2010.

Chapter Review Questions:
1. Name two ways to attach a picture to a new e-mail in Windows Live Mail and explain the advantages of each method?
2. What feature of SkyDrive can be used to access files on your PC that are not being synced in your SkyDrive folder?
3. Describe the process of scanning a photograph into Windows Photo Gallery.

Chapter 9 – Microsoft Office 2010

Microsoft Office 2010 was released around the launch time of Windows 7 and is one of the most frequently used program suites for the operating system. Microsoft Office 2010 is a separate program from Windows 7, just as it has been with all previous versions of Windows. Microsoft Office 2010 is compatible with Windows XP, Windows Vista, Windows 7, and Windows 8. The Home and Student versions of Microsoft Office 2010 include Word, Excel, PowerPoint, and OneNote. Other versions of the Microsoft Office 2010 Suite include the programs in the Home and Student version, as well as some of the other Office programs like Outlook, Access, Publisher, and Lync.

If Microsoft Office 2010 is not already installed on your PC, you will need to install it with a retail disc or by downloading the installer from the office.com website. Some Windows 7 computers may have a trial preinstalled or a Microsoft Office 2010 link on the Start Menu, like in Figure 9.1.

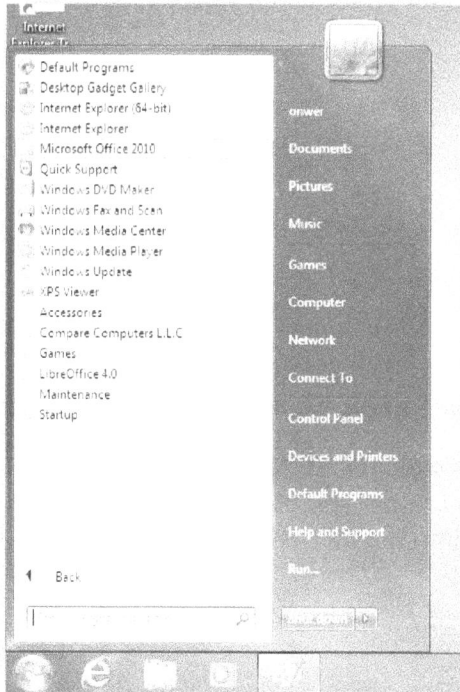

Figure 9.1: Microsoft Office 2010 Preinstalled Link

Clicking on the Start Menu link (see Figure 9.1) will launch the Microsoft Office 2010 window (see Figure 9.2). If you have already purchased Microsoft Office 2010, you can activate the software by clicking the Activate button. If you wish to purchase Microsoft Office 2010, you can click the Purchase button. The Use button will allow you to use Microsoft Office Starter

2010, which is a very basic version of Microsoft Word and Microsoft Excel. Not all features are present in this version of Microsoft Office and there will be a small ad on the side of the screen.

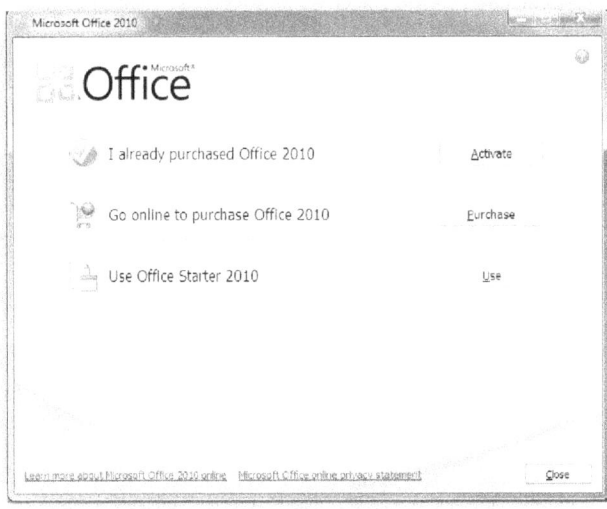

Figure 9.2: Preinstalled Microsoft Office 2010 Window

When beginning the Microsoft Office 2010 installation from the Use link, from a CD, or from a download installer, you must type in the product key and agree to the End User License Agreement in order to use and install the software. Click the checkbox and Continue button to agree to the terms.

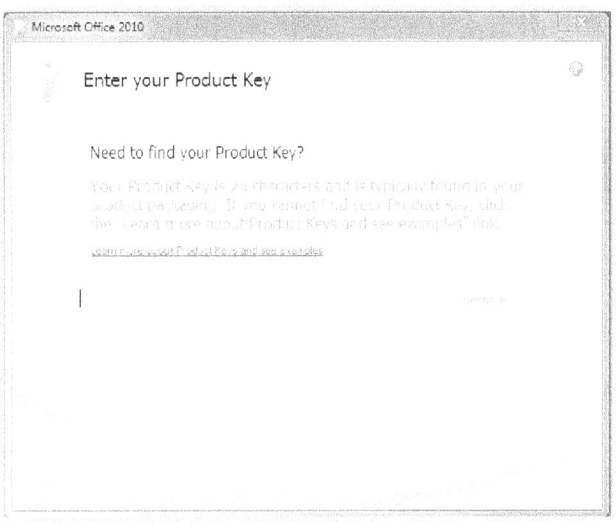

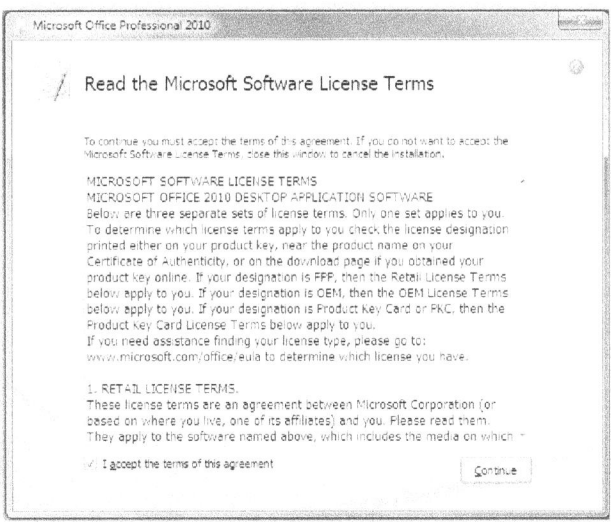

Figure 9.3: Office 2010 End User License Agreement

Click the Install Now button in the following window to begin the installation, or you can click the Customize button to change default installation settings.

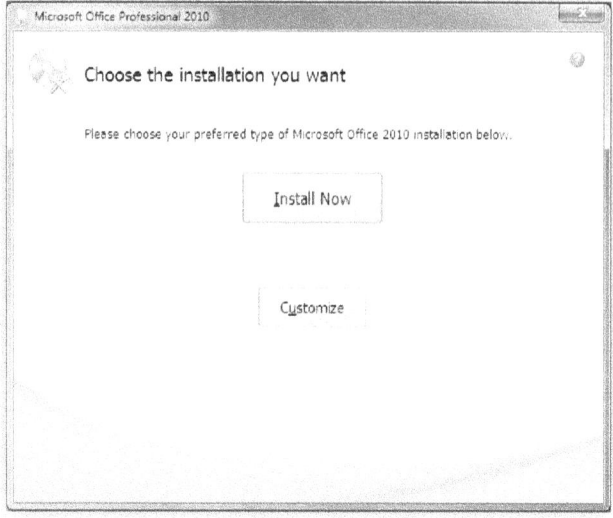

Figure 9.4: Choose Installation Window

It will take a few minutes for the software to install. The progress bar will advance during the installation.

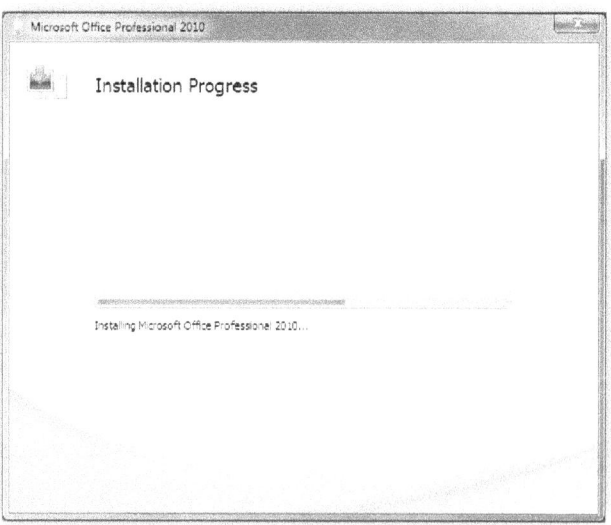

Figure 9.5: Installation Progress

When the installation is complete you will see the window in Figure 9.6. Click the Close button to finish the installation. Programs installed during the setup process will now be located in a folder on your Start Menu.

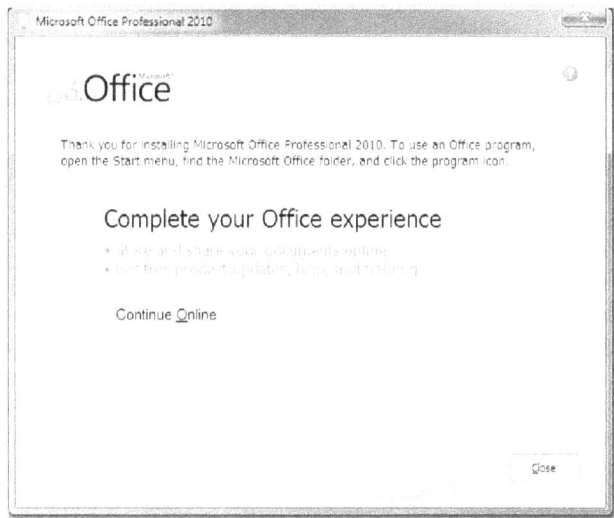

Figure 9.6: Installation Complete Window

Chapter Review Questions:

1. Name the three ways that Microsoft Office 2010 can be installed on your PC?
2. Describe the differences between Office Starter 2010 and the full version of Microsoft Office 2010.

Chapter 10 – Word 2010

Microsoft Word is one of the most commonly used programs in the Office Suite. It is used for word processing, mailings, and creating basic printouts. Click on the Microsoft Word link under the Microsoft Office 2010 folder on the Start Menu to launch the program.

First Use Setup and Activation

During your first use of an Office Suite program you will be prompted to activate the software. After activation is complete you will need to choose an option for keeping the Office software secure and up-to-date. I recommend selecting the first option to use the recommended settings. You can also choose to install only updates, or to be prompted for an answer at a later time.

Figure 10.1: Office Update Options

Word 2010 Window Layout

Now that the initial setup process is complete, we can start to use Microsoft Word. On the initial screen when you open the program you will find a blank document. You can also open a template by clicking the File menu and selecting a template under the New option. For now we will just use the blank document to get started.

Figure 10.2: Word Blank Document

Along the top of the screen, you will notice the tabbed Ribbon UI with tabs and icons for performing various tasks in the program. Common tasks are located in the Home tab, which is open by default. Other tabs allow you to insert pictures and content, review page layout, and change a number of formatting options. In the pictures that follow we will break down some of the features in each tab.

Word 2010 Ribbon User Interface

Under the Home tab, you can cut, copy, and paste from the clipboard; adjust the font, font size, and font style options; adjust text layout and formatting; and select a style for titles, headers, and regular text. Styles allow you to change similar sections throughout your text (such as a heading) by only changing one setting. This saves you from having to manually change the format of each occurrence of a type of text. You can also find and replace specified text in a document from the Home tab.

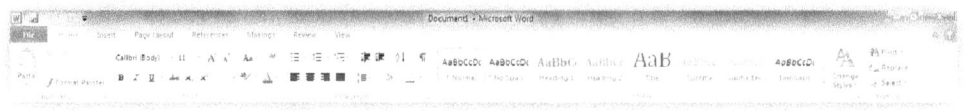

Figure 10.3: Home Tab

In the Insert tab you can insert items into the document. You can insert types of pages and page breaks; insert tables, pictures, text, and shapes; insert headers, footers, and page numbers;

and insert objects, equations, and symbols.

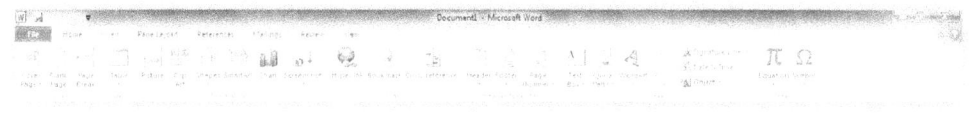

Figure 10.4: Insert Tab

The Page Layout tab allows you to choose document formatting options for the document. You can adjust theme colors and fonts, and also adjust spacing for document text. Watermarks, page colors, and page borders can also be changed through this tab.

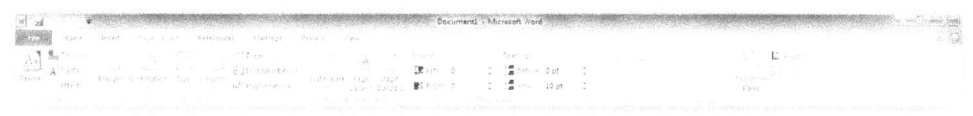

Figure 10.5: Page Layout

Under the References tab you can set up a table of contents, add footnotes, set up citations and bibliography, and add captions. This tab also allows you to add an index reference for specific page numbers and add a table of authorities to your document. When you add content to your paper, features like the table of contents and index references will be automatically updated.

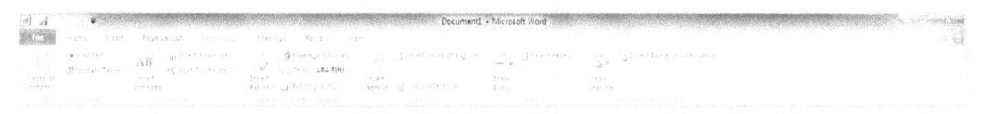

Figure 10.6: References Tab

The Mailings tab is used to create envelope and label printouts. From this tab you can import contacts from a contacts list into a mailing list.

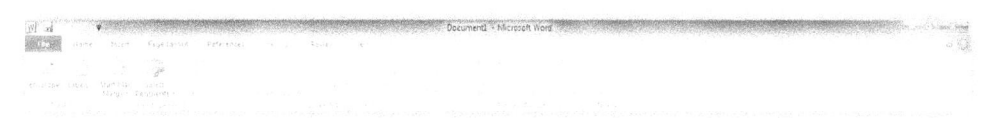

Figure 10.7: Mailings Tab

Under the Review tab you can check spelling and grammar, check definitions, and check synonyms for a word. Language and translation options are available for modifying selected text. You can also use the comments, changes, and markup options to keep track of document notes and modifications, then accept or reject those changes. You can use the Review tab's compare feature to view differences between two versions of a document. Editing can be limited by using the Restrict Editing option as well.

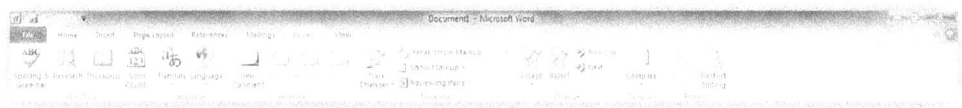

Figure 10.8: Review Tab

The View tab lets you configure the reading mode and layout of the document onscreen. You can add onscreen components, such as the ruler bar and gridlines, to the window. The view can be modified to include multiple pages on the screen at the same time, or multiple windows on the screen.

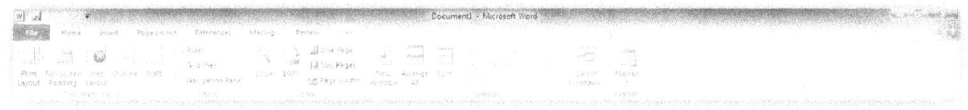

Figure 10.9: View Tab

Word 2010 File Menu Interface

Clicking on the File tab on the Ribbon UI will open the File Options window. From here you can perform many file tasks, like opening, printing, saving, and modifying properties for the document.

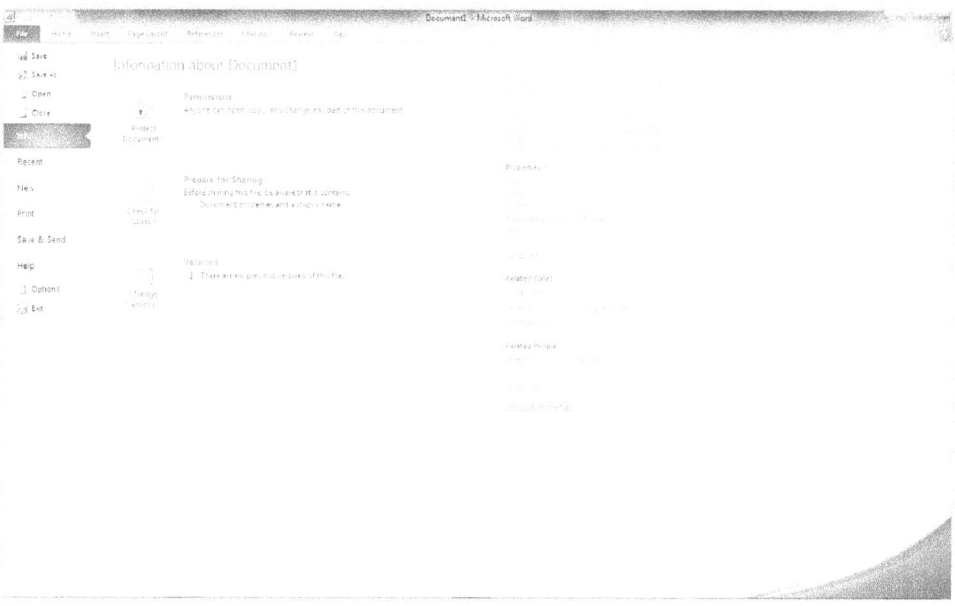

Figure 10.10: File Options

The Save As option in the File menu lets you choose how and where to save the current document. You can browse for a location to save your document by using the links in the left-pane or navigating with the Address Bar. To change the filename simply position your cursor in the File Name text box and type the name you desire. The file type can be changed by clicking on the drop-down file type box and choosing the type of file you want from the list.

Figure 10.11: Save As

The Open link will open a new window where you can browse for documents stored locally on your PC. You can also browse for documents stored on your HomeGroup or network by using this option.

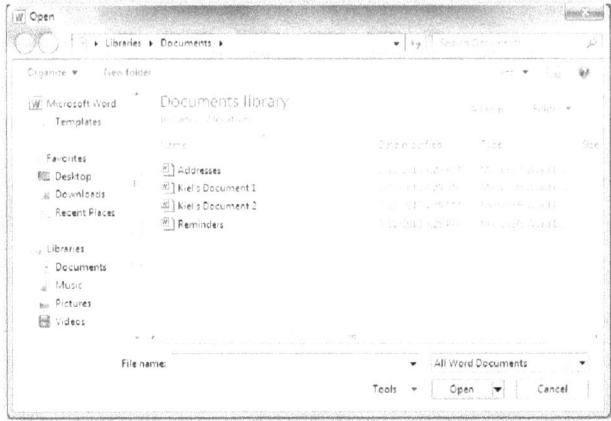

Figure 10.12: Open File Dialog Box

The next entry in the File Options left pane is the Info screen. Clicking on this link will display information about the currently open file. You can view properties, such as title and author for the file, as well as view previous versions and protect the document from modifications.

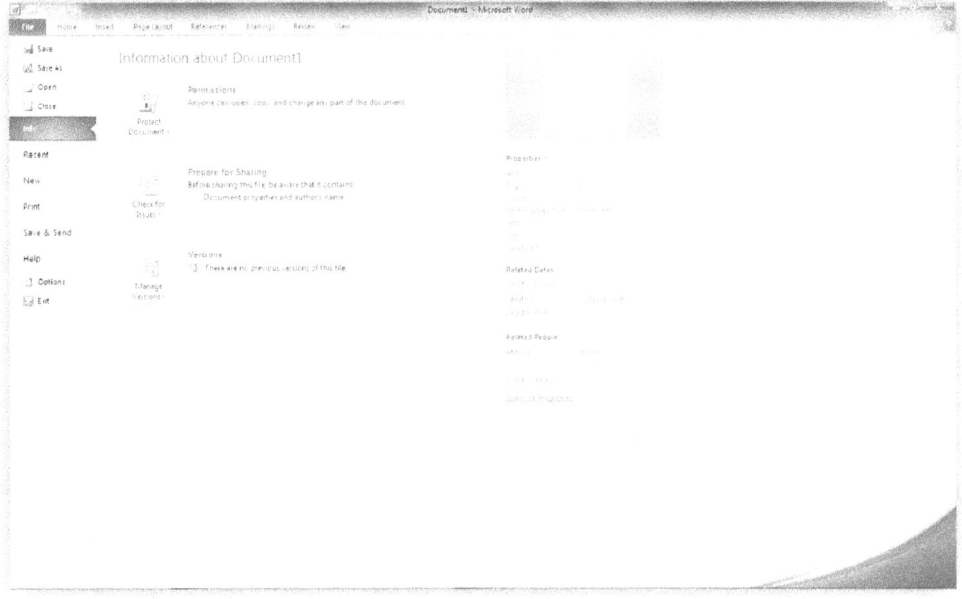

Figure 10.13: Info Screen

The next option down from New is the Open option. From this screen you can open a recent file or other document stored on your PC.

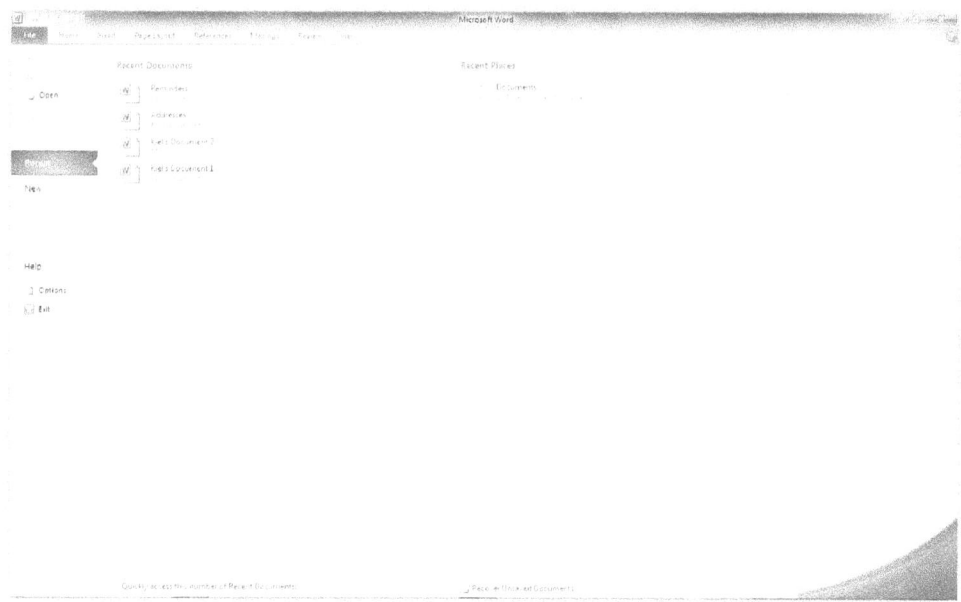

Figure 10.14: Open File Screen

The New link allows you to open a new blank file or one of the many preformatted templates on the screen. You can search for terms to find a template available on office.com.

Figure 10.15: New Document Screen

Under the Print option you will see a print preview of the current document on the right and various print options to the left. From here you can choose the printer, number of copies, and page options for the print.

Figure 10.16: Print Options

The Page Setup link will open the Page Setup window. From here you can adjust settings relating to page margins, layout, and the type of paper being used for printing. Figure 10.17 shows the options available.

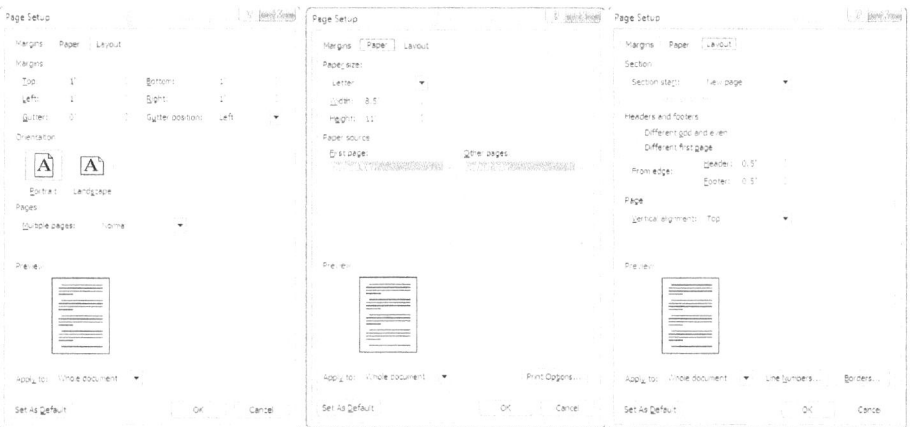

Figure 10.17: Page Setup

To print to a printer other than your default printer, click on the printer drop-down box and select the desired device from the list. Virtual devices like an electronic fax, XPS Document Writer, and PDF printers may appear in the list. Often these virtual devices will "print" to a document file on your PC, such as printing to create a PDF document.

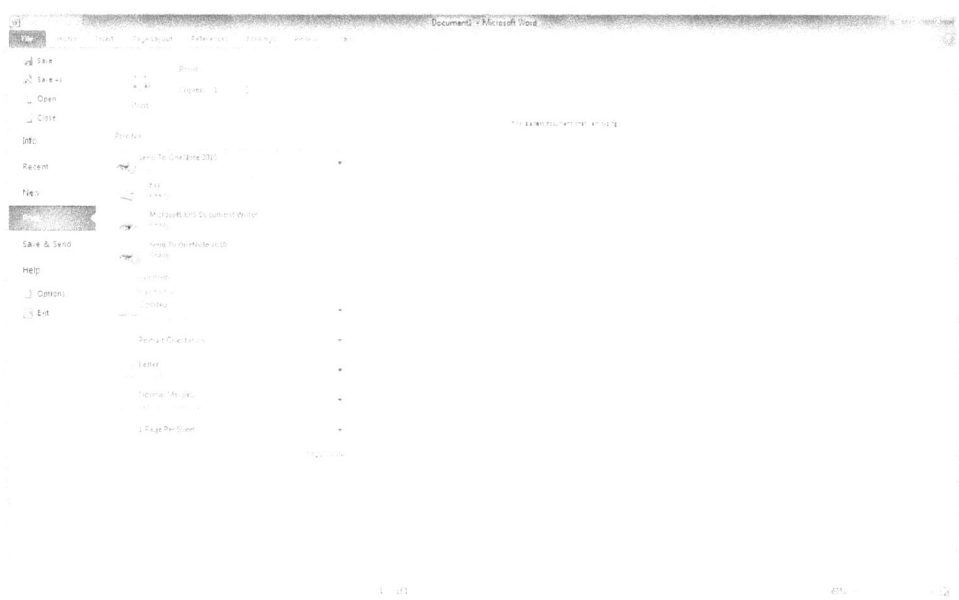

Figure 10.18: Select Printer

The Save & Send option allows you to share your document by e-mail to a contact, or to post online or to a blog. The e-mail options include sending the file as an attachment using your default mail program, sending a link to a file stored in a shared location like a public cloud folder, creating a PDF or XPS document, or faxing the document using internet fax.

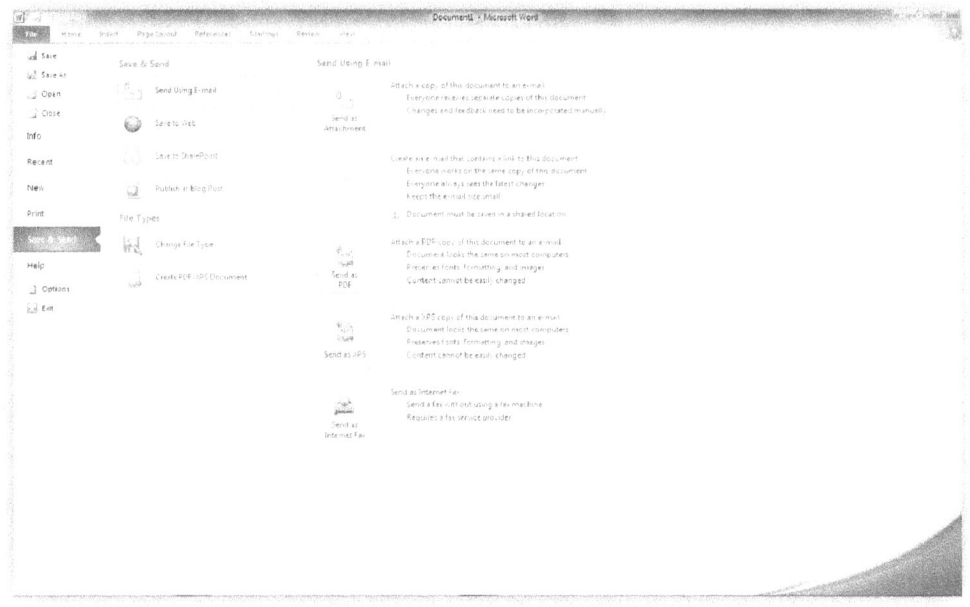

Figure 10.19: E-mail Sharing Options

The Save to Web option allows you to access the document from another PC and to share the file with others by using you Windows Live ID/Microsoft Account.

Figure 10.20: Save to Web

For business users with access to a SharePoint site, you can save the file to the shared location for others to access and collaborate on the document.

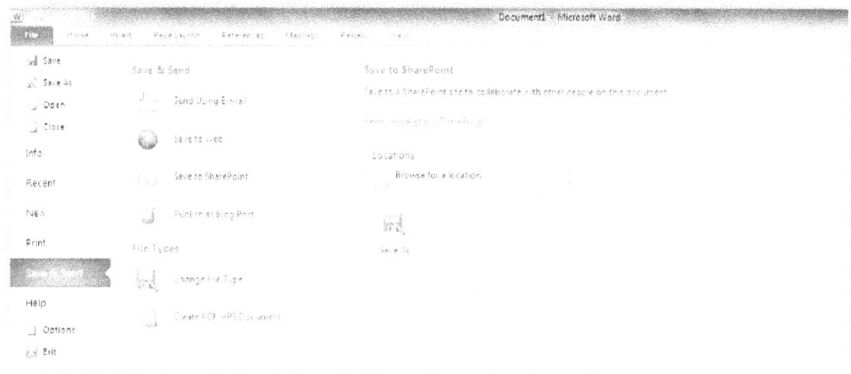

Figure 10.21: Save to SharePoint

The Publish as Blog Post feature can create a new blog post using the current document and supports a number of different blogging services.

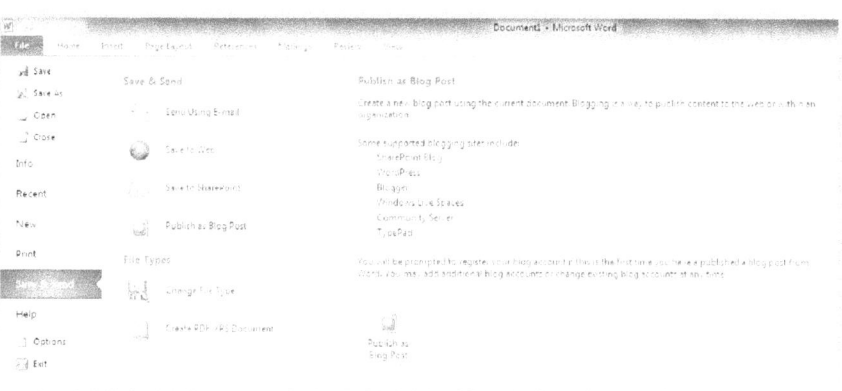

Figure 10.22: Publish To Blog

The Save & Send Change File Type option allows you to save the document in a different format, such as a PDF and XPS document, or in a format for use with an earlier version of Word or an entirely different program.

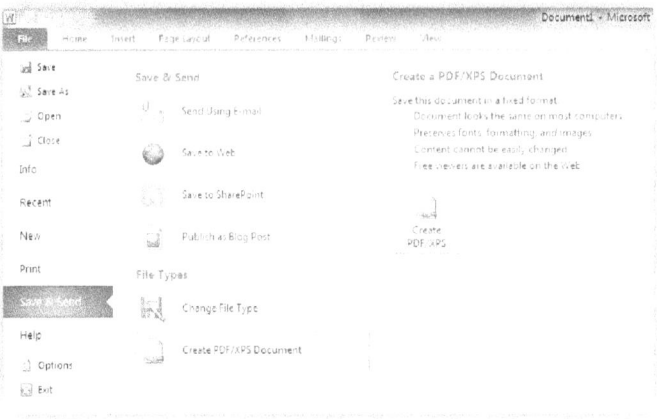

Figure 10.23: Export Options

Next we will look at how to perform some common tasks in Word 2010.

Word 2010 Basic Tasks

To change the font style or size, simply highlight the text you wish to modify. Then choose the desired font style or size from the dropdown list on the Home tab. You can also make the font and size changes before you start typing.

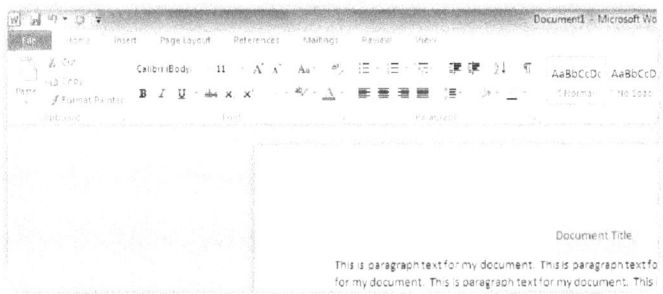

Figure 10.24: Select Text

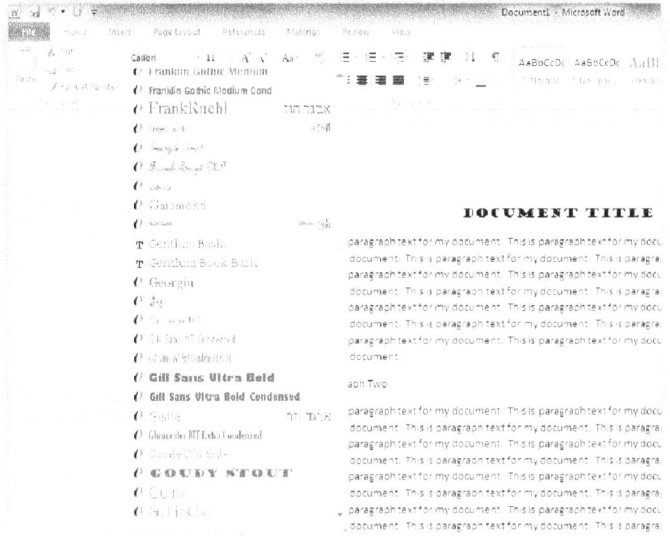

Figure 10.25: Change Font

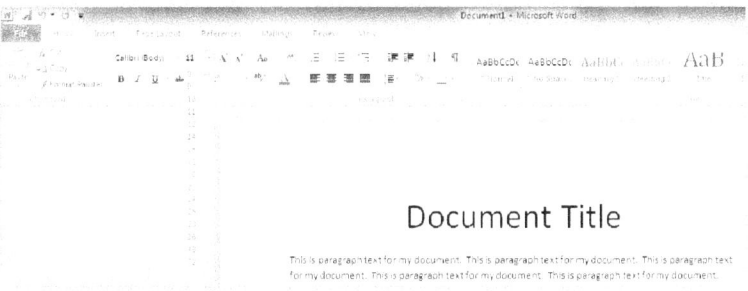

Figure 10.26: Change Font Size

To change the orientation of text on the page you can use the left align, right align, or centering options as seen in Figure 10.27.

Figure 10.27: Text Centering Options

To modify the tabs, line and paragraph indentions, and line spacing, click the Paragraph dialog box button. This button is located in the lower-right corner of the Paragraph section on the Home tab.

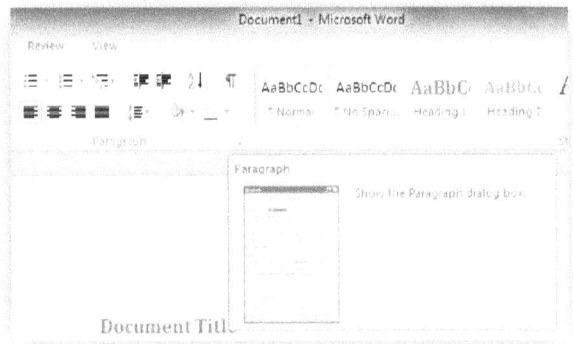

Figure 10.28: Paragraph Dialog Box Button

This dialog box will allow you to adjust the text alignment, line spacing, and configure first-line paragraph indents and hanging indents. You can also set up tab spacing by clicking the Tabs button at the bottom of the window.

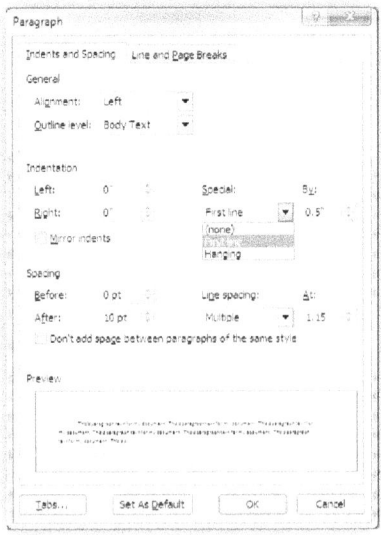

Figure 10.29: Paragraph Dialog Box

Setting styles for types of text in a document is another common task in Microsoft Office 2010 and previous versions. Instead of having to manually change the font, size, and color of every individual header, title, and paragraph in a document, you can set up styles that update each type of text with the font, color, and size you set. So if you wanted to change the color of every header in your document, you only need to change the color of the header in the style, instead of each instance of a header.

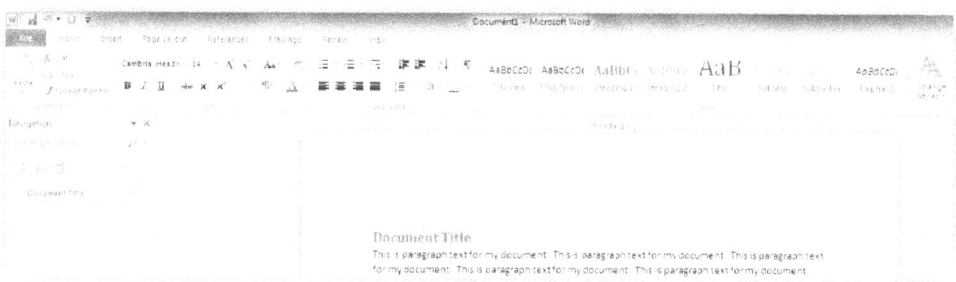

Figure 10.30: Heading 1 Style

To modify the default settings for a particular style, click the Styles dialog box button. This button is located in the lower-right corner of the Styles section of the Home tab.

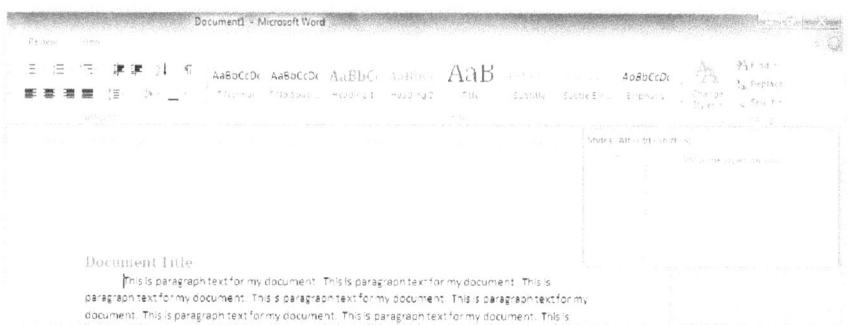

Figure 10.31: Styles Dialog Box Button

Select the Modify option from the drop-down list on the style you wish to modify. This will open a new window allowing you to change numerous settings for the selected style.

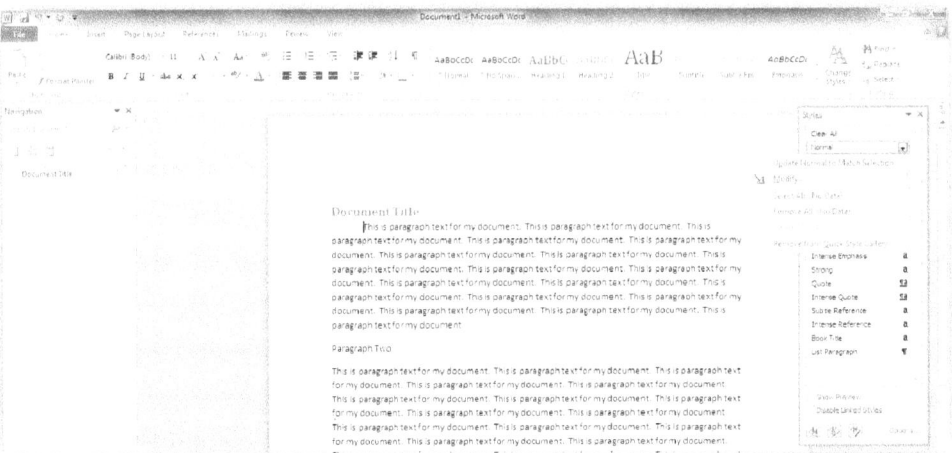

Figure 10.32: Styles Dialog Box

As an example, we may want to create a rule for the Normal style that creates a first-line paragraph indentation. In the Modify Style box, click the Format button in the lower-left corner. Select Paragraph from the list. This will open the Paragraph Indents and Spacing window that was previously discussed. However, these settings will only apply to any text in the document with the selected style.

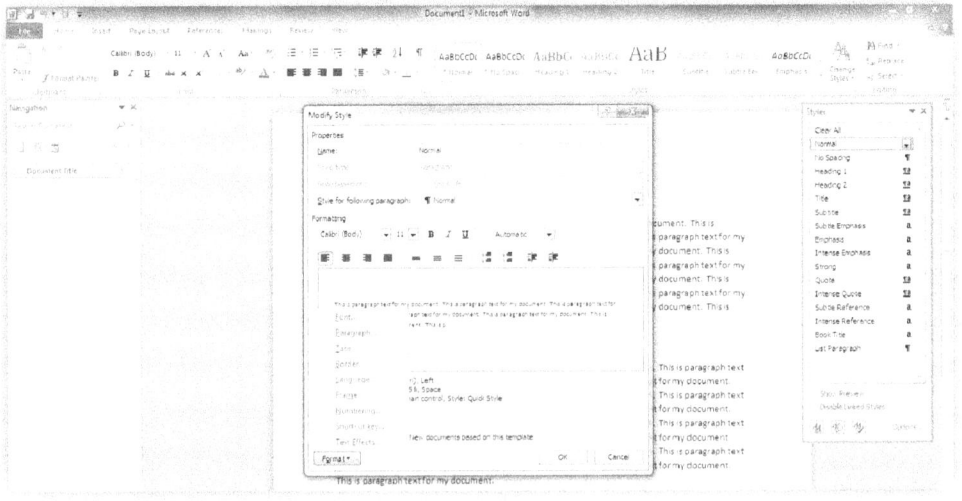

Figure 10.33: Modify Styles Formatting

Choosing the First Line indent option will change all of the text in the document with the

Normal style to have a first line indentation while leaving all other styles formatted the way they were.

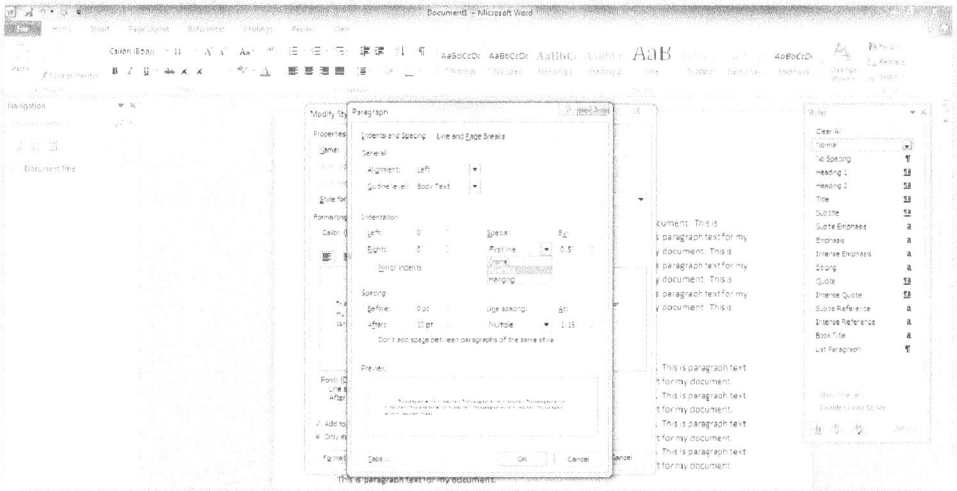

Figure 10.34: Paragraph Dialog Box

In Figure 10.35 we can modify the color, font size, and layout of the Heading 2 style. There are many options that can be adjusted for each style. You will find that these options let you quickly format a document to have the layout you want.

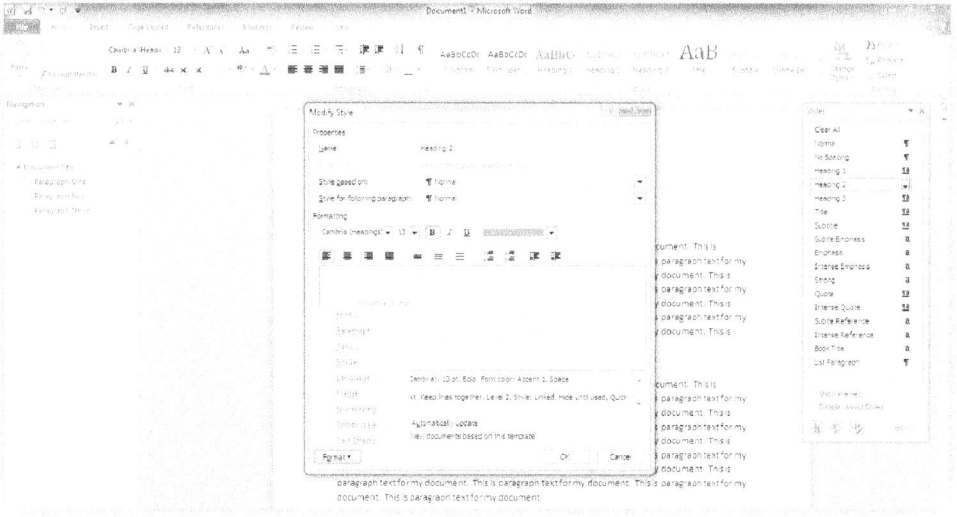

Figure 10.35: Modify Styles Formatting

> Use Styles to easily make quick changes to a variety of text formats throughout your document.

Inserting tables, pictures, and clip art are all common tasks in word processing. Click on the Insert tab and select Picture to browse your available pictures to add to the document.

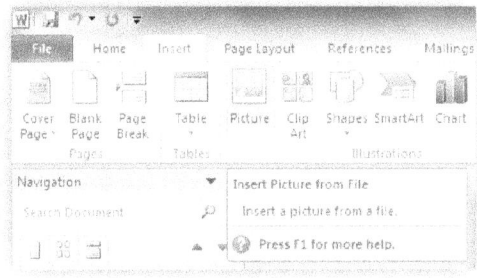

Figure 10.36: Insert Picture Button

After choosing the Insert Picture option you can browse to the location where your pictures are stored (normally your Pictures Library). Select the image you wish to add, then click the Insert button.

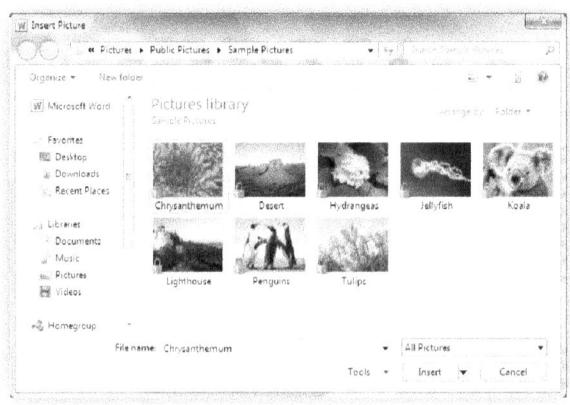

Figure 10.37: Browse for Picture

The image will be added to the document. When the image is selected with your cursor in the document, you will see the Picture Tools tab on the Ribbon. This tab can be used to resize, crop, and style the image.

Figure 10.38: Add a Picture

To adjust the margins in Word 2010, click on the Page Layout tab and then select the Margins button. You can select a preset margin from the dropdown box or click on the Custom Margins link to manually enter margins.

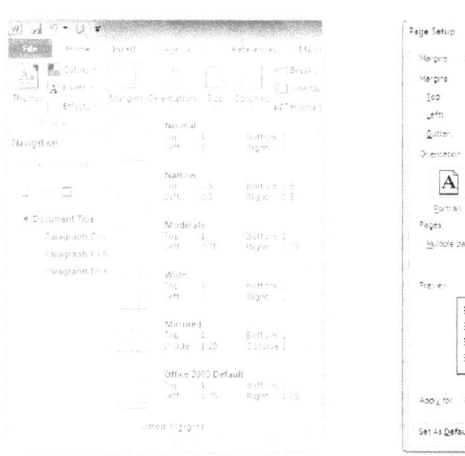

Figure 10.39: Set Page Margins

To check spelling and grammar in the document, click the Review tab, then click the Spelling & Grammar button on the left. Word will scan your document for any problems and prompt you if any corrections may need to be made. You will see a message that the check is complete once all errors have been addressed.

Figure 10.40: Check Spelling & Grammar

At times you may need to either locate a specific word or replace one word with another. The Find feature can be used to locate each instance of a word in the document. The Replace feature will allow you to enter a search term to locate in the document, and also the text you would like to use to replace that search term.

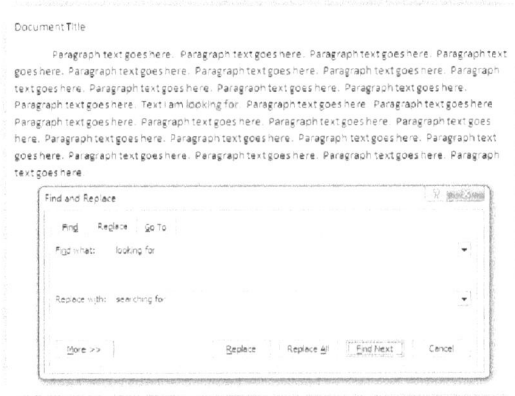

Figure 10.41: Find and Replace Feature

One last common task in Microsoft Word is printing envelopes and labels. To begin printing an envelope, click the Mailings tab followed by the Envelopes button. In the window that opens you can type the mailing address to be printed in the top box and the return address in the bottom box. If you need to print envelopes for a number of contacts on your PC, you can select the contacts button located above the delivery address section. You can then choose multiple contacts from your contacts list instead of manually typing each address separately.

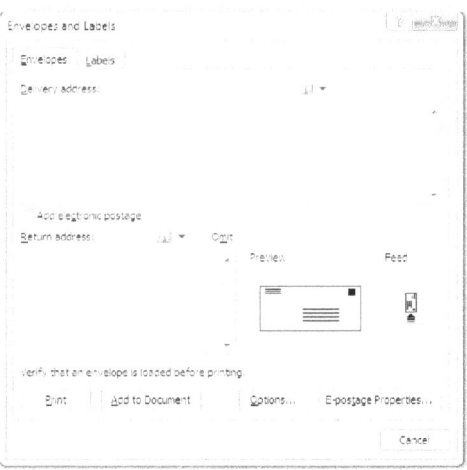

Figure 10.42: Envelopes and Mailings

Next we will take a look at the features of Excel 2010 and how to use the program.

Chapter Review Questions:
1. Explain the advantages for using Styles instead of manual adjustments in order to manage formatting in a large document.
2. Describe the steps for inserting a picture from your Pictures Library into a document.
3. Explain the steps for adding a page number header to each page in a document.

Chapter 11 – Excel 2010

Another commonly used Office Suite program is Microsoft Excel. Excel is used for creating spreadsheets, tables, and graphs. Data can be input into forms and manipulated using formulas. That data can then be used to create visual content for tables, charts, and graphs, to more easily interpret data than just numbers.

Excel 2010 Window Layout

When you open Excel 2010 you will find a blank spreadsheet with a grid for entering in columns and rows of data, the Ribbon UI along the top of the screen, and a formula bar underneath the ribbon. To add or rename spreadsheets to the workbook click the tabs in the lower left corner of the window. We will take a look at the Ribbon UI for Excel and explore some of the program's features.

Figure 11.1: Excel Blank Spreadsheet

Excel 2010 Ribbon User Interface

The Home tab contains common tools used in Excel. You can cut, copy, and paste from the clipboard; adjust the font, font size, and font style options; adjust text layout and formatting; and format cells. The Number section lets you format the type of data in the cell as a number, percentage, or currency, as well as set the number of decimal places shown. A series of entries can be totaled with the AutoSum feature. The Fill option can fill a cell entry down a specified number of rows. You can also find and replace specified text in a document from the Home tab.

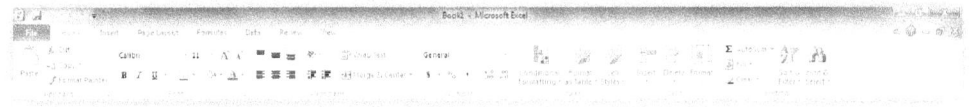

Figure 11.2: Home Tab

In the Insert tab you can insert items into the document. You can insert charts and pivot tables; insert pictures, text, and shapes; insert headers and footers; and insert objects, equations, and symbols.

Figure 11.3: Insert Tab

In the Page Layout tab you can adjust the margins, page orientation, size, and themes. This tab can configure the print area, width and height, and sheet options, as well as object orientation on the page.

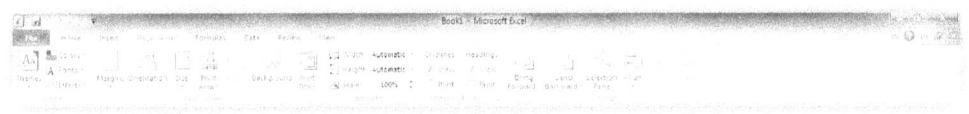

Figure 11.4: Page Layout

The Formulas tab provides links to the many functions available in Excel, grouped by their category. Click on the function category for a dropdown list of common functions. Name Manager is used to manage each of the cell names used as reference points in the spreadsheet. The formula auditing section of the Formulas tab can track cells used in calculations and show formulas for those calculations. The calculation options let you change when formulas in a spreadsheet are calculated.

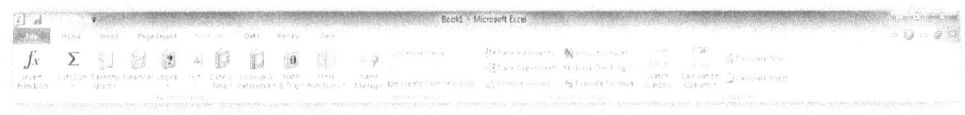

Figure 11.5: Formulas Tab

The Data tab has items relating to data in the spreadsheet. The External Data options on the left side of the Data tab are for importing information from an external source. The Connections section shows and refreshes the connections to the external data sources. The Sort and Filter section lets you sort or filter information in the spreadsheet. The Data Tools group lets you separate text in one cell into separate columns, remove duplicate entries, and validate data is within specified constraints. You can also use the What If Analysis to check the effect different values have on a formula. The Outline group allows for grouping cells together for consolidation.

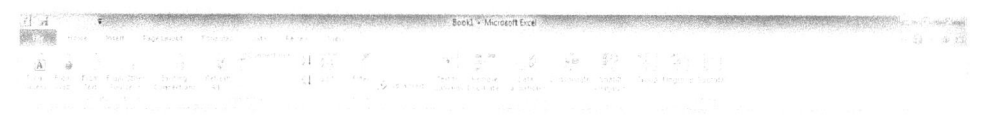

Figure 11.6: Data Tab

Under the Review tab you can check spelling and grammar, check definitions, and check synonyms for a word. Translation options are available for modifying selected text. You can also use the comments, changes, and markup options to keep track of spreadsheet notes and modifications, then accept or reject those changes. Editing can be limited by using the Protect Sheet and Protect Workbook options.

Figure 11.7: Review Tab

The View tab lets you configure the reading mode and layout of the spreadsheet onscreen. You can add onscreen components, such as headings and gridlines, to the window. The view can be modified to include multiple pages on the screen at the same time, or multiple windows on the screen.

Figure 11.8: View Tab

Excel 2010 File Menu Interface

Clicking on the File tab on the Ribbon UI opens the File Options window. From here you can perform many file tasks, like opening, printing, saving, and modifying properties for the spreadsheet.

The Save As option will open a window allowing you to choose the location and file type for the current workbook. You can type in a different file name in the File Name box. Choose a different file type by clicking on the File Type dropdown box and select the desired type from the list.

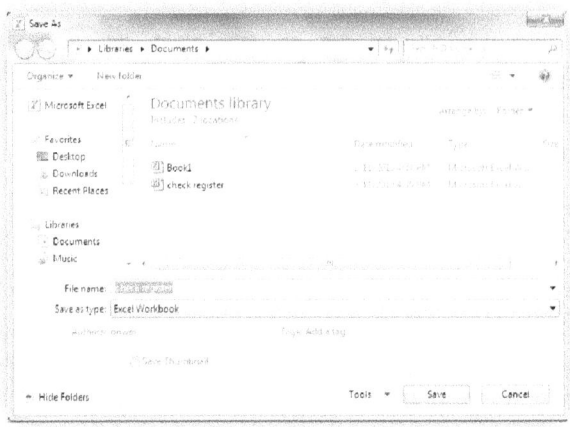

Figure 11.9: Save As Window

The Open option will allow you to browse your system for the Excel Workbook you wish to open. You can navigate the directories by using the links in the left pane or the Address Bar at the top of the window. Select the document you wish to open and click the Open button.

Figure 11.10: Open Window

The next entry in the File Options left pane is the Info screen. Clicking on this link will display information about the currently open file. You can view properties, such as title and author for the file, as well as view previous versions, inspect metadata, and protect the document from modifications.

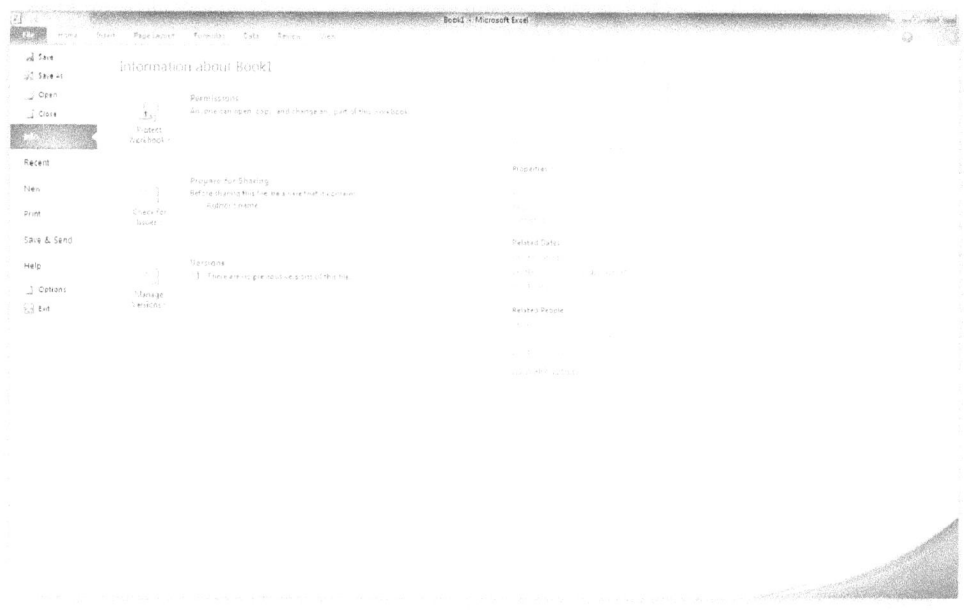

Figure 11.11: Info Screen

The Recent option will display recently opened workbooks and places, as well as items you have pinned to the list. Clicking on one of the items in the list will open the workbook in Excel.

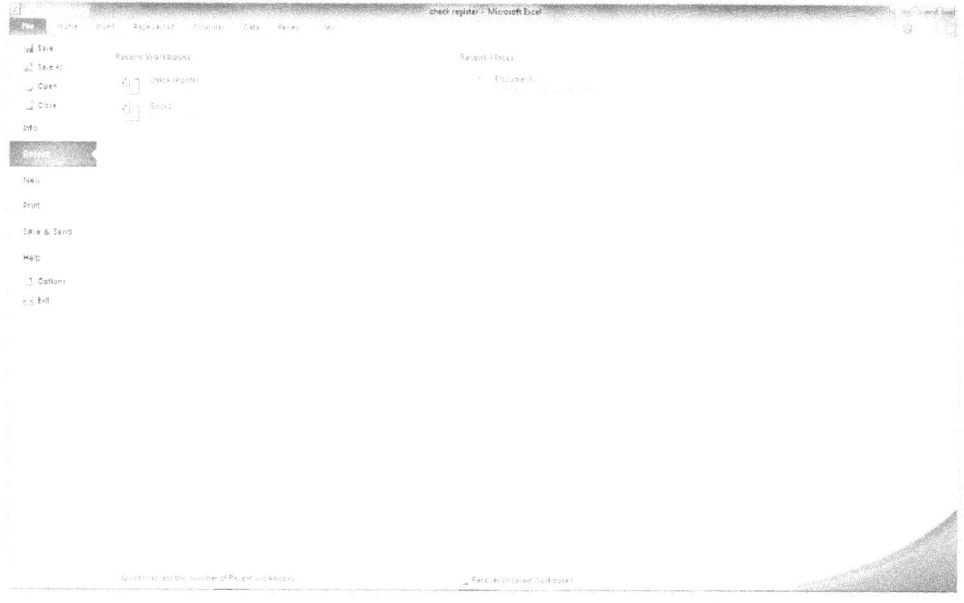

Figure 11.12: Recent Workbooks Screen

The New link can be used to open a new blank spreadsheet or one of the many preformatted templates on the screen. You can search for terms to find an online template that matches keyword search.

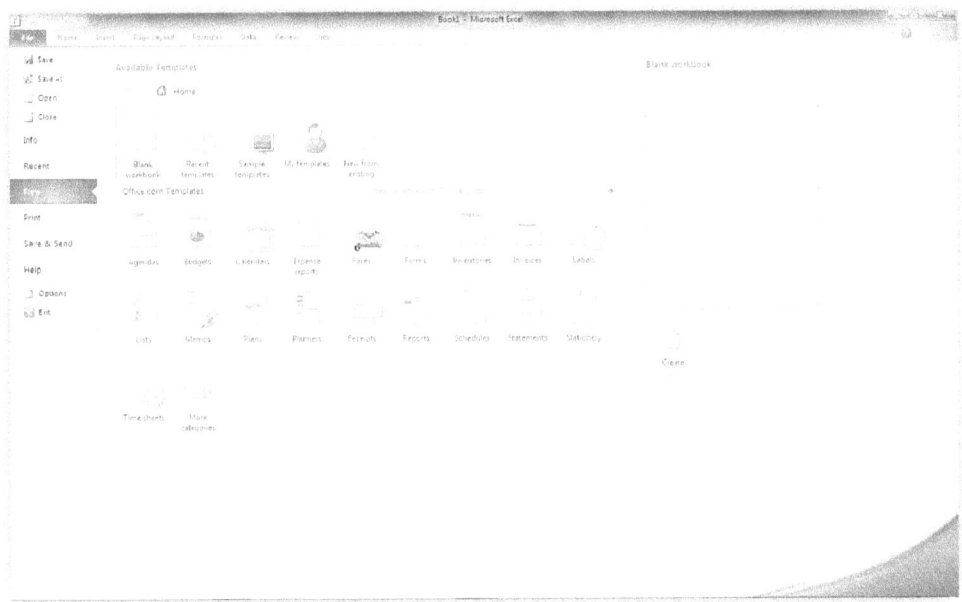

Figure 11.13: New Spreadsheet Screen

Under the Print option you will see a print preview of the current spreadsheet on the right and various print options to the left. From here you can choose the printer, active sheets to print, number of copies, and page options for the print job.

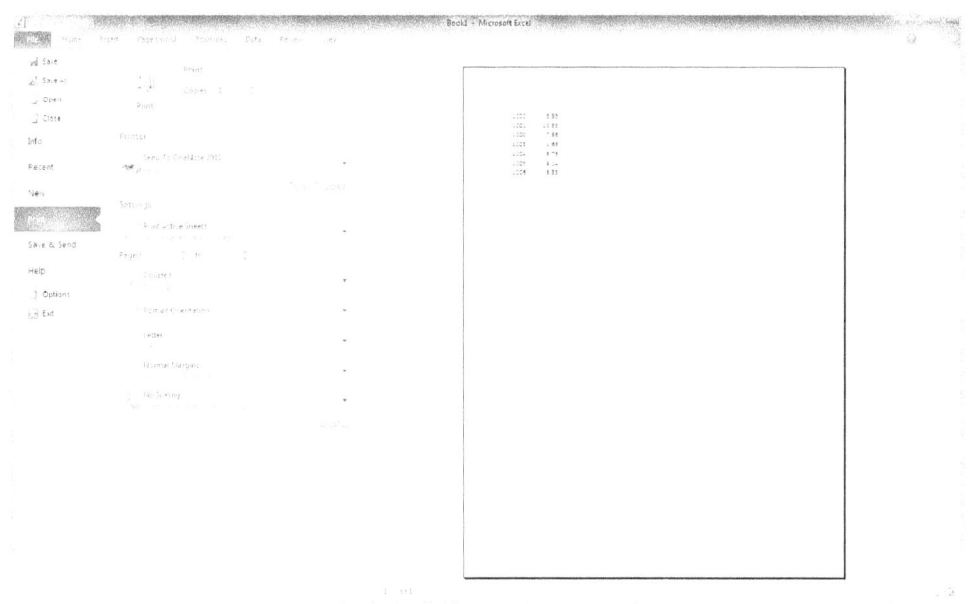

Figure 11.14: Print Options

Clicking the Page Setup link will let you adjust print options, margins, and print layout. From this screen you can choose to print headings, gridlines, and comments.

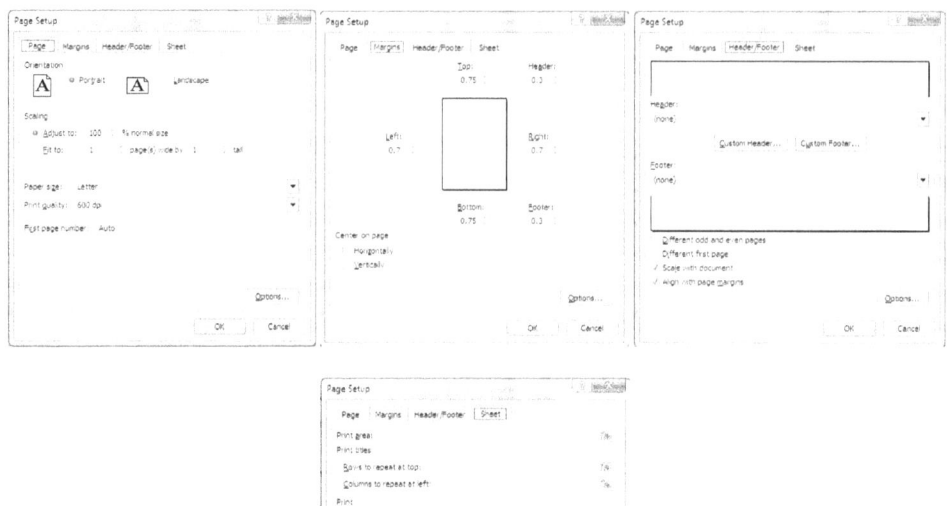

Figure 11.15: Page Setup Screen

The Save & Send option provides options for saving the workbook as different file types and options for sharing the file with others. The Send Using E-Mail link allows the document to be sent as an attachment through your default e-mail client. You can also send the document as a PDF or XPS document, or send the file as an Internet Fax.

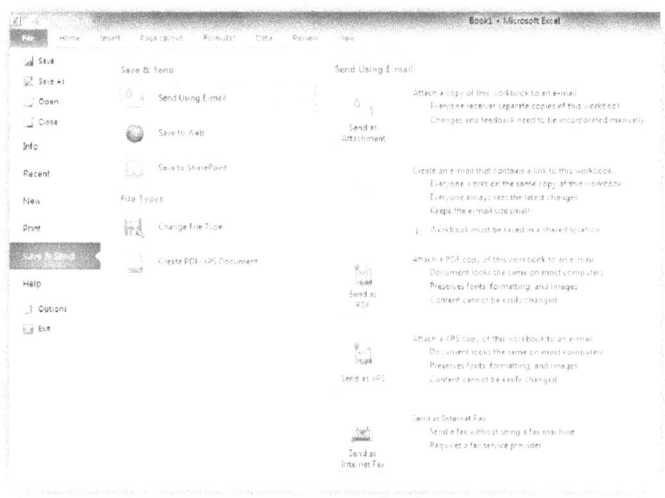

Figure 11.16: Send Using E-Mail

The Save to Web option allows you to access the workbook from another PC and to share the file with others by using your Windows Live ID/Microsoft Account.

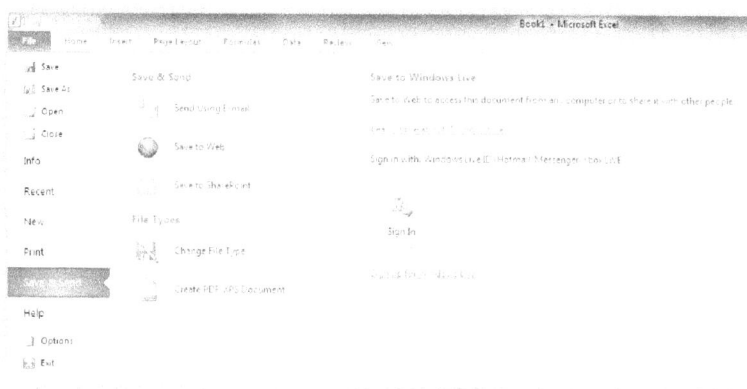

Figure 11.17: Save to Web

For business users with access to a SharePoint site, you can save the file to the shared location for others to access and collaborate on the workbook.

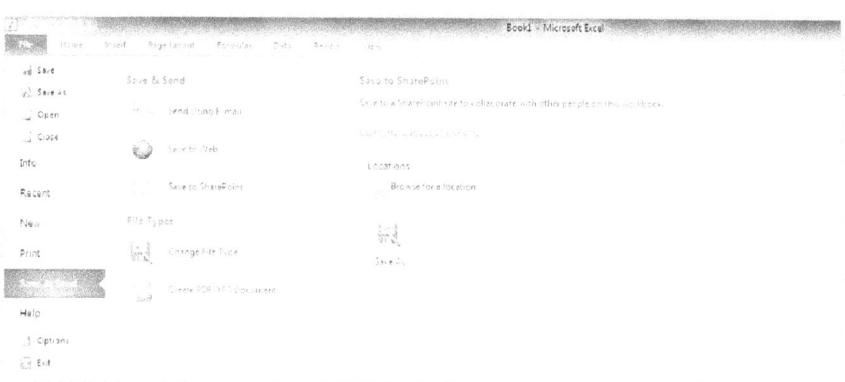

Figure 11.18: Save to SharePoint

The Change File Type option allows you to save the file in a different format or in a format compatible with previous versions of Excel. You can save the file as an OpenDocument Spreadsheet; a comma, tab, or space delimited file; or as another type of file.

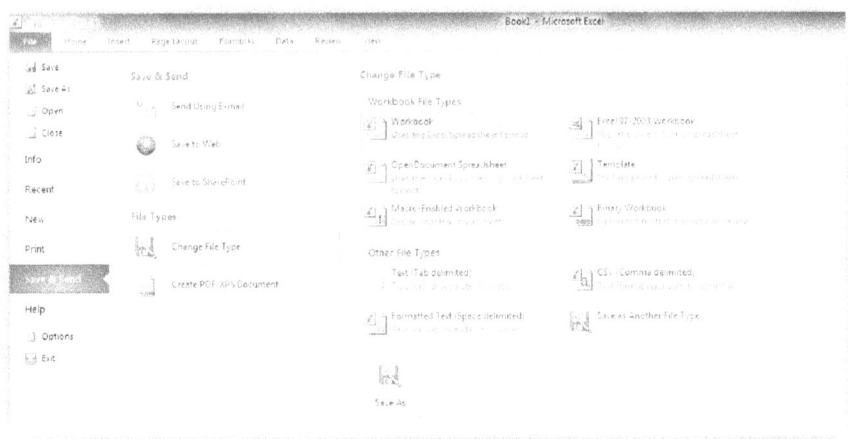

Figure 11.19: Change File Type

Your Workbook can be saved as a PDF or XPS document by clicking the Create PDF/XPS Document button. This will create a digital version of your workbook as the specified file type.

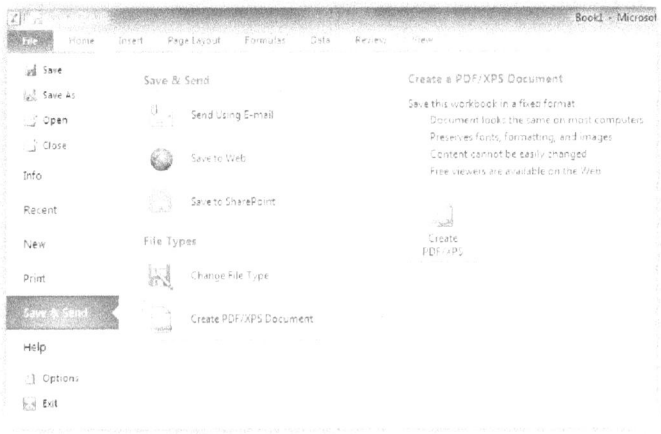

Figure 11.20: Create PDF or XPS Document

The Help option will provide access to the Microsoft Office Help feature, the Getting Started Guide, and options for the program. In the right-pane you can view information about the program.

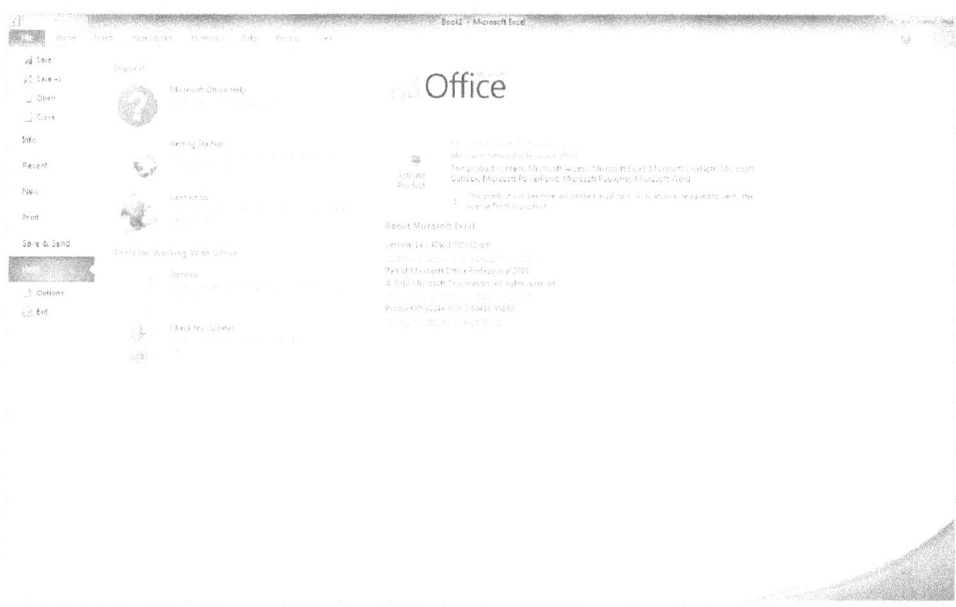

Figure 11.21: Office Help Window

Next we will look at how to perform some common, basic tasks in Excel 2010.

Excel 2010 Basic Tasks

Excel 2010 workbooks support multiple sheets of data. To navigate between the sheets, click on the Sheet tabs located in the lower-left corner of the Excel window. You can rename the sheets by double-clicking on the name and typing. You can configure formulas in Excel to utilize data from one sheet in another. For instance, if you had a sheet for each month of the year, you could pull the total balance from the previous month's sheet and use that value as the starting balance in the current month's sheet.

Figure 11.22: Rename Sheets

The first basic task we will look at is filling information down a column or across a row. Simply type a number in a cell followed by the Enter or Tab key. Select the cell with the text you just entered and hover your cursor in the lower-right corner of the cell. You will notice the cursor icon changes to a black "+" symbol. When you see that symbol in the cell's corner, click and drag with your mouse. Release your cursor when you reach the end of the range you wish to fill.

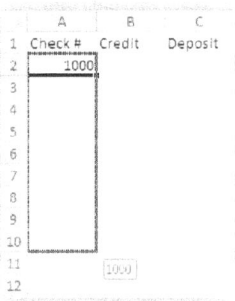

Figure 11.23: Fill Data

To fill items in a series you will go through the same steps, but when you have filled all of the desired cells, move your cursor to the lower-right corner of the filled range. A small box will appear with a dropdown list. In the dropdown list select the Fill Series option. The values in the list will then auto-increment from the preceding value.

184

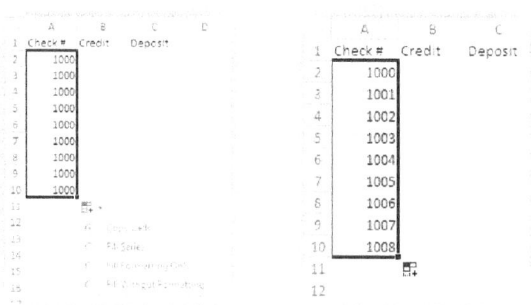

Figure 11.24: Fill Series

The next basic task will involve entering in numeric values and formatting them as currency. In the following example we will enter check amounts for the listed checks.

	A	B	C
1	Check #	Credit	Deposit
2	1000	115.26	
3	1001	32.12	
4	1002	5	
5	1003	27.14	
6	1004	128.01	
7	1005	95.75	
8	1006	36.63	
9	1007	12.09	
10	1008	72.13	
11			

Figure 11.25: Random Values Entered

After the values have been entered, highlight the cells we want to format as currency by clicking in the center of the top cell and dragging the cursor to the last cell to be formatted.

	A	B	C
1	Check #	Credit	Deposit
2	1000	115.26	
3	1001	32.12	
4	1002	5	
5	1003	27.14	
6	1004	128.01	
7	1005	95.75	
8	1006	36.63	
9	1007	12.09	
10	1008	72.13	
11			

Figure 11.26: Select Cells for Formatting

Once all the cells have been selected, click the dollar sign button located in the Number section of the Home tab. This will format each value as currency by adding a dollar sign and two

185

decimal places to the value.

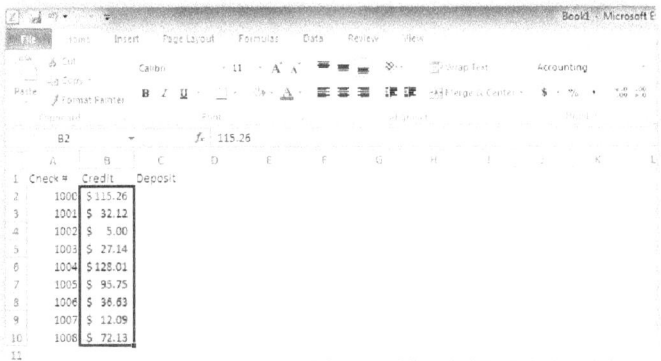

Figure 11.27: Select Cells to Total

Next, we will look at using the AutoSum formula feature to automatically calculate the total for a specified range of values. Select an empty cell for displaying the total. We will use the empty cell at the end of our check values to store the total for that column. Click the AutoSum button in the Editing section of the Home tab. The formula will appear in the cell and formula bar, and a box will appear around the cells to be added together. If you need to change the formula to modify the cells being summed, you can either manually edit the column and row values in the formula, or drag the box with the dotted lines to additional cells.

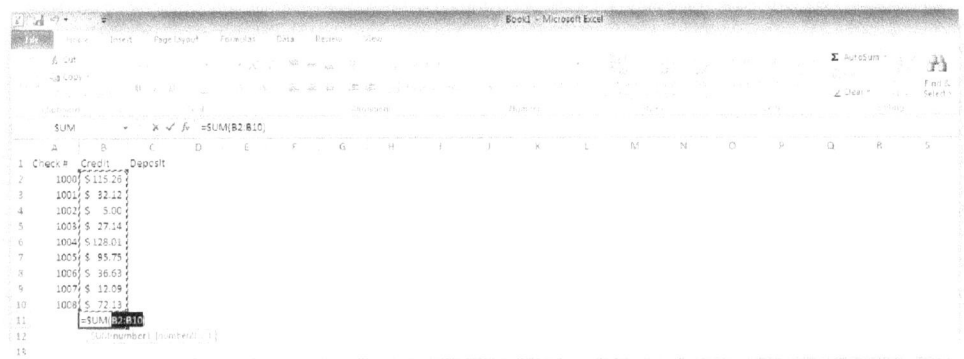

Figure 11.28: AutoSum Formula

Once the desired cells are included in the formula you can press Enter on your keyboard to calculate the total for the cell. The text in the cell will change to the sum value. To modify the formula click the cell and change the formula in the formula bar.

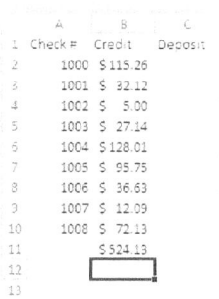

Figure 11.29: Total Value Calculated

Tip AutoSum a series of rows by highlighting the cell following the series and clicking the AutoSum button. Verify the formula includes the desired cells and press Enter.

Next, we will look at creating charts and graphs from data entered into a spreadsheet. Highlight the data you wish to add to the chart or graph.

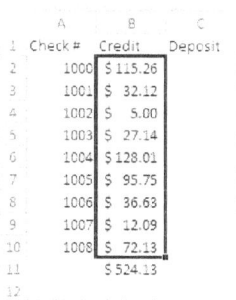

Figure 11.30: Select Data to Graph

Select the type of chart you wish to use from the Charts section on the Insert tab. We will use the data to create a pie chart.

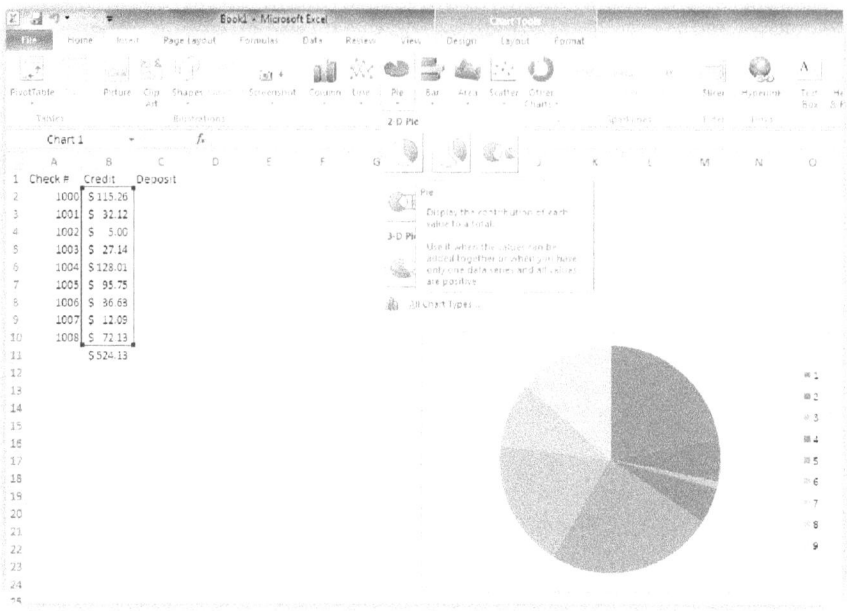

Figure 11.31: Pie Chart from Data

Selecting the column chart option will plot the data as a column chart.

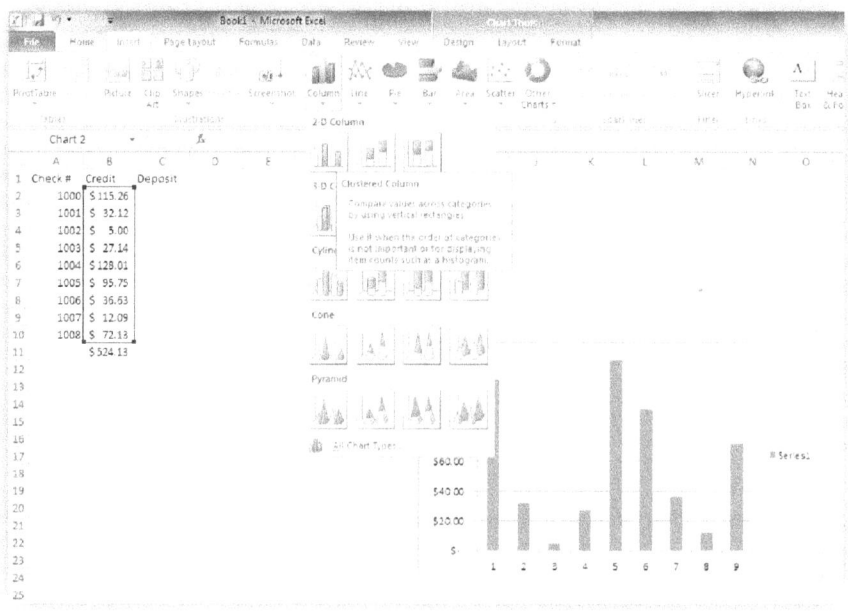

Figure 11.32: Column Chart from Data

Selecting the line chart option plots the data as a line chart. Under the Chart Tools tabs you can change the design and format options for the chart. You can modify the style and color of items in the chart to suit your needs.

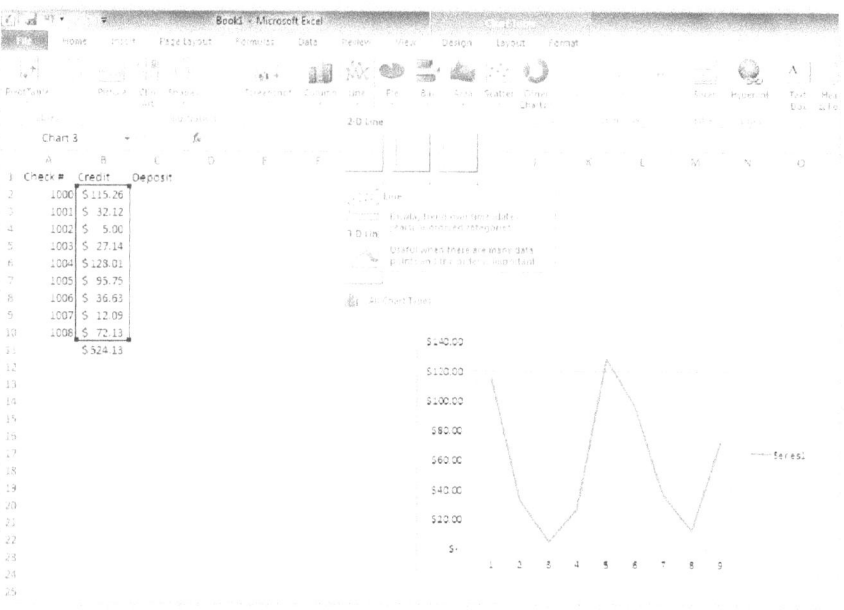

Figure 11.33: Line Chart from Data

If additional rows are needed between rows of data, right-click on the row heading that will be beneath the row we are going to add. Select Insert in the context menu that appears. This will add a new row and will shift all items in the rows beneath down one row. Be sure any formulas are correct after the shift in row numbers.

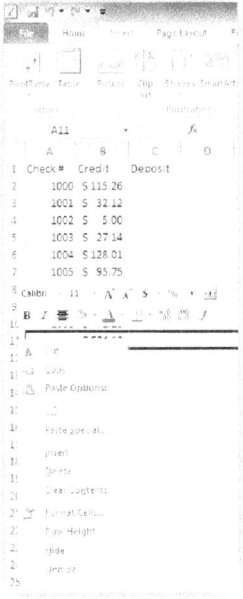

Figure 11.34: Insert Row

In Figure 11.35 you can see the AutoSum total we previously calculated will need to be modified to add in the value in the new row. Change the row number in the AutoSum formula to add the new row value into the total.

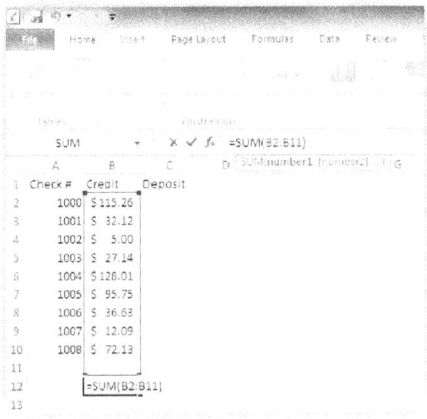

Figure 11.35: Modify Formula

 After adding rows or columns, verify your formulas reference the correct cells.

The formula has now been updated to include the new row values in the AutoSum formula. Enter in a value for a deposit that was made into the new row. Use the AutoSum feature to get a total for the Deposit column. You can then use the totals in the Credit and Deposit columns to calculate a total for both. In cell D12 we will type the formula "=SUM(C12-B12)", without quotes. This will find the sum of the values stored in cells C12 and B12. Since the value in C12 will be deposits (a positive value) and B12 will be checks written (a negative value), subtract B12 from C12 to get our total.

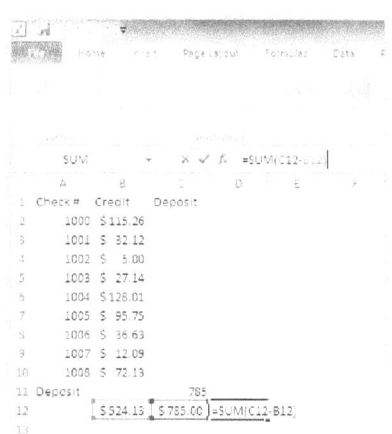

Figure 11.36: Calculate Grand Total

The next task we will look at is the insert function feature. Excel has a number of common functions for math, statistics, and other commonly used formulas. First choose an empty cell, and then click the "*fx*" button on the formula bar. This will open the Insert Function window. From here you can scroll through the lists of available functions in Excel. Select the AVERAGE function in the list and click OK.

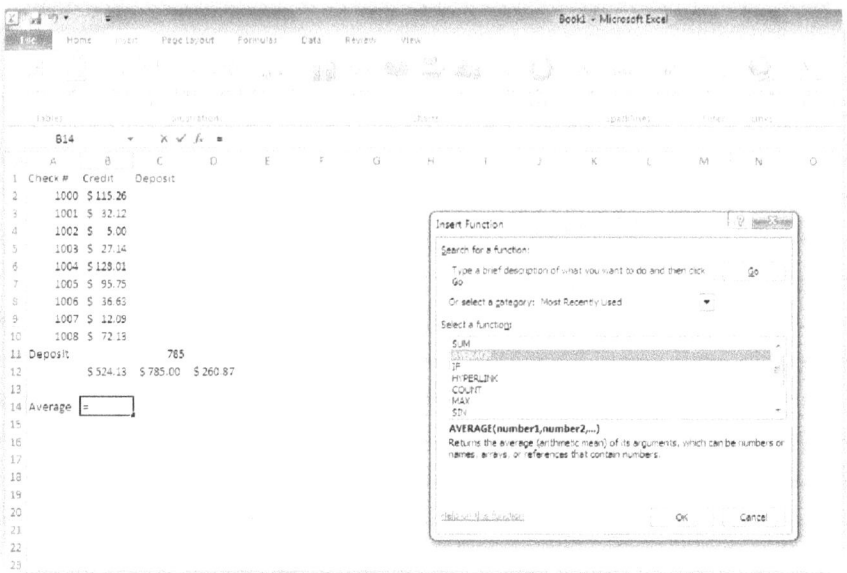

Figure 11.37: Insert Average Function

In the next window choose the cells used for the function calculation. In the Number 1 box we will enter the cell range for the values used to calculate an average. Enter "B2:B11" so that all values in cells B2 through B11 are added together and divided by the number of values totaled. Click the OK button to finish.

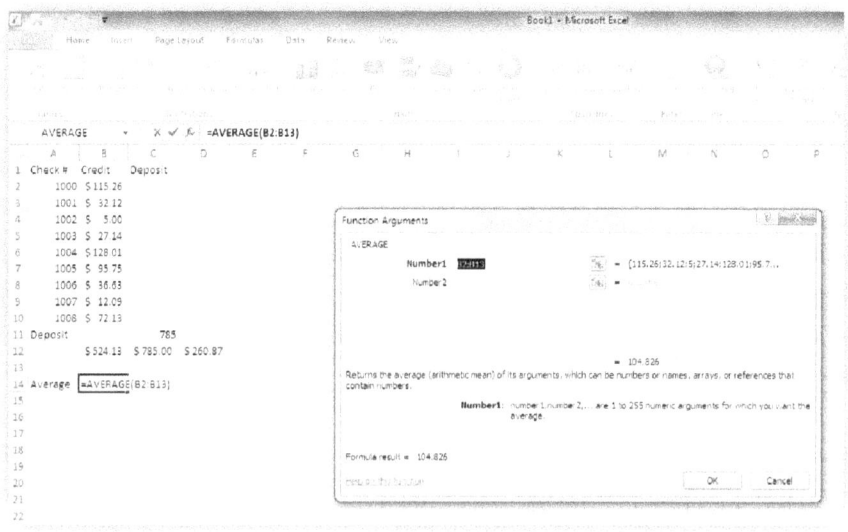

Figure 11.38: Set Function Arguments

The next commonly used feature we will explore is the Sort feature. If we have a table of data like the check register in Figure 11.39, we may want to sort out the information in descending order by check amount. Highlight the related fields that will be sorted, then click the Sort button on the Data tab.

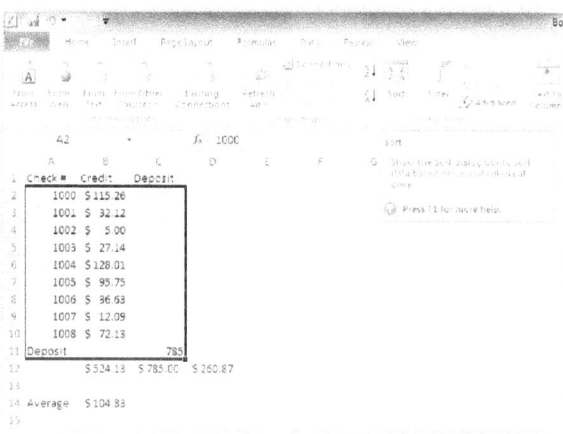

Figure 11.39: Select Fields to Sort

In the Sort window that opens choose the options for what field and data to sort by. We will sort by the Credit columns values.

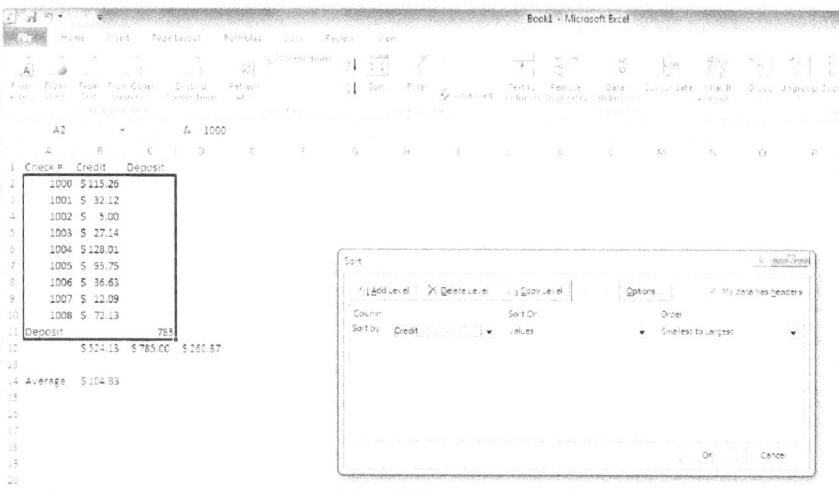

Figure 11.40: Sort Options

Once you press the OK button, Excel will sort the rows by the specified options. In Figure 11.41 you can see the rows are now sorted by the Credit column in descending order.

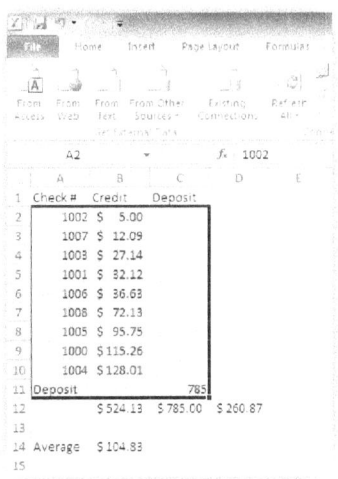

Figure 11.41: Sorted Data

> 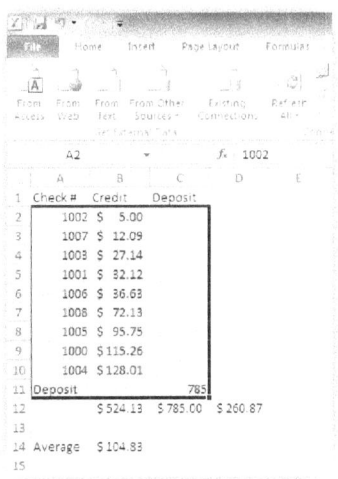 Be sure to select the entire group of data to be sorted so that related data is moved together.

Now that you have learned how to perform some of the most common tasks in Excel, you should have a good foundation for working with the program. In the next section we will learn how to use PowerPoint—a program widely used for presentations at school and work.

Chapter Review Questions:

1. Describe how to fill a series of cells in a column from 1 to 100.
2. How would we add a row between row 50 and 51?
3. Describe the steps for adding up the series of cells in the column.
4. If we wanted to determine the average of our series of cells, what steps would we take to calculate the average?
5. How do we change a number in a cell to a dollar amount?

Chapter 12 – PowerPoint 2010

With PowerPoint 2010 you can produce slide shows and presentations which can be played back on a PC, DVD player, or viewed online. In the next section we will provide an overview of some of available features in PowerPoint.

PowerPoint 2010 Window Layout

When you open PowerPoint 2010 you will see a blank presentation and slide. Along the top of the screen you will notice the tabbed Ribbon UI with tabs and icons for performing various tasks in the program. Common tasks are located in the Home tab, which is open by default. Other tabs allow you to insert pictures and content, review layout, and change a number of formatting options. In the pictures that follow we will break down some of the features in each tab.

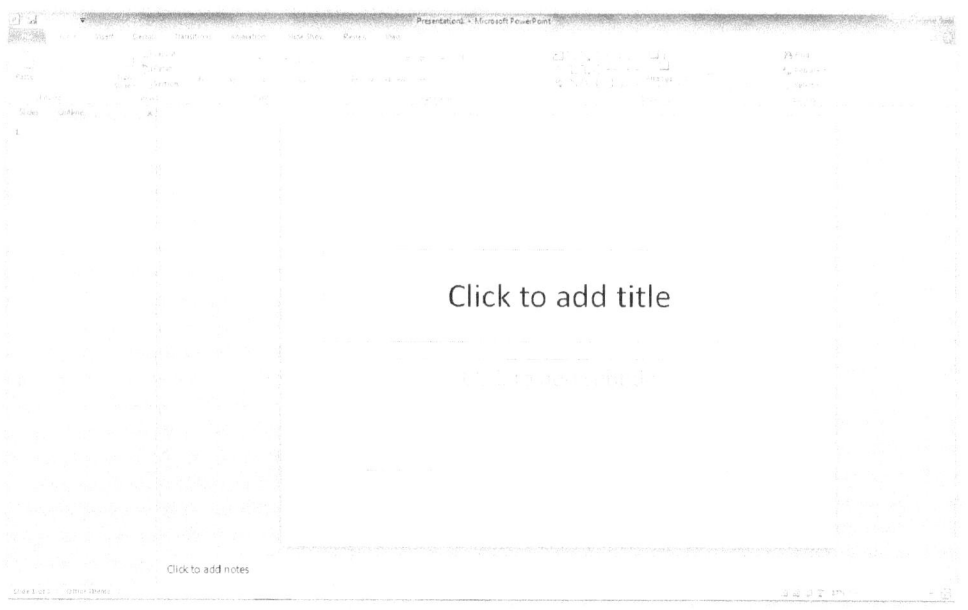

Figure 12.1: Blank Presentation Screen

PowerPoint 2010 Ribbon User Interface

Under the Home tab you can cut, copy, and paste from the clipboard; insert a new slide and adjust the layout; adjust the font, font size, and font style options; adjust text layout and formatting; and add SmartArt to the slide. You can also find and replace specified text in a document from the Home tab.

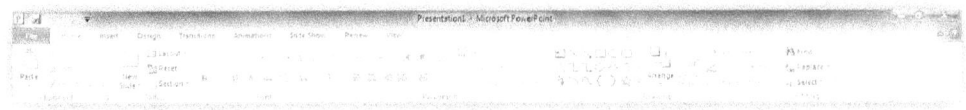

Figure 12.2: Home Tab

In the Insert tab you can insert items into the slide and presentation. You can insert new slides, tables, pictures, text, and shapes; insert audio and video; insert headers, footers, and comments; and insert objects, equations, and symbols.

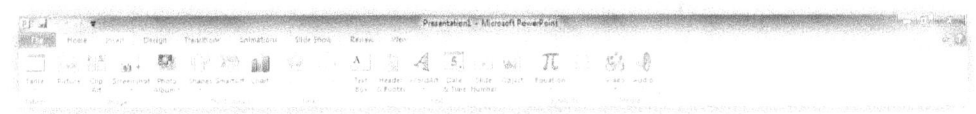

Figure 12.3: Insert Tab

The Design tab allows you to choose document formatting options for titles, headings, and text in your presentation. You can adjust the background, colors, fonts, and theme design for presentation text. Watermarks and page size can also be changed through this tab.

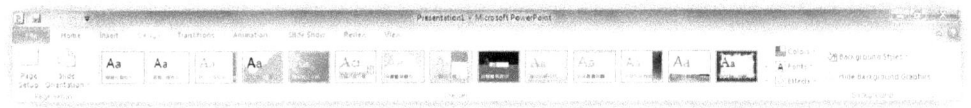

Figure 12.4: Design Tab

In the Transitions tab you can select transition effects for navigating between slides in your presentation. You can also add sound effects to the slide show and change settings for when to advance slides.

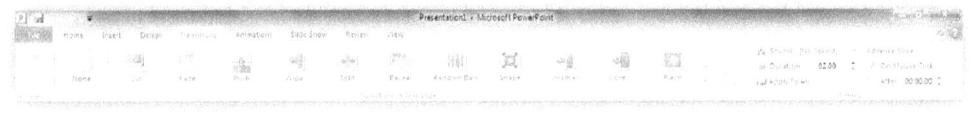

Figure 12.5: Transitions Tab

The Animations tab contains animation effects for moving text and other content into position on each slide. Duration, delay, and order of animation effects can be set in this tab.

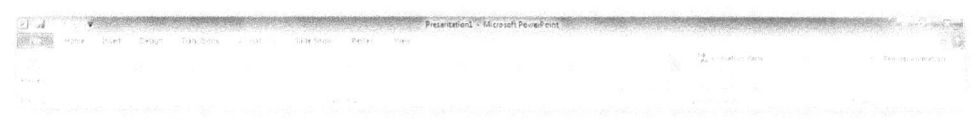

Figure 12.6: Animations Tab

In the slide show tab you can preview the slide show, configure slide show options, and record the slide show. You can also present online and manage monitors for use with the presentation.

Figure 12.7: Slide Show Tab

Under the Review tab you can check spelling and grammar, check definitions, and check synonyms for a word. Language and translation options are available for modifying selected text. You can also use the comments, changes, and markup options to keep track of slide notes and modifications, then accept or reject those changes. You can also use the Review tab's Compare feature to view differences between two versions of a presentation.

Figure 12.8: Review Tab

The View tab lets you configure the reading mode and layout of the presentation onscreen. You can add onscreen components, such as the ruler bar and gridlines, to the window. The view can be modified to include multiple pages on the screen at the same time or multiple windows on the screen.

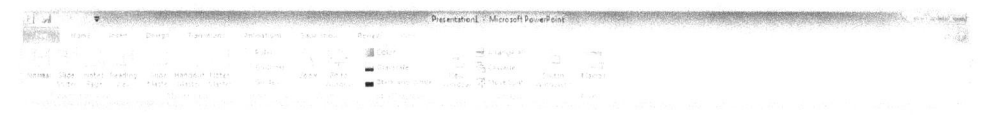

Figure 12.9: View Tab

PowerPoint 2010 File Menu Interface

Clicking on the File tab on the Ribbon UI opens the File Options window. From here you can perform many file tasks, like opening, printing, saving, and modifying properties for the presentation.

The New link can be used to open a new blank presentation or one of the many preformatted templates on the screen. You can search for terms to find a template that matches keywords in your search.

Figure 12.10: New Presentation Screen

Under the Print option you will find a print preview of the current presentation on the right, and various print options to the left. From here you can choose the printer, number of copies, and page options for the print job. You can choose how you want the presentation to print-only the current slide; all slides; or as an outline, handout, or individual pages.

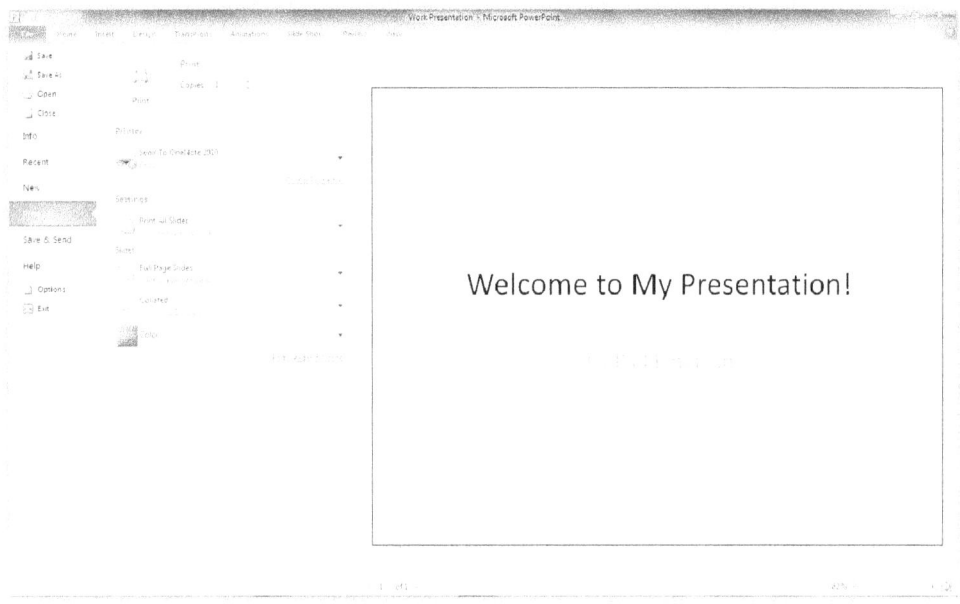

Figure 12.11: Print Presentation Screen

The first drop-down item under Settings allows you to print all slides, print selected slides, print the current slide, or specify a range of slides to print.

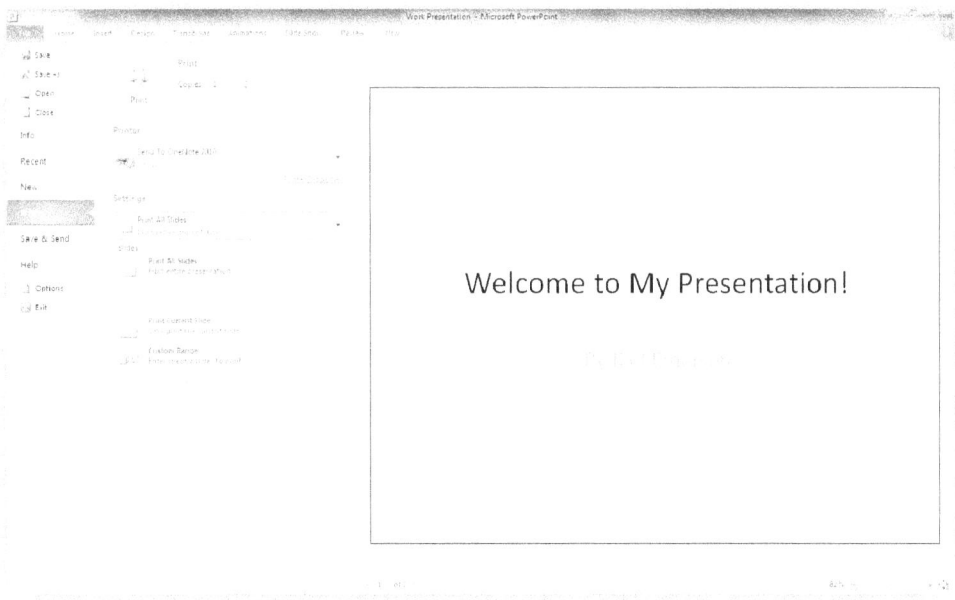

Figure 12.12: Print Slide Options

The second drop down item under Settings allows you to choose how the slide is printed. You can choose to have the slide printed as a full page, print a certain number of sides per page, or to print the slides as notes or an outline.

Figure 12.13: Print Options

The Send Using E-Mail option under the Save & Send section can be used to send the presentation as an e-mail attachment using your default e-mail program. It can also be used to send the presentation as a link via e-mail if the presentation is saved to a shared location. You can send the presentation as a PDF, XPS, or as an internet fax as well.

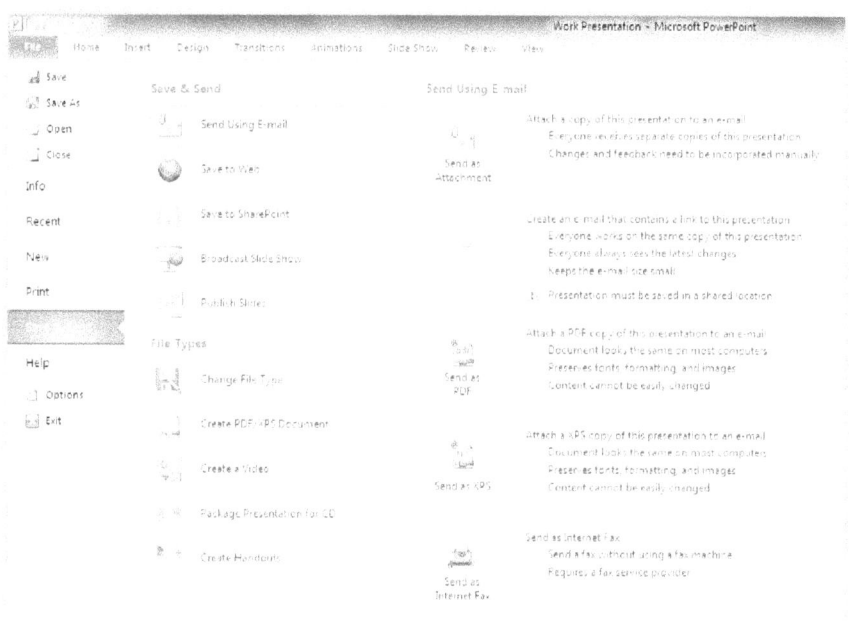

Figure 12.14: Send Using E-Mail

The Save to Web option allows you to access the presentation from another PC and to share the file with others by using your Windows Live ID/Microsoft Account.

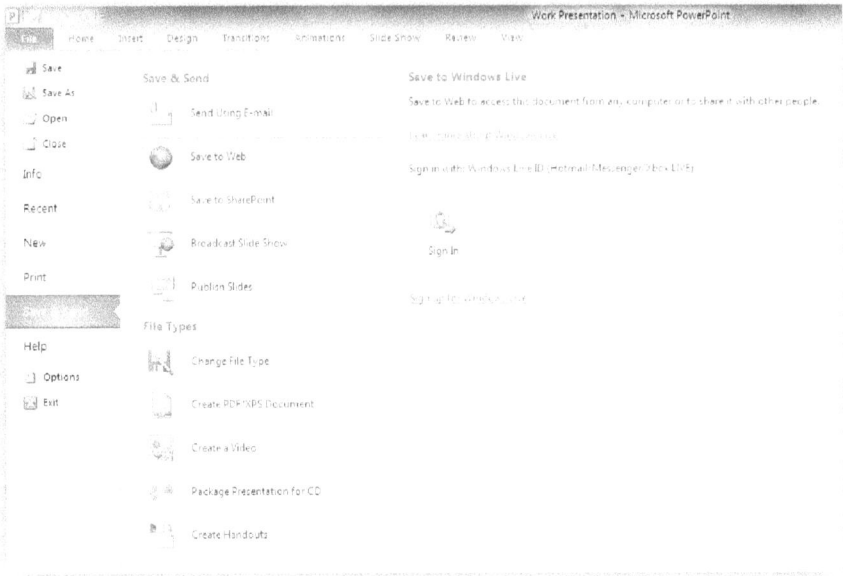

Figure 12.15: Save to Web

For business users with access to a SharePoint site, you can save the presentation to the shared location for others to access and collaborate on the presentation.

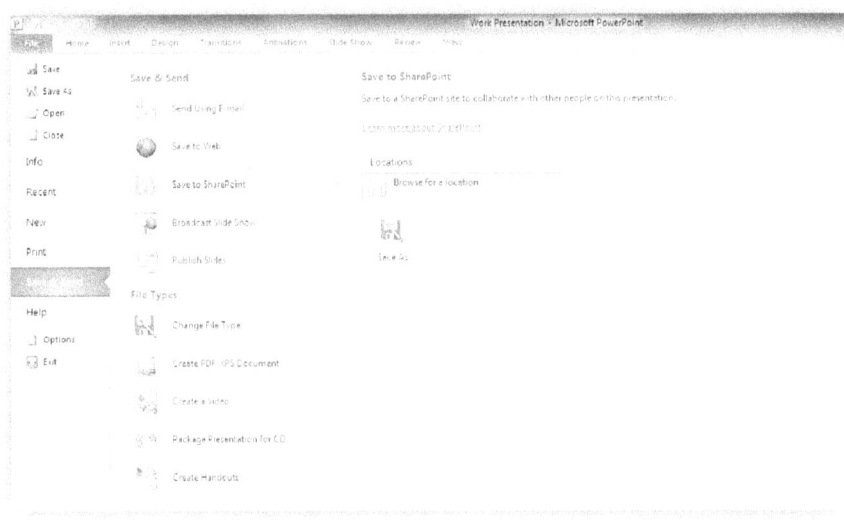

Figure 12.16: Save to SharePoint

The Broadcast Slide Show feature can be used to present the slide show to others online.

The presentation doesn't require an installation and can be viewed by clicking on a link you provide.

Figure 12.17: Broadcast Slide Show

The Publish Slides option can be used to upload the presentation to a shared slide library or SharePoint location for others to access and modify. You can be alerted via e-mail when changes have been made to the presentation.

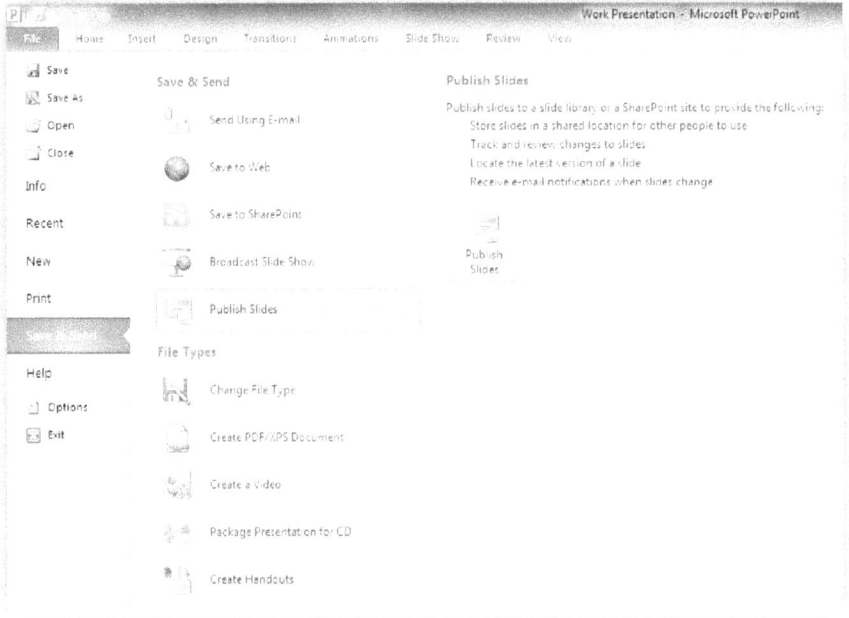

Figure 12.18: Publish Slides

The Change File Type option allows you to save the presentation in a different format. You can save the file in a format for use with an earlier version of PowerPoint or an entirely different program.

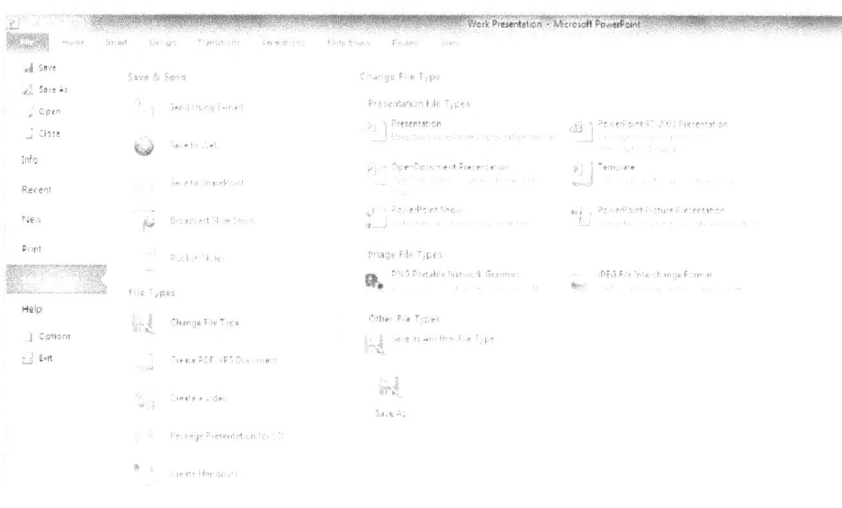

Figure 12.19: Change File Type

To create a digital document from the PowerPoint presentation, select the Create PDF/XPS Document option. The PDF or XPS document can then be viewed on most computers that have a PDF viewer installed. Pictures, fonts, and layout will be saved in the file and remain consistent when viewed on different computers.

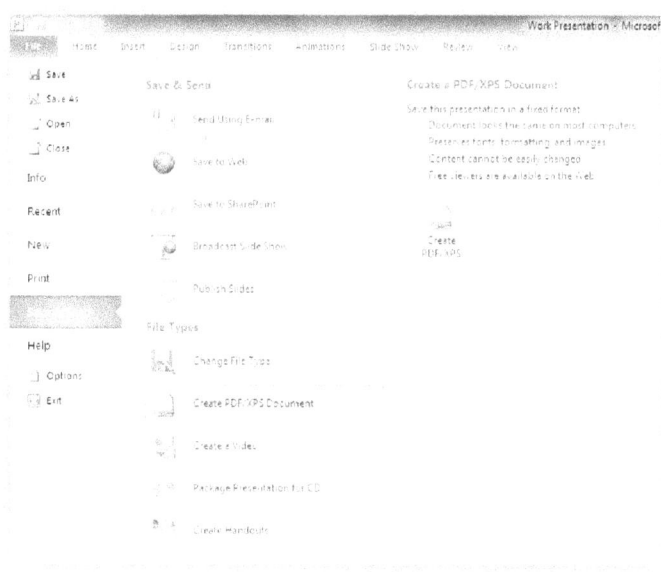

Figure 12.20: Create PDF or XPS Document

Other export options include creating a video from the presentation. You can configure the options for timing, narration, and the quality of the video rendered. The video can then be uploaded online, burned to a disc, or e-mailed.

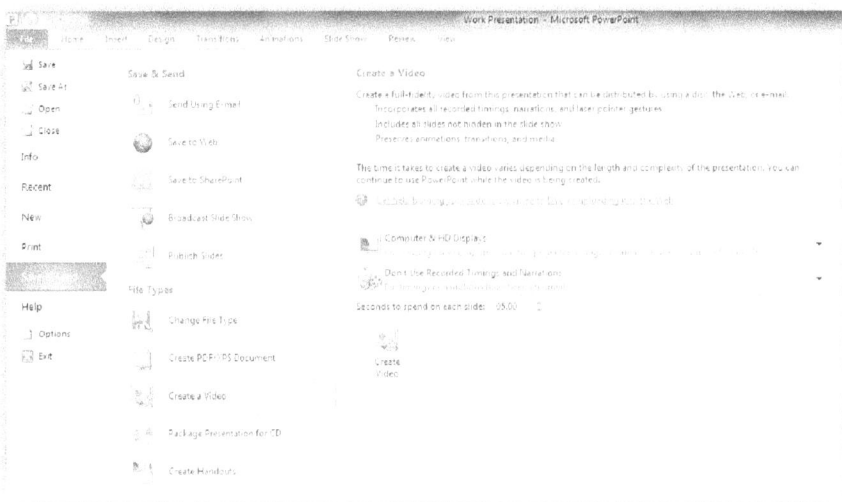

Figure 12.21: Create a Video

You can also use the Package Presentation for CD option to make a disc containing the images, sounds, videos, and fonts, along with the presentation. This way all media for the slide show is available when viewed on a different computer than where the presentation was produced.

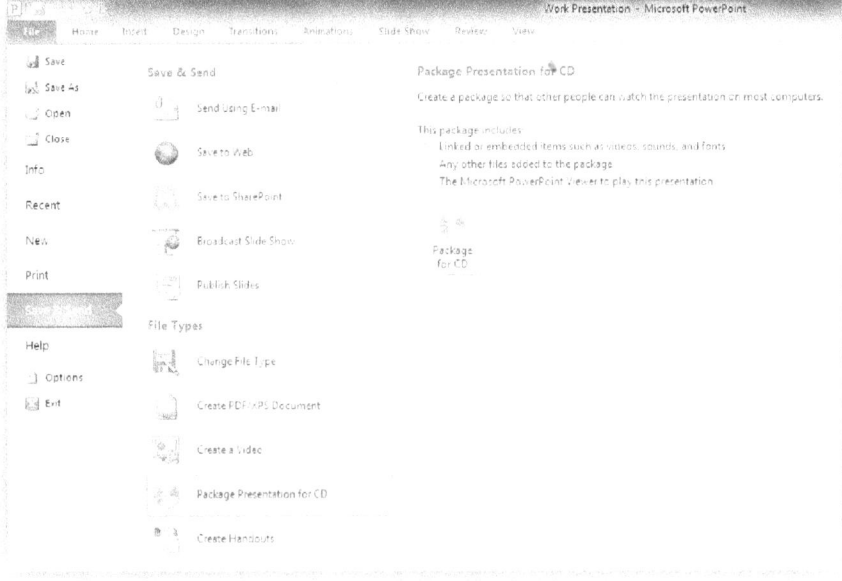

Figure 12.22: Package Presentation for CD

The Create Handouts option will create a Microsoft Word document that contains the slides and notes from the presentation. When you make changes to the slide presentation, the information in the Word document will automatically be updated.

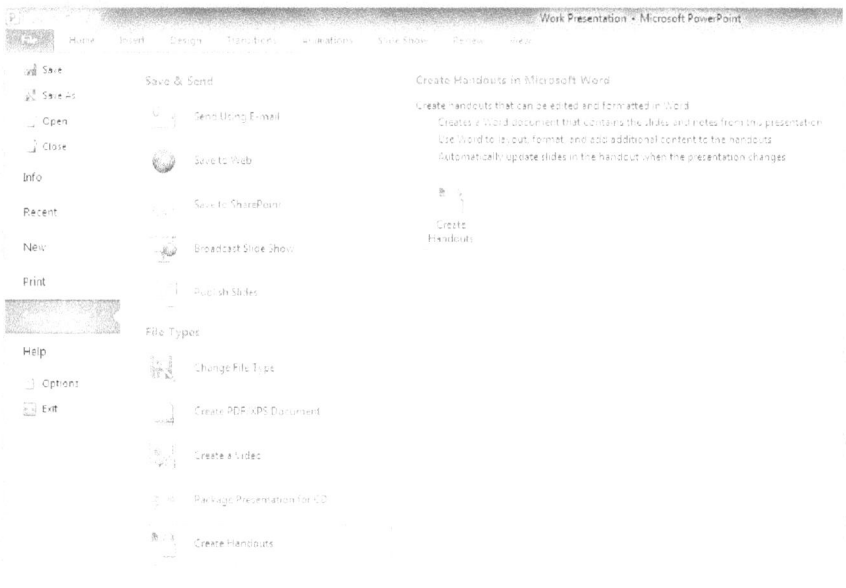

Figure 12.23: Save & Send Options

Next we will look at how to perform some common tasks in PowerPoint 2010.

PowerPoint 2010 Basic Tasks

Entering titles, text, and modifying font style and size are all common tasks for working in PowerPoint. To enter text in our blank slide template, click in the textbox that contains the text Click to Add Title. Once the cursor is in the textbox you can begin typing. Do the same for the subtitle textbox. To adjust the font or the size, select the text you wish to modify and select the font and font size you wish to use from the dropdown menus.

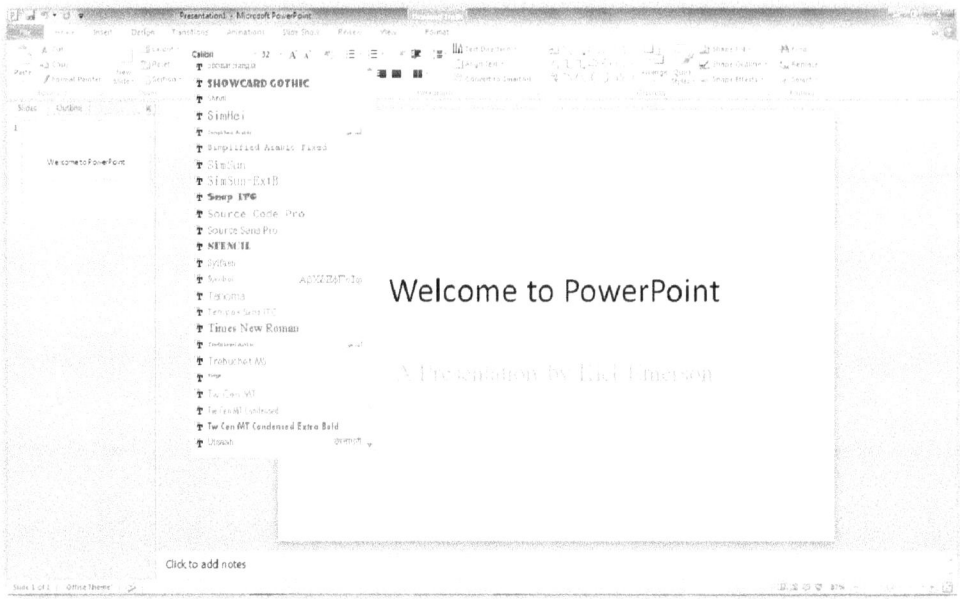

Figure 12.24: Enter Text, Modify Font

To insert a slide after our first title slide, click the New Slide dropdown button on the Home tab. It will expand out with several slide choices. Choose the slide that matches the content layout you will want for the slide. The slide will then be added to the presentation.

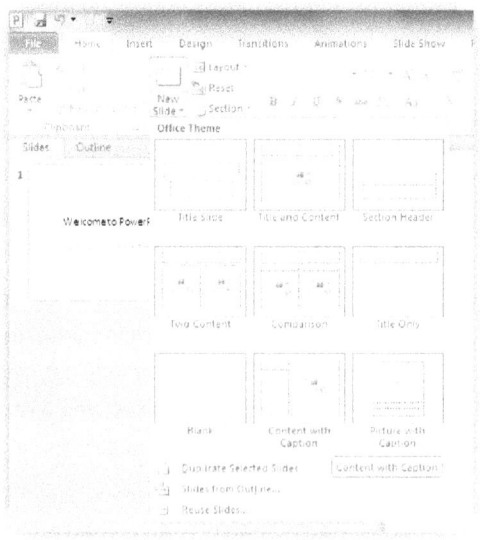

Figure 12.25: Insert Slide

Clicking the new slide in the left pane will display the slide in the right pane. From here we can add the slide title, text, and content to the slide. We can delete the textboxes and items from this slide if we choose or we can add additional content.

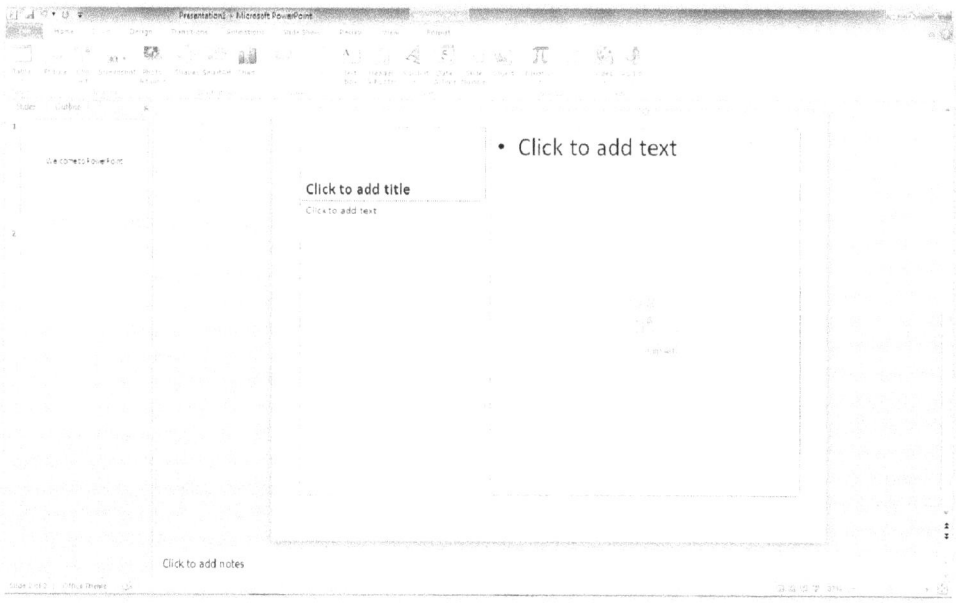

Figure 12.26: Insert Text

Now we will add an image to the slide. If we wanted to use a picture stored on the PC we can choose the Pictures button on the Insert tab. In this case we want to use an image from the Office.com Clip Art gallery. Click the Clip Art button on the Insert tab. Then search the Office.com clip art gallery for a picture to add.

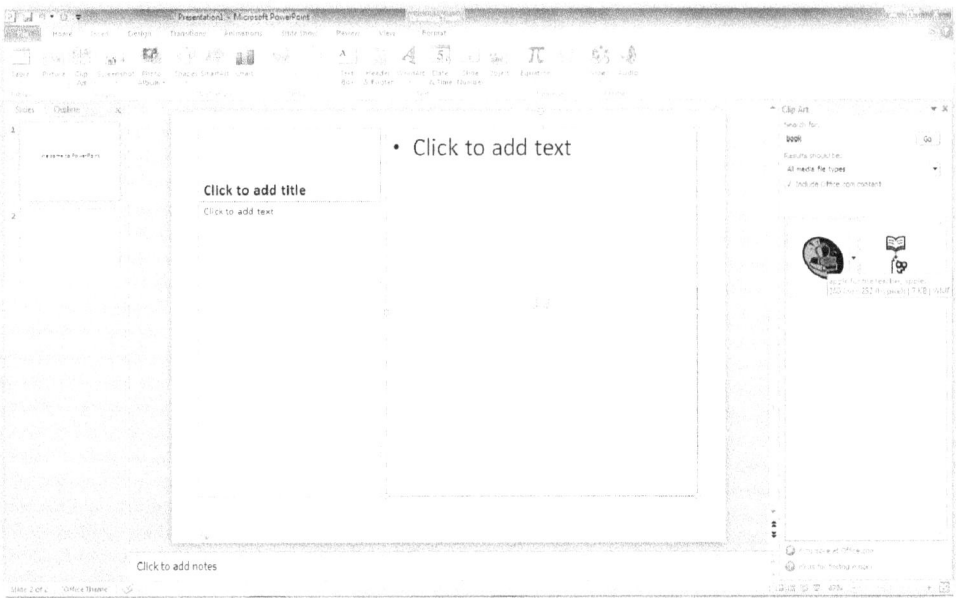

Figure 12.27: Insert an Image

After you have found the picture you wish to add, click the Insert button. The picture will then be added to the slide. You can drag the picture to position it on the slide. Use the corners of the selected image to change the size of the image.

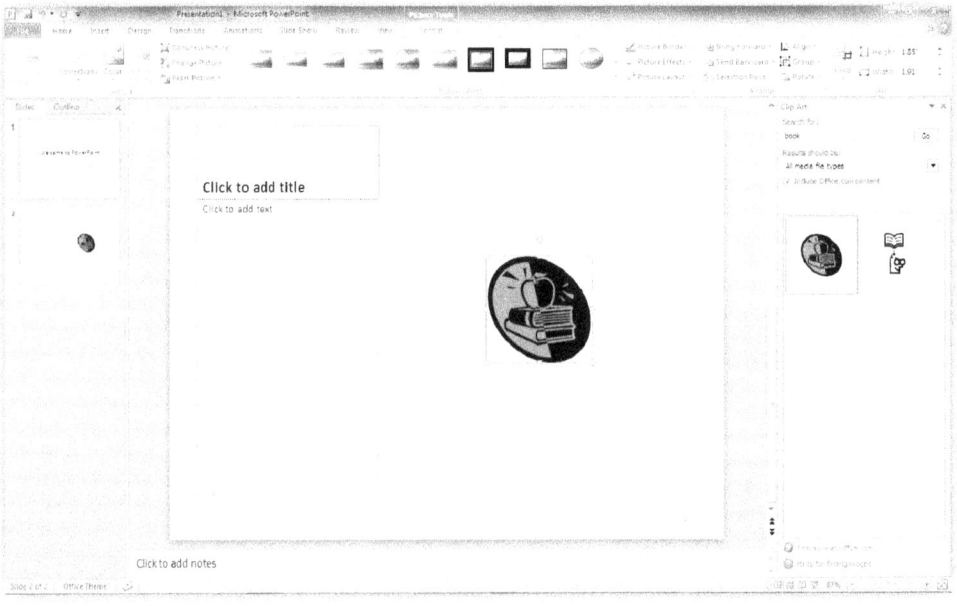

Figure 12.28: Picture Added to Slide

The next common PowerPoint task we will explore is using transitions and animations. Transitions are the graphical changes that occur between slides in a presentation. They are used to help liven up a presentation. Animations refer to the text, images, and other elements appearing on each slide. An animation may involve a line of text floating into position on the slide.

To add a transition to a slide we will select the slide we are transitioning to from the left pane. Click the Transitions tab and browse for a transition that you would like to use. When you click the transition you will see a preview of what it will look like with the selected slide.

Figure 12.29: Add Slide Transitions

To add an animation to a slide element, choose the element you wish to modify. Then select an animation to use from the Animations tab. You will see a preview of what the selected option will look like on the current slide.

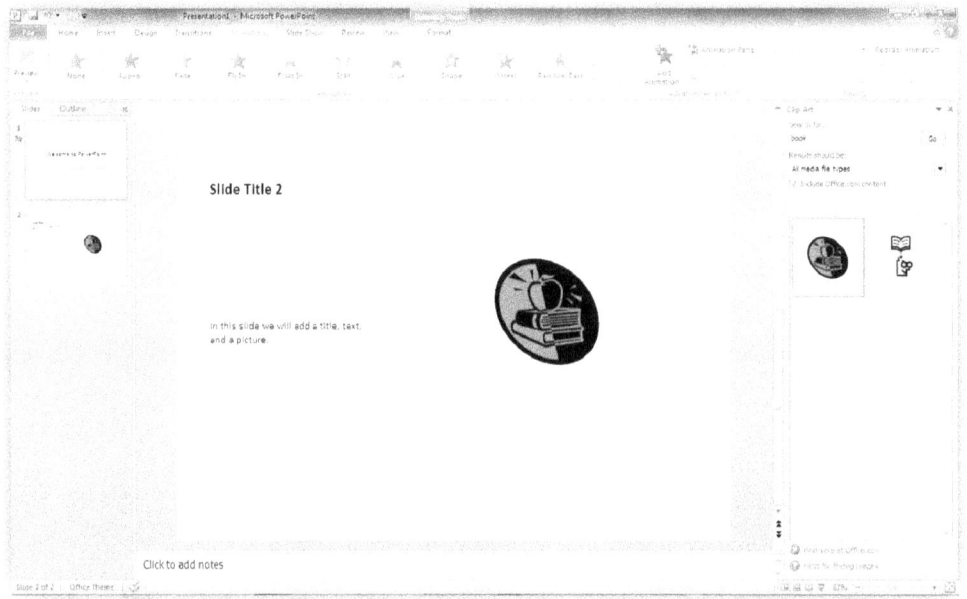

Figure 12.30: Add Animations

Now that we have learned a few basic tasks in PowerPoint, you should be more comfortable working with the program and creating presentations for home, school, and work. In the next section we will look at OneNote 2010. OneNote is the last of the four programs in the Microsoft Office 2010 Home and Student version of the Suite (Word, Excel, PowerPoint, & OneNote). All other Microsoft Office 2010 applications are part of either a premium business version of the suite or sold individually.

Chapter Review Questions:
1. How do we add a new slide to the presentation?
2. How do we add a picture from our Pictures Library to a slide?
3. Describe the steps for adding an animation to the picture we added to the slide, and for adding a transition between slides one and two.

Chapter 13 – OneNote 2010

OneNote is a program designed to keep track of notes, pictures, videos, reminders, and much more – all in one easy to use location. With OneNote you can use the integrated search feature to locate information quickly. You can type, embed, and move items anywhere on the screen.

OneNote 2010 Screen Layout and Basic Tasks

In OneNote, your Notebook is a major category, like school, work, or home. From there you can add pages for more refined categories, such as Science, Math, Chemistry, etc. On each page you can type notes, write with your touch screen, paste webpage content, and insert pictures and video.

To begin, select your notebook or create a new one. Then click the "+" tab to create a new page.

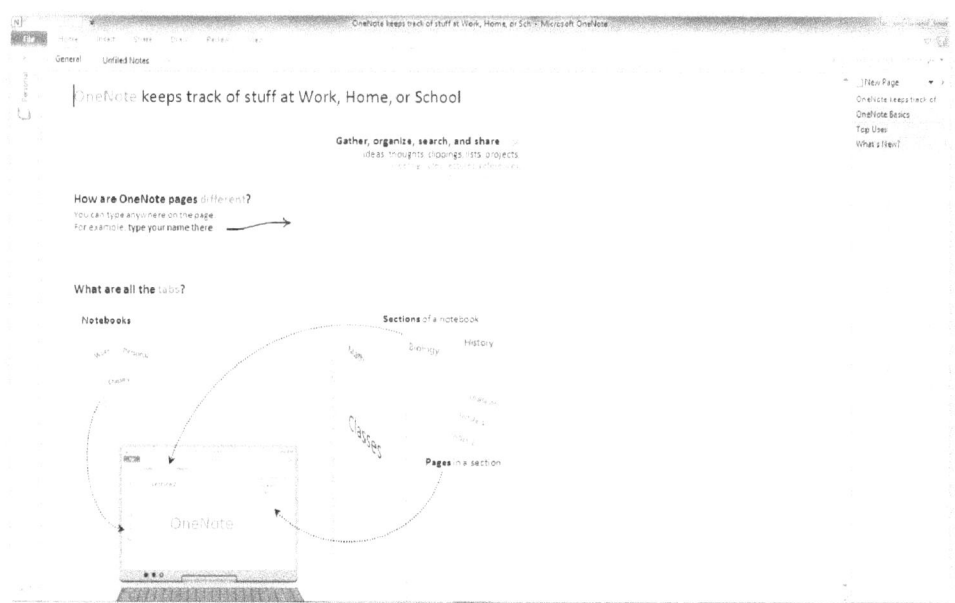

Figure 13.1: OneNote 2010 Start Page

Title the page by typing in the top section. The name listed in the right pane will reflect the new page name. You can start typing anywhere on the screen below the title or start adding content to the page.

While browsing online, you can add a screen clipping or link to OneNote by using the Send To OneNote tool. This tool is usually running as an active program window or running in the Taskbar. The Send To OneNote tool makes it easy to add sections of websites to your notebook pages. If you click the Screen Clipping option you will see the balloon in Figure 13.2. This balloon will prompt you to select an area of the webpage to add to OneNote.

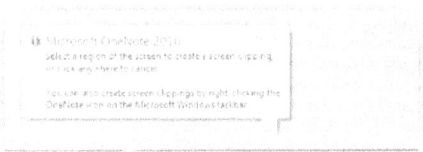

Figure 13.2: OneNote Screen Clipping Balloon

Once the area of the website has been selected, you will see the option in OneNote to select a location for the content. Choose where you want the screen clipping to go and click the Send To Selected Location button.

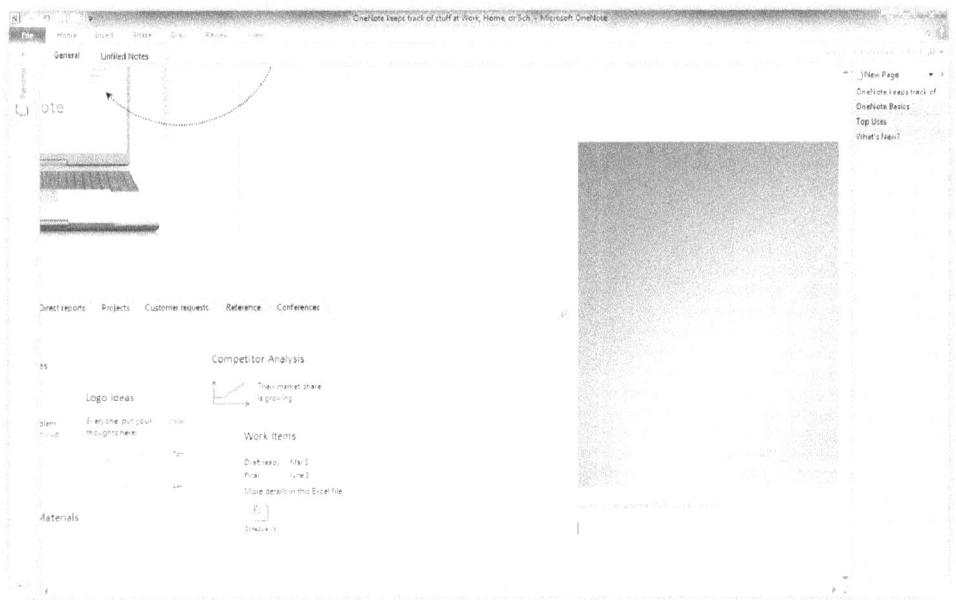

Figure 13.3: Select Location in OneNote

Webpages, pictures, text, and other items onscreen can be captured with the OneNote Screen Clipping TaskBar program.

OneNote 2010 Ribbon User Interface

Under the Home tab you can cut, copy, and paste from the clipboard; adjust the font, font size, and font style options; adjust text layout and formatting; and select a style for titles, headers, and regular text. Styles allow you to change similar sections throughout your text (such as a heading) by only changing one setting. This saves you from having to manually change the format of each occurrence of a type of text. Tags can be added through the Home tab. Tags are used to mark items as important or as a To Do item.

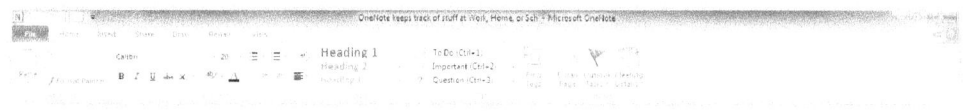

Figure 13.4: Home Tab

In the Insert tab you can insert items into the notebook. You can insert tables, pictures, text, and shapes; insert audio and video; and insert dates, equations, and symbols.

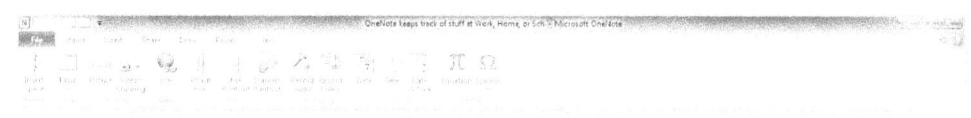

Figure 13.5: Insert Tab

The Share tab can be used to e-mail the page with your default e-mail program or share the notebook with others. Other items on the Share tab allow you to view read and unread notes, track changes by specific authors, and view previous revisions of the notebook.

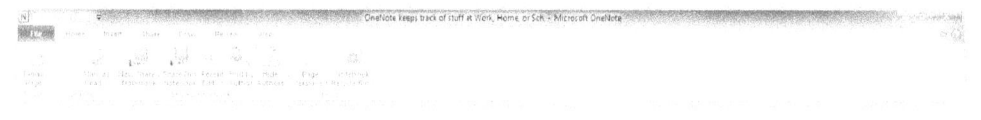

Figure 13.6: Share Tab

The Draw tab lets you choose your cursor, brush and color, and shapes for drawing on the page. You can also arrange content onscreen and convert drawing ink into text or math.

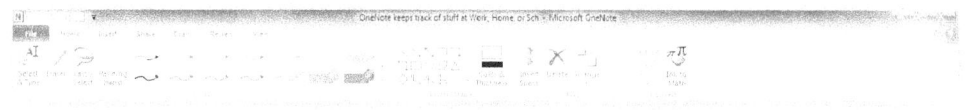

Figure 13.7: Draw Tab

Under the Review tab, you can check spelling, check definitions, and check synonyms for a word. Language and translation options are available for modifying selected text. You can also view linked notes from the Review tab.

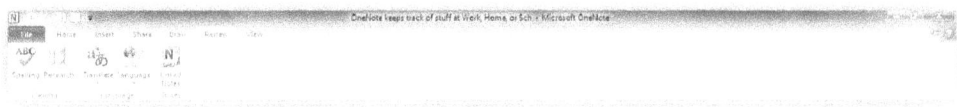

Figure 13.8: Review Tab

The View tab lets you configure the reading mode and layout of the file onscreen. You can change the onscreen format's color, page lines, and hide the titles.

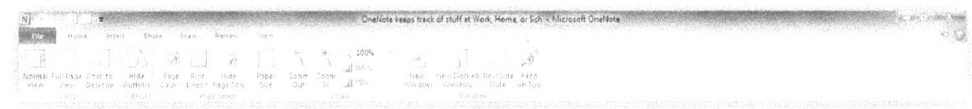

Figure 13.9: View Tab

OneNote 2010 File Menu Interface

Clicking on the File tab on the Ribbon UI opens the File Options window. From here you can perform many file tasks, like opening, printing, saving, and modifying properties for the notebook.

The top entry in the File Options left pane is the Info screen. Clicking on this link will display information about the currently open file. You can share and sync the notebook from this page or view the file's properties.

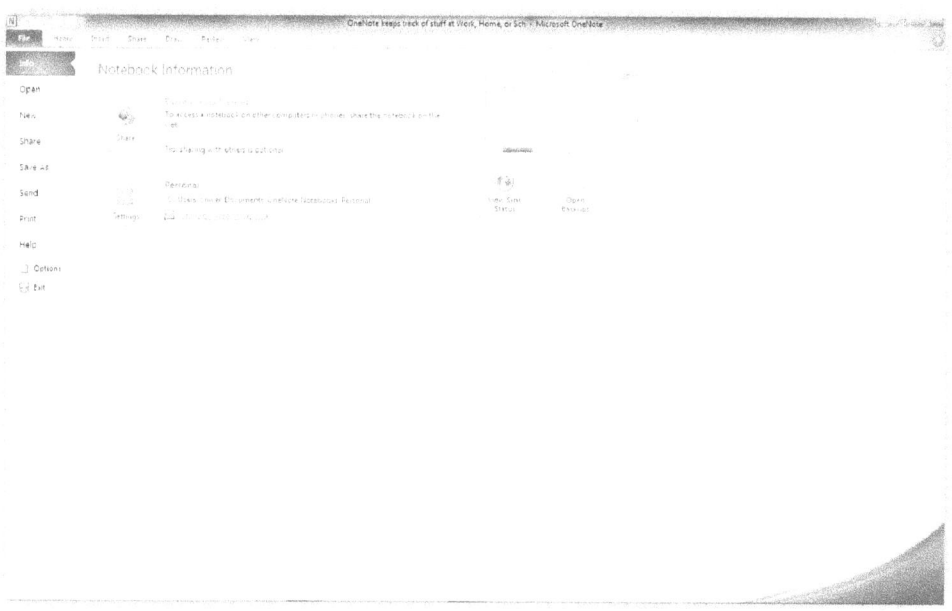

Figure 13.10: Info Screen

The Share option allows you to share a link to your notebook to contacts and friends.

Figure 13.11: Share Option

The Save As option allows you to save a page, section, or notebook in a different format. You can export as a PDF and XPS document, earlier version of OneNote, or as a Microsoft Word document.

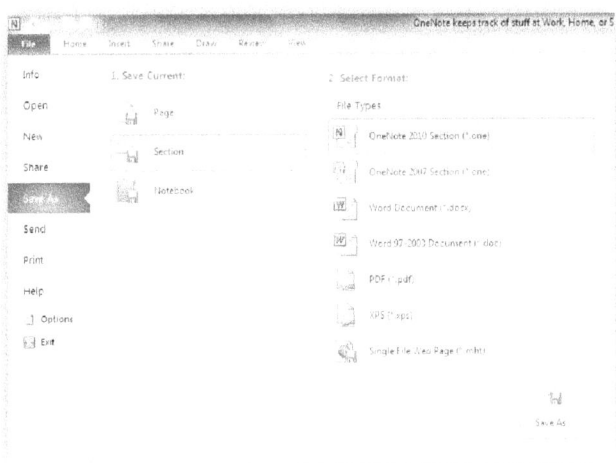

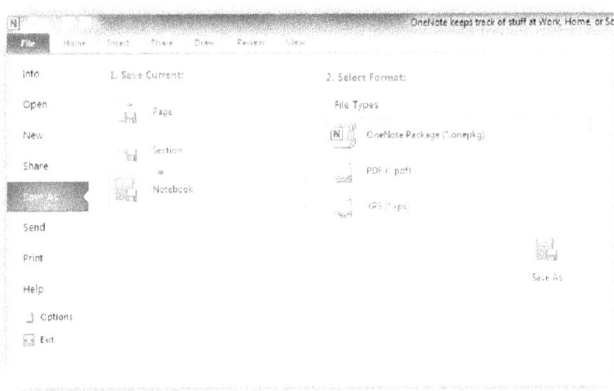

Figure 13.12: Save As

The Send option lets you e-mail the page, attach the page as a document or PDF to an e-mail, or to send to a blogging account.

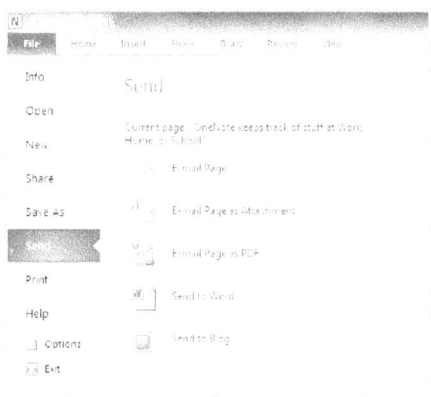

Figure 13.13: Send Notebook Options

In the Outlook 2010 section we will explore the business e-mail and scheduling application and its many features.

Chapter Review Questions:
1. Describe the differences between a Notebook, Page, and Note.
2. What tool can be used to capture on-screen pictures, text, and content?
3. What option allows you to e-mail your Notebook, attach as a PDF, or upload to a blog?

Chapter 14 – Outlook 2010

Outlook is a widely used e-mail and scheduling program that is used predominantly in business environments. Outlook allows for accessing multiple e-mail accounts, managing contacts, and setting appointments and reminders in the calendar section.

Outlook 2010 Initial Setup

When Outlook 2010 first opens, you will be presented with a wizard for configuring your e-mail account in the program. You will need to know your e-mail address, password, and possibly mail server settings for your account. Click the Next button to proceed with the wizard.

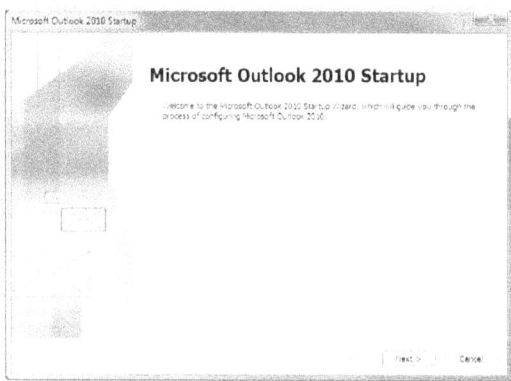

Figure 14.1: Outlook 2010 Setup Wizard

Type your name as you would like it to appear on outgoing messages, your e-mail address, and your e-mail password in the spaces provided. If you need to manually configure your mail server settings, select that option and click Next.

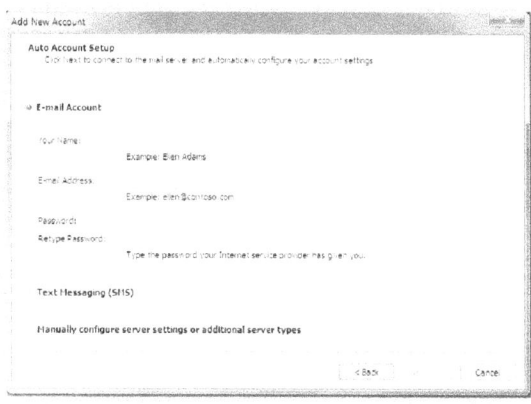

Figure 14.2: Add An E-mail Account Option

221

When manually configuring mail server options you will be asked if you are using an Exchange Server, outlook.com or ActiveSync service, or if you are using POP or IMAP. Check the recommended settings with your e-mail provider for the option you should select. Click the Next button to continue.

In the following window you will be prompted for your name, e-mail address, password, and mail server settings. Please consult your e-mail provider for the settings you will need to enter. After you have entered the information and clicked the Next button, Outlook will attempt to validate that the account settings are correct. If the settings appear to be correct you will complete the wizard and find downloaded messages in your inbox folder.

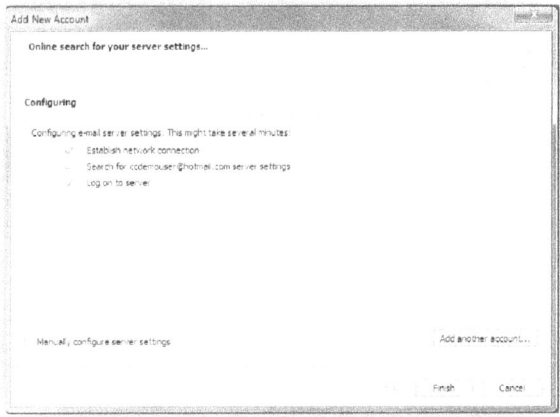

Figure 14.3: Validating Account Settings

 Be sure to verify your mail server settings with your e-mail provider.

Outlook 2010 Start Window and Layout

In the main Outlook window you will see the Ribbon UI running along the top of the screen, your e-mail folders in the left pane, messages in the center pane, and a preview of the selected message in the right pane. In the lower-left corner you can switch between categories in Outlook. Options include viewing mail, calendar, contacts, and task.

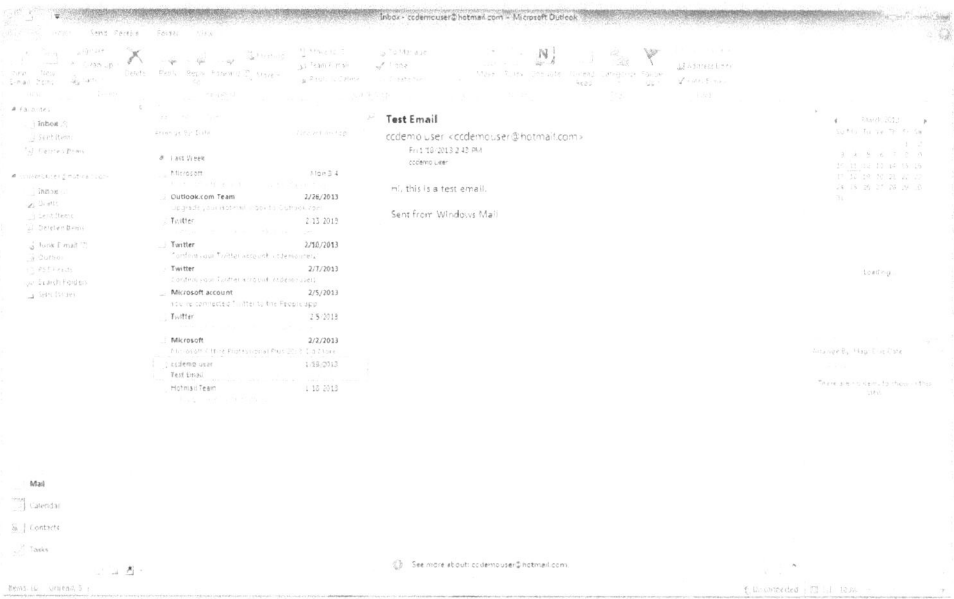

Figure 14.4: Outlook 2010 Main Window

Outlook 2010 Mail Ribbon User Interface

The Outlook Mail Home tab is the initial Ribbon UI tab that will be open in Microsoft Outlook. The Home tab contains many of the common e-mail tasks. From this tab you can create a new e-mail message or other item; mark messages as junk or mark for deletion; reply to and forward e-mails; and move, tag, and locate e-mails.

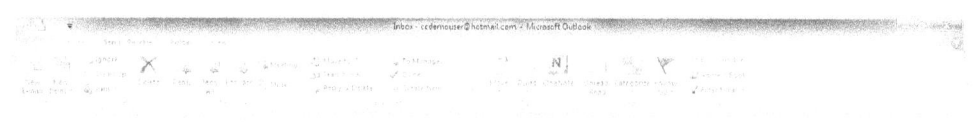

Figure 14.5: Mail Home Tab

In the Mail Send/Receive tab you can check for new e-mail and sync folders. There are also options for downloading only message headers, working offline, and viewing or canceling the message download process.

Figure 14.6: Main Send/Receive Tab

The Mail Folder tab has options to manage and add new storage folders and options for messages stored in folders.

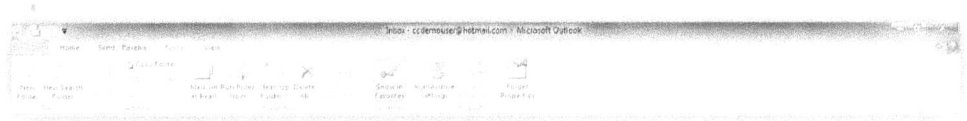

Figure 14.7: Mail Folders Tab

The Mail View tab has options for the onscreen layout of the window panes and e-mails in the folder pane. Messages can be arranged by sorting according to selected options. Items can also be opened in new windows for more screen space.

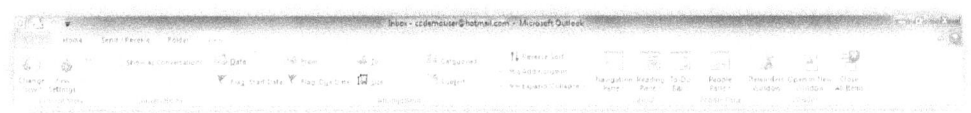

Figure 14.8: Mail View Tab

Outlook 2010 File Menu Interface

Clicking on the File tab on the Ribbon UI opens the File Options window. From here you can perform several tasks, like viewing account information, opening and exporting data files, and saving or printing e-mails.

One of the top entries in the File Options left pane is the Info screen. Clicking on this link will display information for the e-mail accounts configured in Outlook. You can configure settings for the account, add social network connections, archive messages and delete trash, and set up rules for incoming messages.

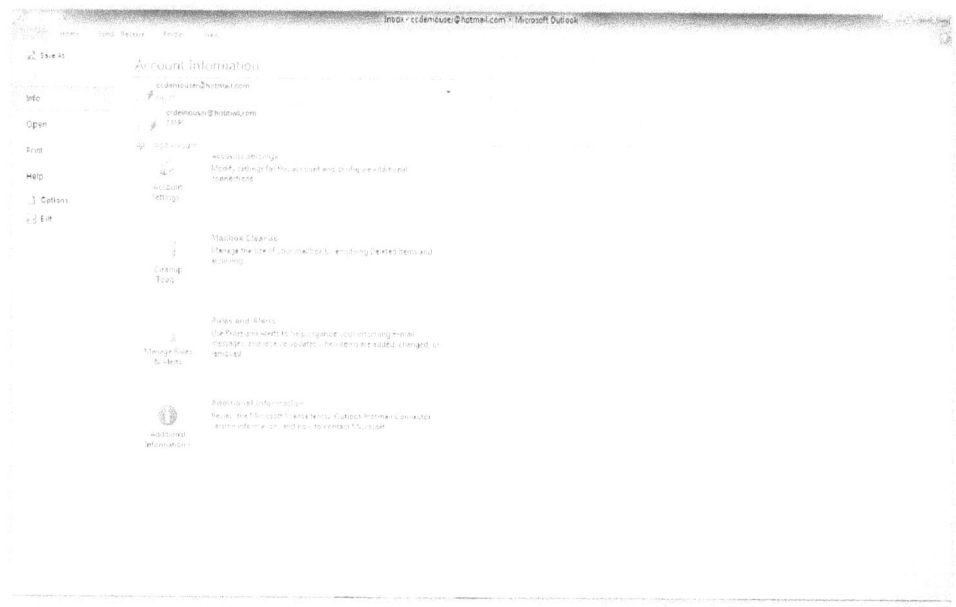

Figure 14.9: Info Screen

Clicking the Account Settings button on the Info tab will open the Account Settings window. You can use this window to edit settings related to the e-mail accounts configured in Outlook.

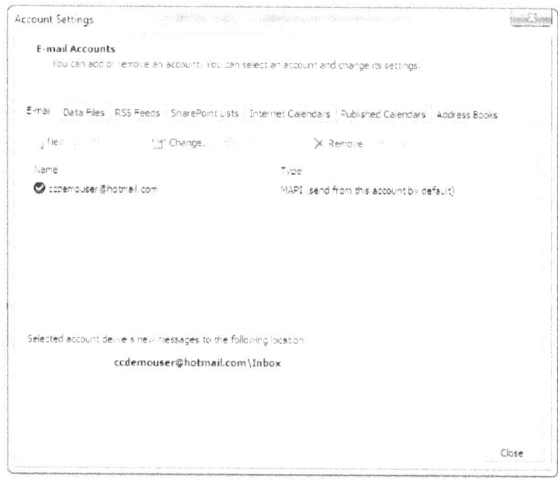

Figure 14.10: Account Settings Window

In the Open option you can open a calendar, an Outlook data file, another user's folder, or import and export files and settings.

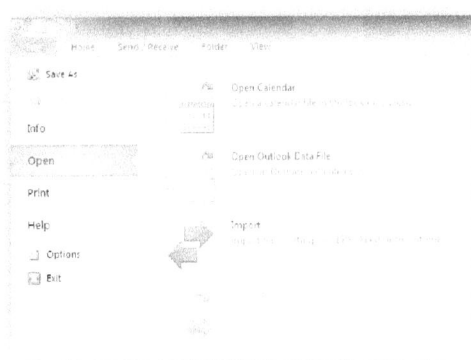

Figure 14.11: Open & Export Screen

The Print Options allows you to print e-mails, choose the printer you wish to use, and select other printer options. In the right pane you can view a preview of the print as it will appear with the current settings.

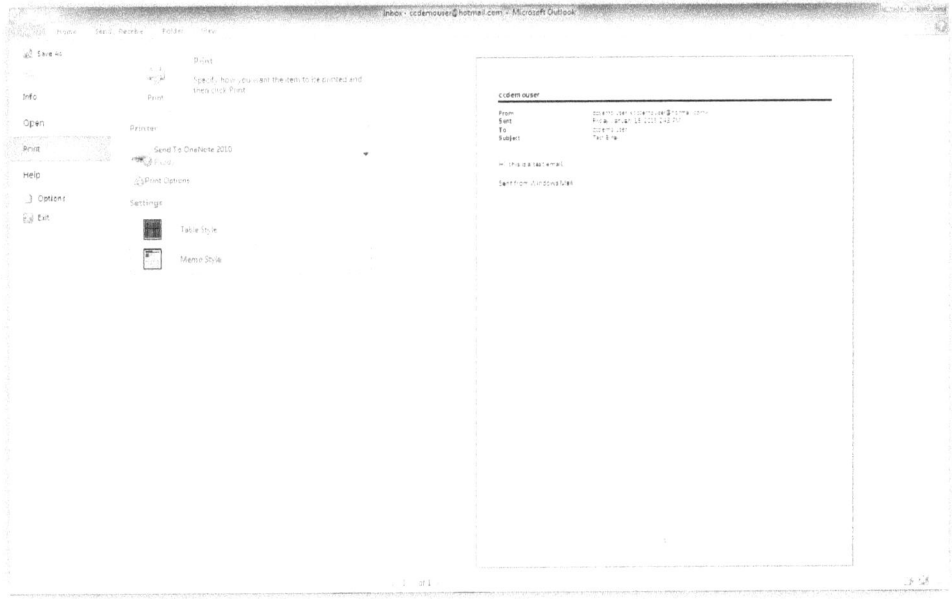

Figure 14.12: Print Options

Outlook 2010 Compose a New Message

To compose a new e-mail message, click the New E-mail button in the Home tab on the main Outlook Mail window. In the new window that opens you can create the e-mail you wish to send. Enter the e-mail address or contact name you wish to send the e-mail to in the "To" section. Add names or addresses of others that should receive a carbon copy in the "CC" box.

You can enter a subject for the e-mail in the Subject box below. Type your e-mail message in the large textbox beneath the subject line. If you are not sure of the e-mail address for a contact, you can either type the person's name in the "To" section, or click the "To" button or Address Book button on the home tab to select from a list of your contacts. To attach a file or picture you can use the Attach File, Attach Item, or other option from the Insert tab. To send the new e-mail click the Send button (located to the left of the "To" and "CC" sections).

Figure 14.13: New Message Window

The Message tab contains options for copying and pasting items from the clipboard, formatting the text and layout, and attaching items to the message. You can open the Address Book and check names against it, and also flag the message's importance level.

Figure 14.14: Message Tab

The Insert tab can be used to attach a file to the e-mail, or to include an Outlook Item, business card, calendar, or signature. You can insert a table, chart, or image to the message, or include advanced text options.

Figure 14.15: Insert Tab

The Options tab provides theme effects for the e-mail message. You can show the Blind Carbon Copy field and the From field, and also request delivery and read receipts for the message. The More Options section allows you to save the sent message to a specific location, delay the delivery of the message, and direct e-mail replies to a specific address.

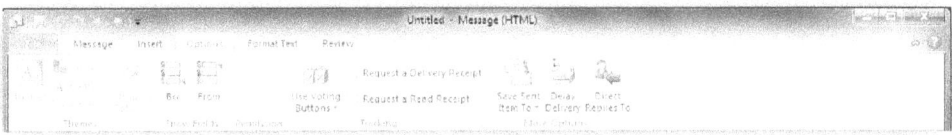

Figure 14.16: Options Tab

The Format Text tab contains many options for formatting the font, color, size, and layout of text in the message.

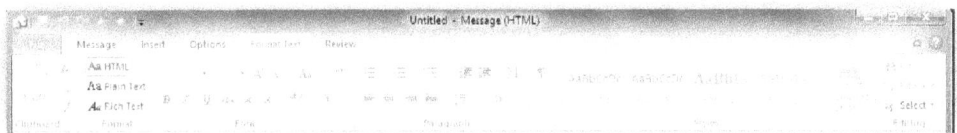

Figure 14.17: Format Text Tab

The Review tab can be used to check spelling and grammar in the message, and to utilize other proofreading tools.

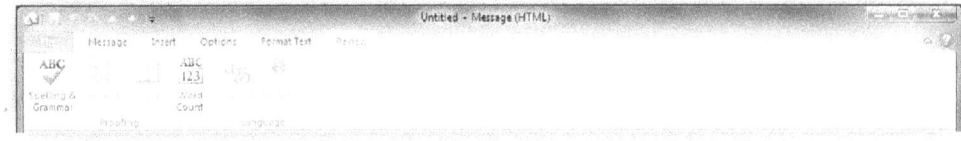

Figure 14.18: Review Tab

To reply or forward messages you receive from others, you can right-click on messages in the middle pane of the Outlook Mail main window. From this context menu you can reply, forward, delete, mark as junk, and select many other message options.

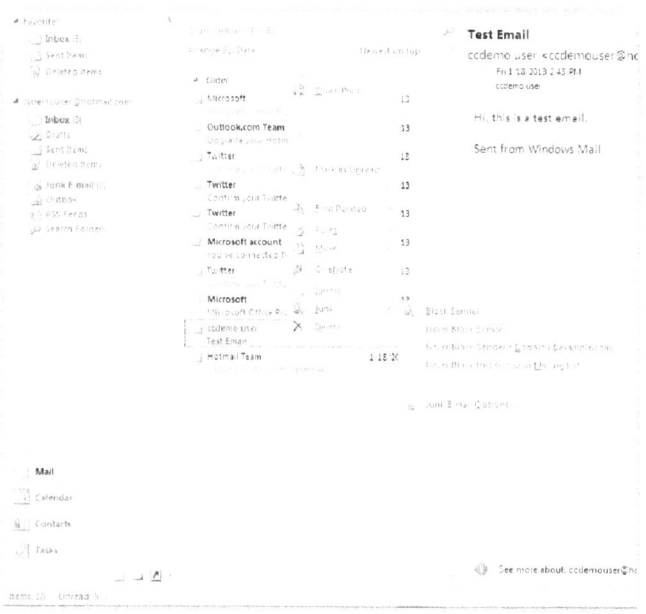

Figure 14.19: Messages Context Menu

When you receive an attachment in an e-mail, you will see the file's icon at the top of the message window (Figure 14.20). Right click the attached file for options to open or save the attachment. Clicking the Open option will open the file with the default program. If no installed program can open that file type, you may be prompted to locate a program that can open the file. The Save As option will allow you to save the selected file with a specified name and location. The Save All Attachments option can be used to save all attached files in the current e-mail message to a location on your computer.

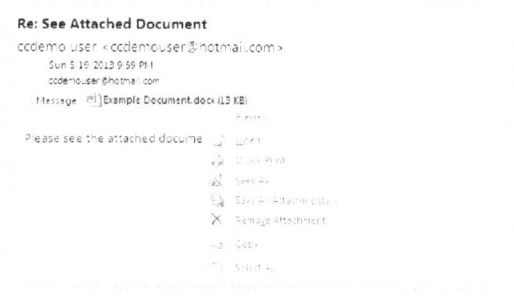

Figure 14.20: Saving Attachments

Running along the bottom left corner of the Outlook window are several links to other Outlook program components. From this menu you can switch between e-mail, your calendar, your contacts, and your tasks.

229

Outlook 2010 Calendar

The Outlook Calendar manages appointments, reminders, and can be used to notify other contacts of meetings and other events.

Outlook 2010 Calendar Window Layout

Along the top you will see the Calendar's Ribbon UI with calendar specific options. In the left pane you will find a condensed calendar for the current and following month, along with options for viewing different calendars. Above the large calendar in the right pane you will see a calendar search bar.

Figure 14.21: Outlook Calendar Main Window

Outlook 2010 Calendar Ribbon User Interface

The Home tab is used to create a new appointment, meeting, or other item; change the view style and view of the current calendar; open a different calendar; and share your calendar with others by e-mail or online.

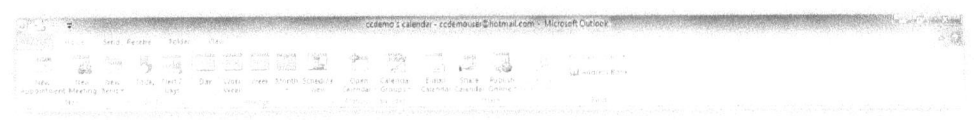

Figure 14.22: Outlook Calendar Home Tab

The Mail Send/Receive tab can send and receive all folders and groups. There are also options for working offline and viewing or canceling the message download process.

Figure 14.23: Outlook Calendar Send/Receive Tab

The Folder tab lets you create, copy, move, and delete calendars. You can share, set permissions, and open other calendars.

Figure 14.24: Outlook Calendar Folder Tab

The View tab allows you to modify the calendar view and layout onscreen. You can change the window layout or open elements in a new window.

Figure 14.25: Outlook Calendar View Tab

Outlook 2010 Contacts List

Clicking the Contacts link at the bottom of the screen will open your Outlook contacts list. Here you can add, view, sort, and modify contacts in your address book. You can create groups for different mailing lists and include contacts in those groups.

Outlook 2010 Contacts Window Layout

Your Contacts folders will be listed in the left pane and individual contact cards will be displayed in the main center pane. You can use the search box to search for a contact or the alphabetical list to the right of the contact cards to filter listed names.

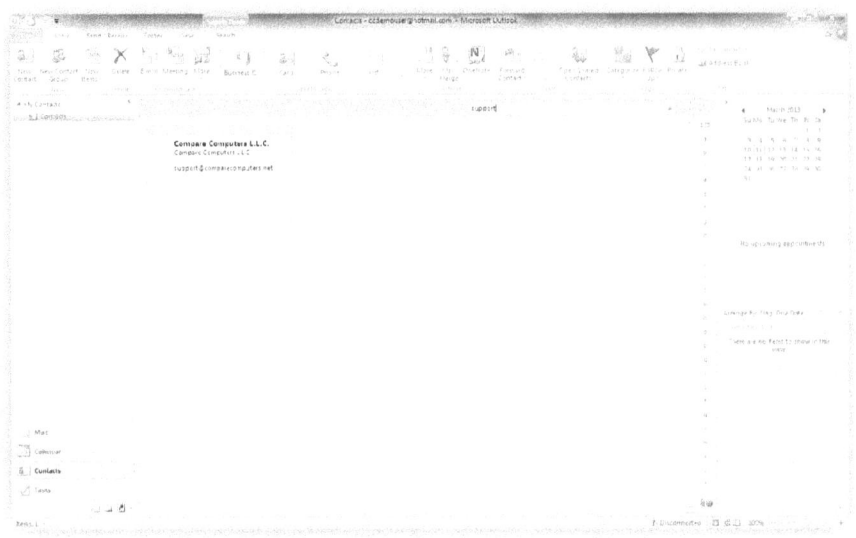

Figure 14.26: Outlook Contacts Main Window

Outlook 2010 Contacts Ribbon User Interface

The Home tab contains options to add a new contact, group contact, or add other items. You can share contacts with others, categorize contacts, and search your contacts.

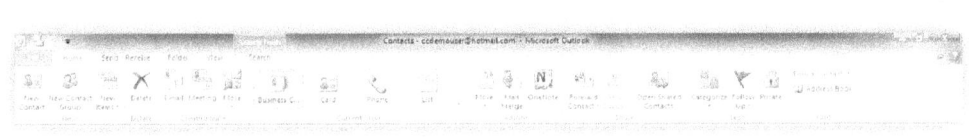

Figure 14.27: Outlook Contacts Home Tab

The Send/Receive tab is used to send/receive all folders or groups, show or cancel progress, and work offline.

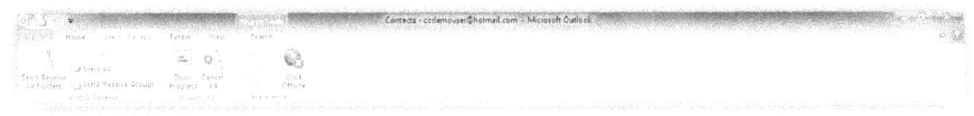

Figure 14.28: Outlook Contacts Send/Receive Tab

The Folder tab can create, copy, move, and delete folders. You can share and manage access to contacts from this tab as well.

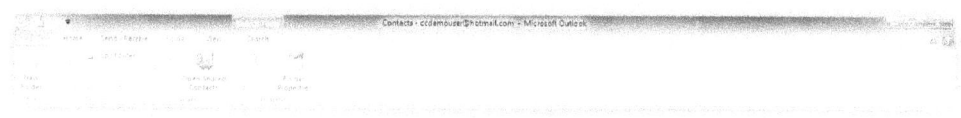

Figure 14.29: Outlook Contacts Folder Tab

The View tab contains options for modifying the onscreen layout of elements and for opening items in a new window.

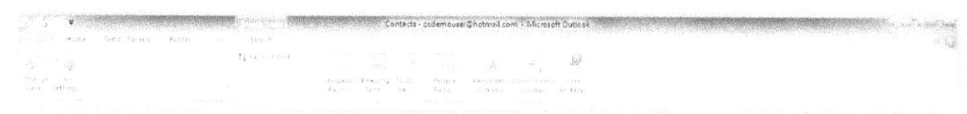

Figure 14.30: Outlook Contacts View Tab

Outlook 2010 Tasks Window Layout

Clicking on the Task link at the bottom of the window will open the Outlook Tasks window, where you can add and manage to-do lists and other tasks you need to track.

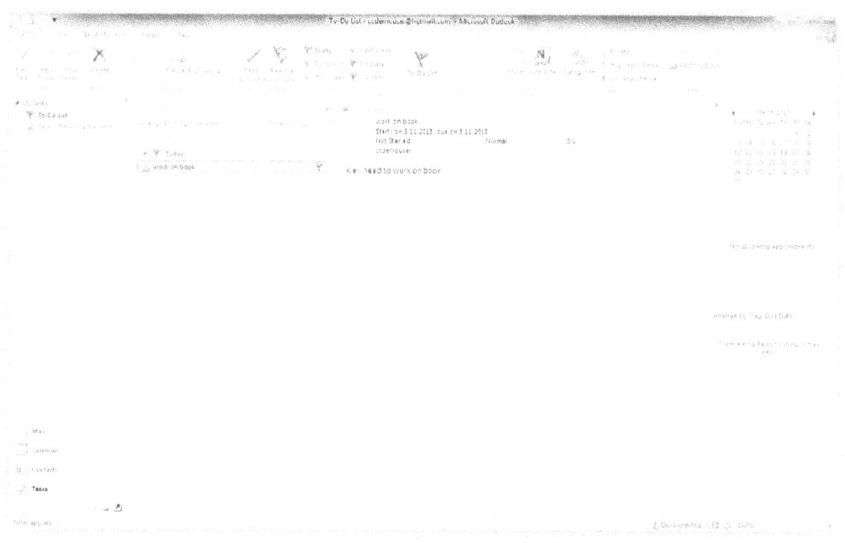

Figure 14.31: Outlook Task Main Window

Outlook 2010 Tasks Ribbon User Interface

The Home tab can create new tasks, e-mails, and other items. You can manage and respond to tasks, flag tasks for follow up, and tag or categorize tasks.

Figure 14.32: Outlook Tasks Home Tab

The Send/Receive tab can be used to send/receive all folders or groups, show or cancel progress, and work offline.

Figure 14.33: Outlook Tasks Send/Receive Tab

The Folder tab can be used to create, copy, move, and delete folders. You can share and manage access to tasks from this tab as well.

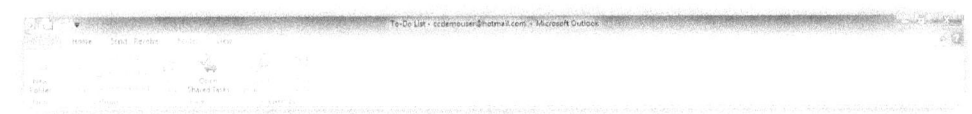

Figure 14.34: Outlook Tasks Folder Tab

The View tab can change the arrangement of items and layout onscreen. You can modify the window layout and open items in a new window.

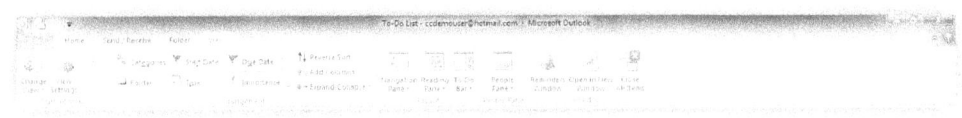

Figure 14.35: Outlook Tasks View Tab

Next we will delve into Publisher 2010 and learn how to work with the program for creating posters and other content.

Chapter Review Questions:
1. Describe the steps for attaching a PDF file in your Documents Library to a new e-mail message.
2. Explain how you would create a new calendar event and invite a contact to the event.
3. Describe how to add a new contact to your Contacts List.

Chapter 15 – Publisher 2010

Publisher is a program in the Office 2010 suite for designing graphics-rich posters, calendars, cards, and designs.

Publisher 2010 Window Layout

Along the top of the screen you will notice the tabbed Ribbon UI with tabs and icons for performing various tasks in the program. Common tasks are located in the Home tab, which is open by default. Other tabs allow you to insert pictures and content, review page layout, and change a number of formatting options. In the pictures that follow, we will break down some of the features in each tab.

Figure 15.1: Blank Project Screen

Publisher 2010 Ribbon User Interface

Under the Home tab you can cut, copy, and paste from the clipboard; adjust the font, font size, and font style options; adjust text layout and formatting; and select a style for titles, headers, and regular text. Text boxes, tables, pictures, and shapes can all be added to the project from the Home tab. You can also find and replace specified text in a document from the Home tab.

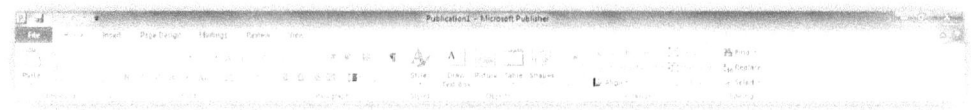

Figure 15.2: Home Tab

In the Insert tab you can insert items into the document. You can insert pages, tables, pictures, and text. Shapes and page building blocks, like calendars and advertisements, can also be added through the Insert tab. You can insert headers, footers, and comments, as well as objects, files, and symbols.

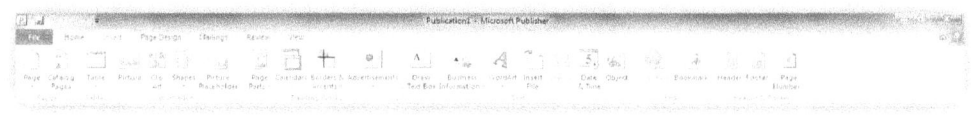

Figure 15.3: Insert Tab

In the Page Layout tab, you can adjust the margins, page orientation, size, and element layout. You can select color schemes for the design of the project and choose background colors and images to add to the page.

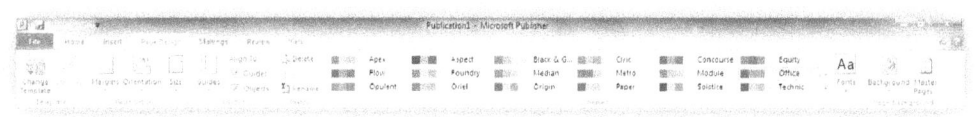

Figure 15.4: Page Design

The Mailings tab is used to create personalized mailings to contacts. From this tab you can import contacts' information from a contacts list into the document.

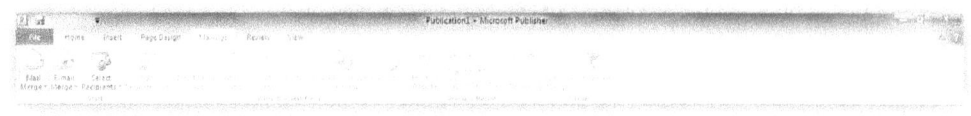

Figure 15.5: Mailings Tab

Under the Review tab, you can check spelling, check definitions, and check synonyms for a word. Language and translation options are available for modifying selected text.

Figure 15.6: Review Tab

The View tab lets you configure the reading mode and layout of the document onscreen. You can add onscreen components, such as the ruler bar and gridlines, to the window. The view can be modified to include multiple pages on the screen at the same time. This tab can also manage multiple windows on the screen.

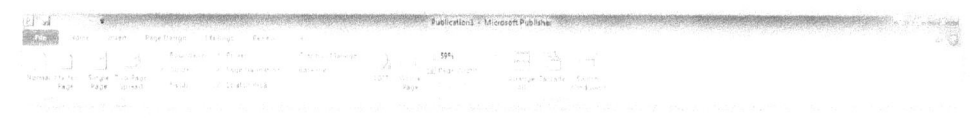

Figure 15.7: View Tab

Publisher 2010 File Menu Interface

Clicking on the File tab on the Ribbon UI opens the File Options window. From here you can perform many file tasks, like opening, printing, saving, and modifying properties for the project.

The Save As file option allows you to save the document in a different format, such as a PDF and XPS document, or in a format for use with an earlier version of Publisher.

The New link allows you to open a new blank file or one of the many preformatted templates on the screen. You can search for terms to find a template that matches search keywords.

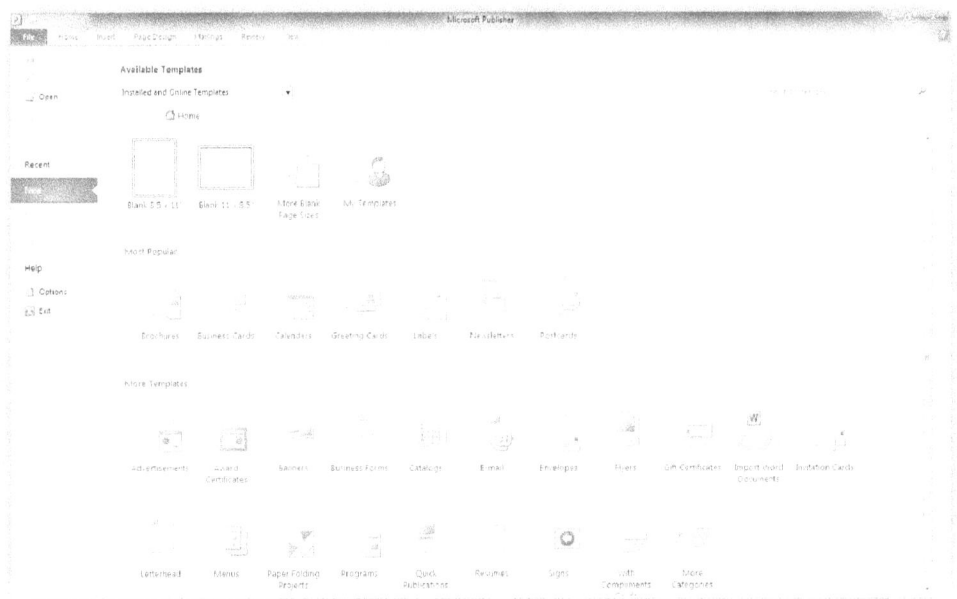

Figure 15.8: New Document Screen

Under the Print option, you will see a print preview of the current document on the right and various print options to the left. From here you can choose the printer, number of copies, and page and color options for the print job.

The Save & Send option allows you to e-mail the design as a publisher file attachment, PDF attachment, or XPS attachment. You can also e-mail the page as html in the e-mail body. This allows the e-mail message to have the same appearance as your publisher document without requiring an attached file to be opened.

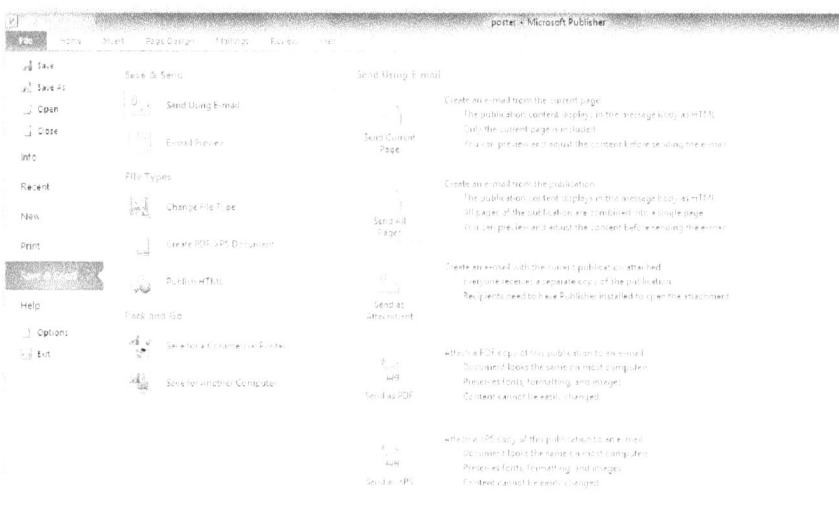

Figure 15.9: Send Using E-Mail

The Change File Type option can save the Publisher file in a format for use in a previous version of the program. It can also save the file as an image file, web page, or as several other file types.

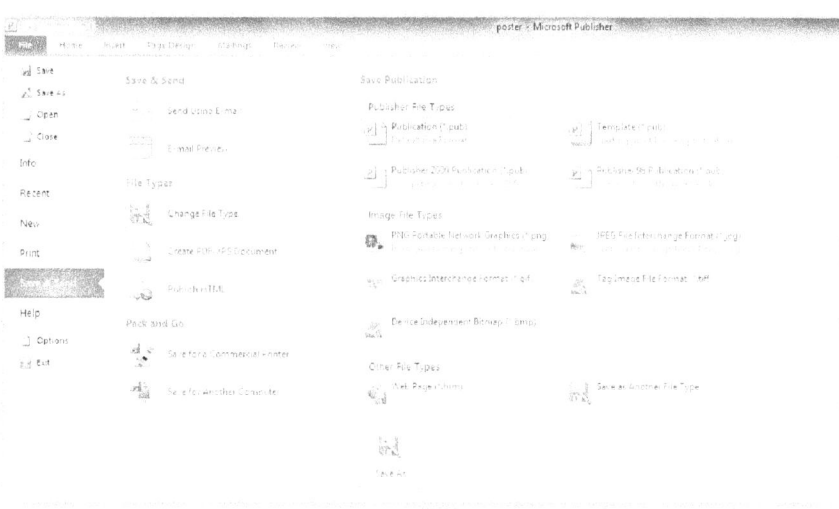

Figure 15.10: Change File Type

A PDF or XPS document can be created from the Publisher file by selecting the Create PDF/XPS Document option.

Figure 15.11: Create PDF or XPS Document

The Publish HTML option will generate an HTML file that can be published to your website. The page can then be viewed in a web browser without requiring Microsoft Publisher to be installed on the client computer.

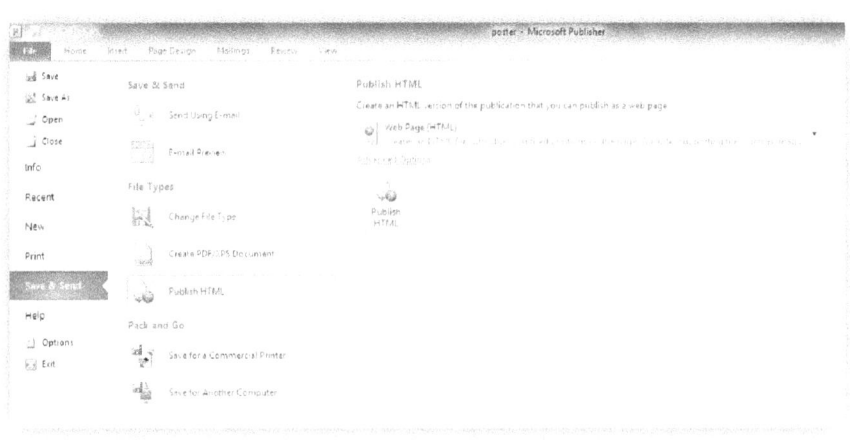

Figure 15.12: Publish HTML

The Pack and Go option can be used to print the file on a different device. This option can create high-quality files for use on commercial printers.

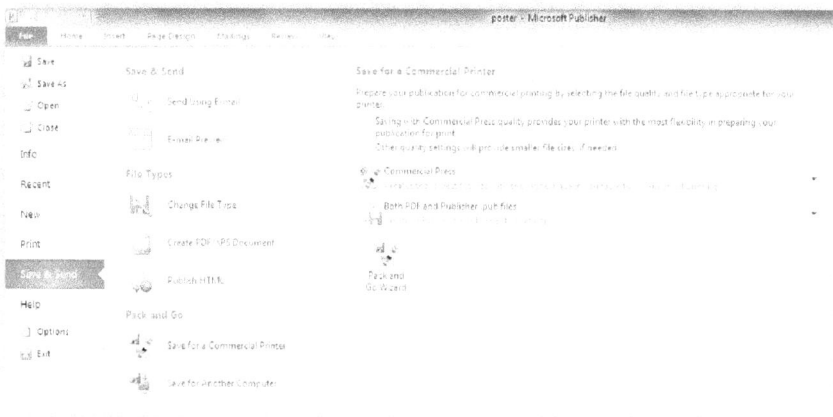

Figure 15.13: Save for a Commercial Printer – Pack and Go Wizard

When using the Save For Another Computer option, the Pack and Go feature can save all of the required resources for the Publisher file and generate copy of the file that can be used on another PC.

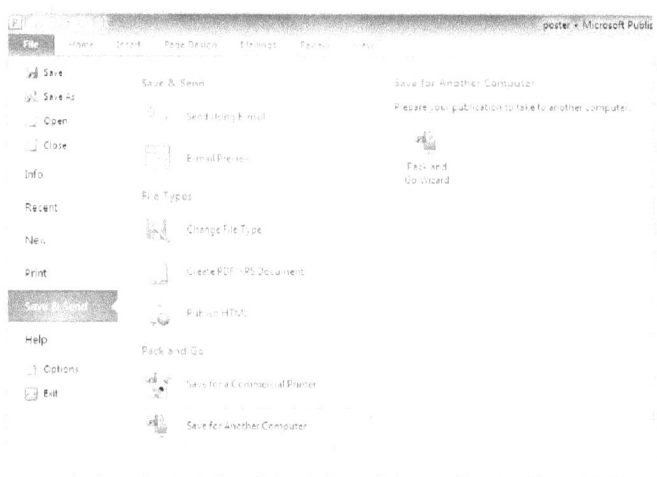

Figure 15.14: Save & Send Options

Next we will look at how to perform some common tasks in Publisher 2010.

Publisher 2010 Basic Tasks

In Publisher, several common tasks can be used to create a variety of different projects. We will briefly look at adding text, images, and shapes to a project, as well as modifying the page design and adding page components.

To insert an online picture into the project, click on the Insert tab and then the Clip Art option. Search for a picture you would like to add to the project. When you have found the image you want, click the Insert button. You can move and resize the image by dragging the borders of the picture.

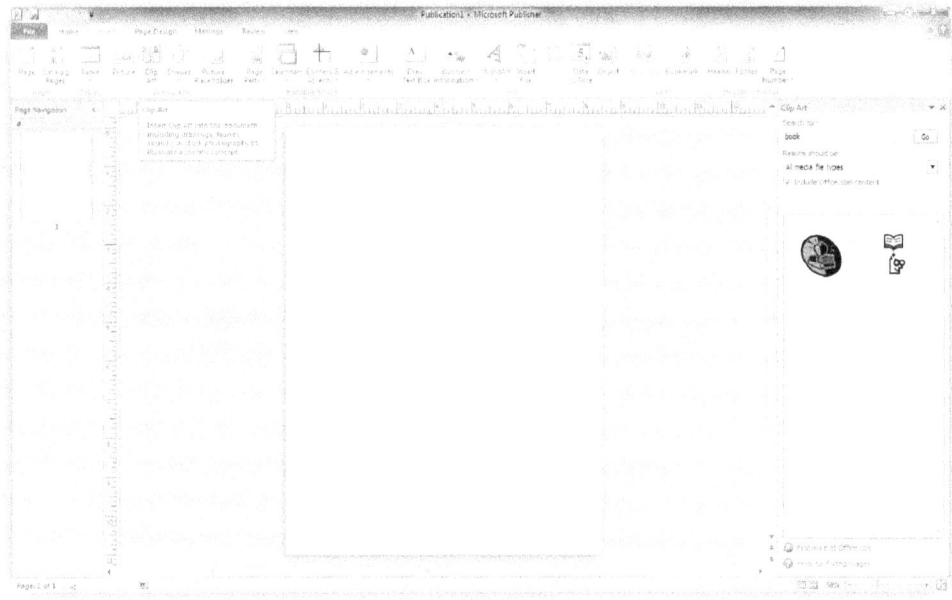

Figure 15.15: Insert an Image

To add text to the project, choose the Draw Text Box option from the Home tab. You will now see a Text Box Format tab on the Ribbon UI, which will allow you to modify the font, font size, and many other options for the text you type in the box.

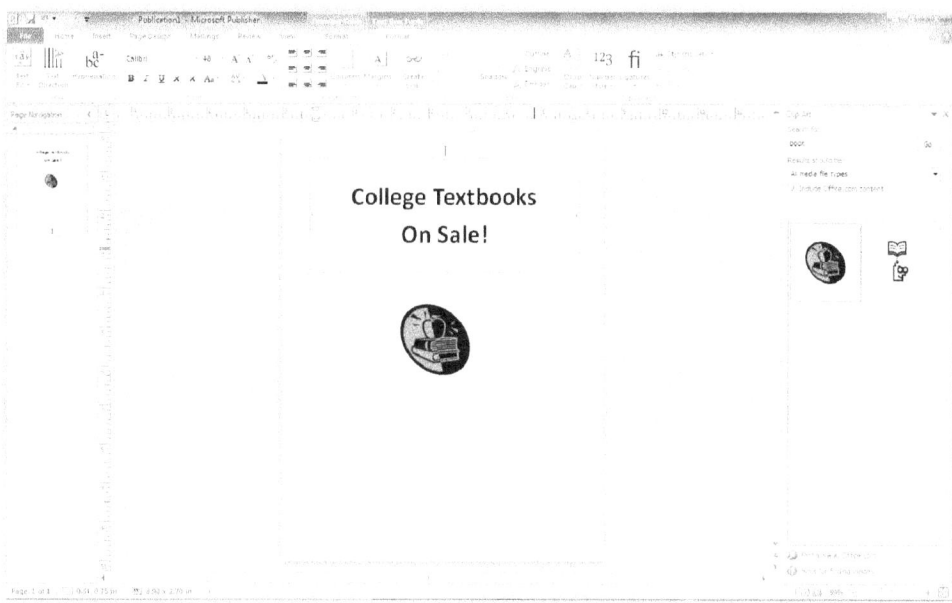

Figure 15.16: Insert a Text Box

To add a shape to the project, choose the shape you want to add from the Shapes dropdown box under the Insert tab. Once the shape is added you can move the item to a new location. Drag the borders of the shape to resize the object.

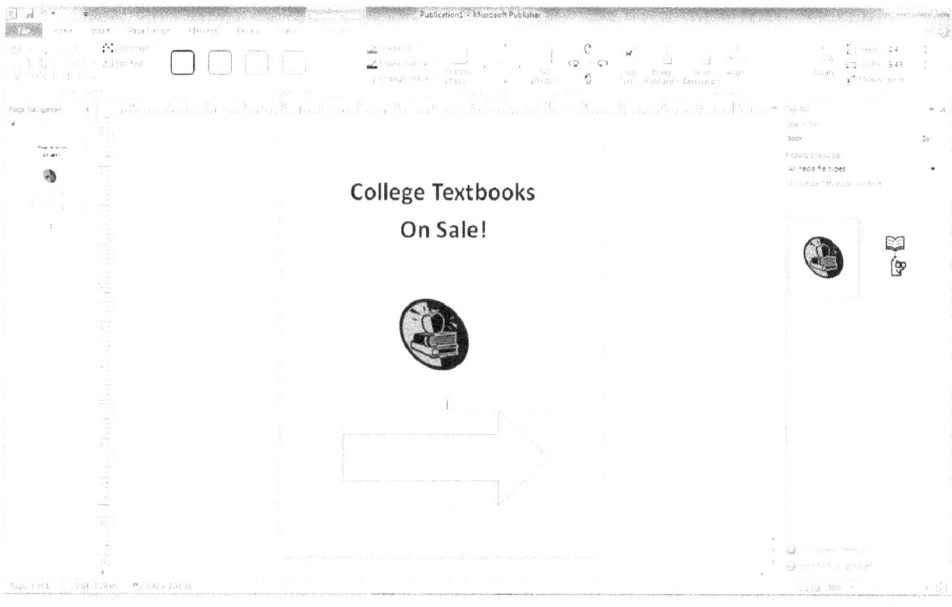

Figure 15.17: Insert a Shape

243

Click on the Page Design tab to modify the design and layout of the page. From here you can choose a color scheme or change the background color for the project. In this example we have changed the background to a gradient.

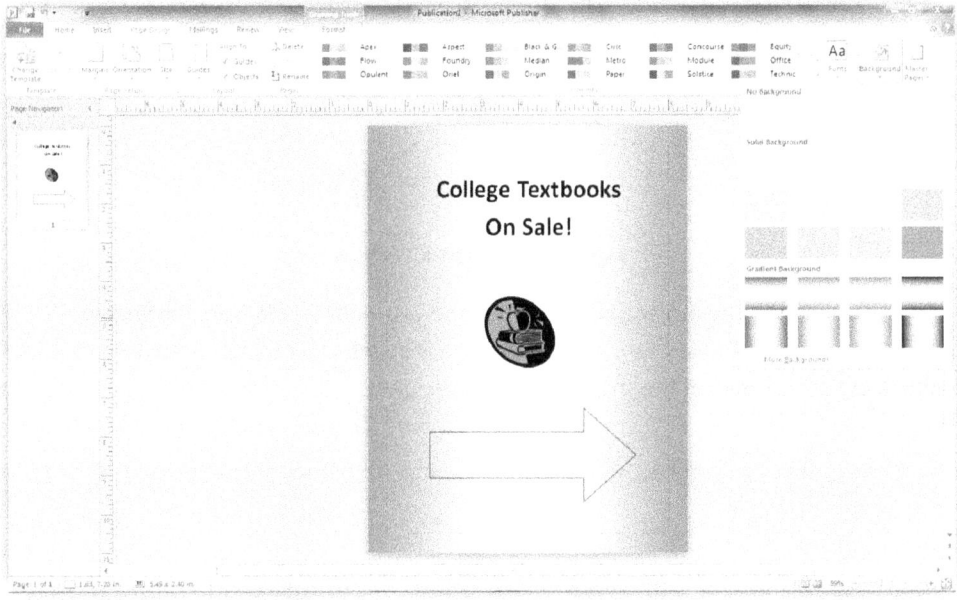

Figure 15.18: Modify Page Design

Adding Page Parts to a project lets you add some preconfigured items to the page. You can add headings, sidebars, and quote boxes, all with preset themes, to hold the text you enter. You could add a quote box to call attention to a customer's recommendation for your services on a poster for your business.

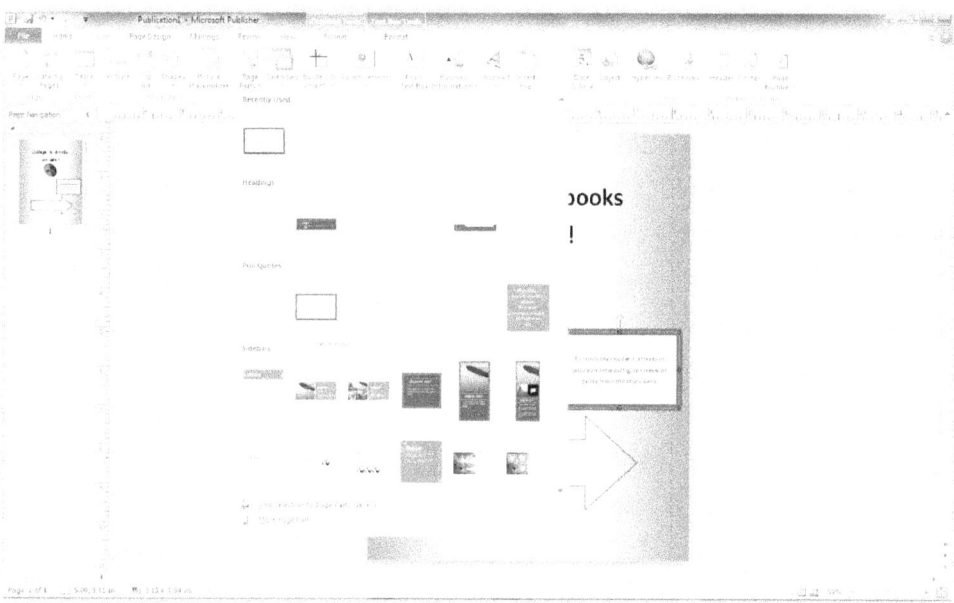

Figure 15.19: Insert Page Parts

These were just a few of the tasks you can perform in Publisher 2010. Now that you have performed several common tasks in Publisher, you should feel more comfortable working with the program to create your own unique designs.

The final Microsoft Office 2010 application that we will briefly look at is a database program called Access 2010.

Chapter Review Questions:

1. How would we add a picture from your Pictures Library to a new document?
2. If we wanted to send a sign we created to a printer, what is the best method for achieving the best quality end result?
3. What is the best method for saving our Publisher document so that we can continue to work on the file on a different PC?

Chapter 16 – Access 2010

Access is a program for creating databases, tables, and queries for working with data. Designing databases and working with features in Access is an in-depth topic and will not be covered in detail in this book. I will briefly show you some of the basics of the program and user interface so that you may become more comfortable with exploring the program further on your own.

Access 2010 Start Window and Layout

When launching Access, you will encounter the start page with options for opening a database file or creating a new database from a template. To start a new desktop database, click the Blank Desktop Database option.

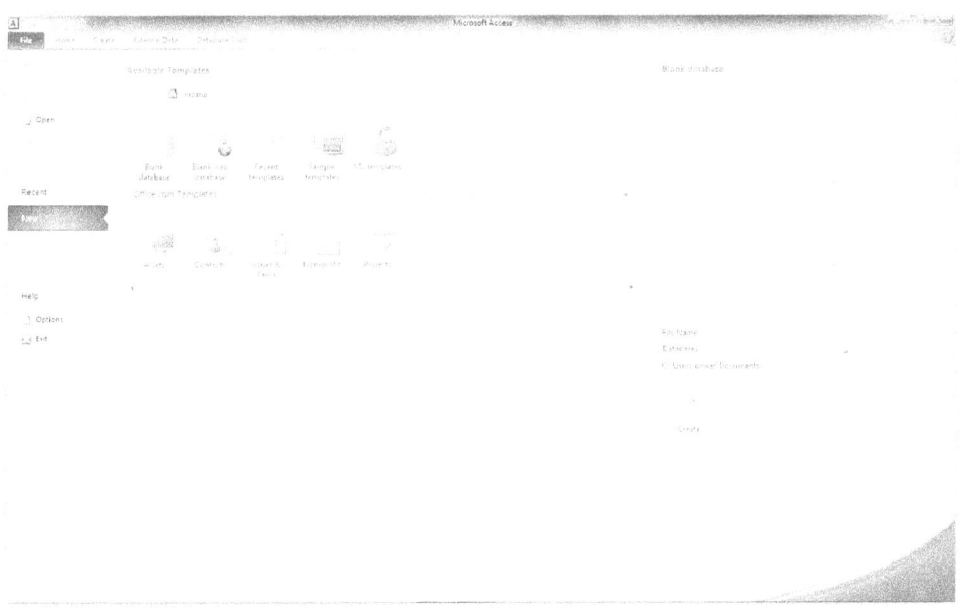

Figure 16.1: Access Start Page

Along the top of the screen you will notice the tabbed Ribbon UI with tabs and icons for performing various tasks in the program. Common tasks are located in the Home tab. Other tabs allow you to import data into a table, modify tables and fields, and configure table relationships. In the pictures that follow, we will break down some of the features in each tab.

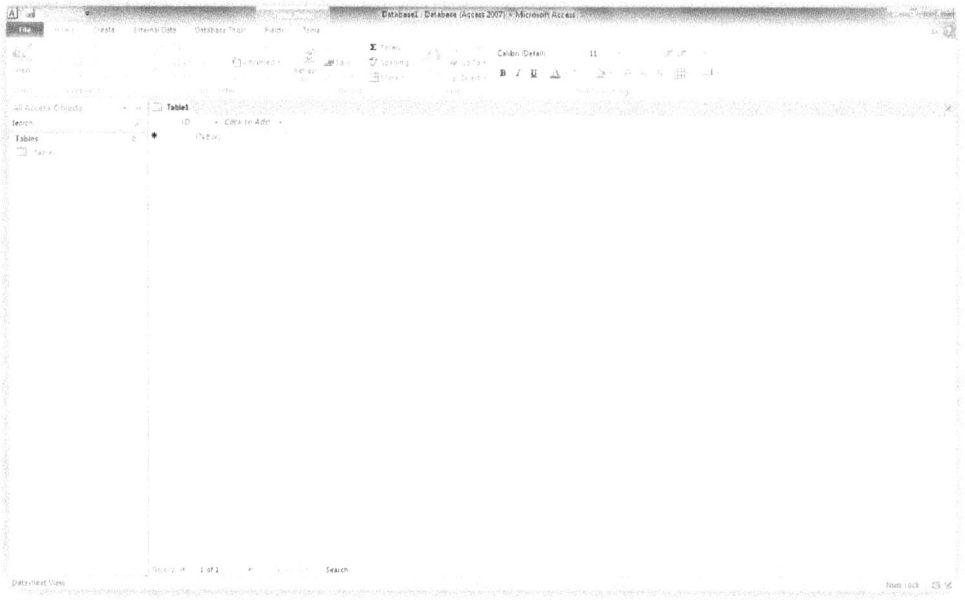

Figure 16.2: Access Main Window

Access 2010 Ribbon User Interface

Under the Home tab you can cut, copy, and paste from the clipboard; adjust the font, font size, and font style options; choose filter options; and switch between view types. You can also find and replace specified text in a document from the Home tab.

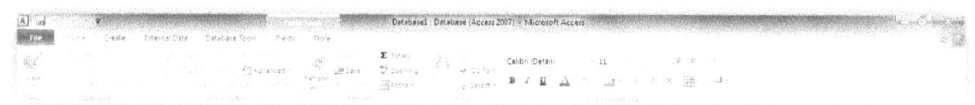

Figure 16.3: Home Tab

In the Create tab you can make tables, queries, forms, and reports. Tables store rows of data fields, forms can be used to streamline entry of data into those tables, queries output records that match criteria, and reports can be generated from queries and tables of data for analysis.

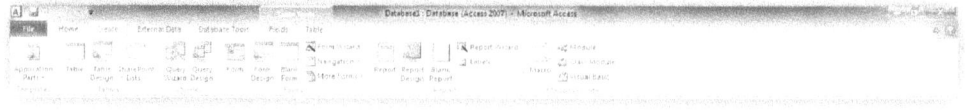

Figure 16.4: Create Tab

In the External Data tab, you can import data from another source into Access. Data can be from an Excel spreadsheet, another Access database, from another database type, or from other types of data files. You can also export data from an Access database into a different file type from this tab. Data can be exported into a spreadsheet, text file, XML file, PDF, XPS, e-mail, or other options.

Figure 16.5: External Data Tab

The Database Tools tab contains features for your database. You can use the Compact and Repair tool to fix issues with the database, run Visual Basic code or Macros, edit data table relationships and dependencies, or to move data to other applications.

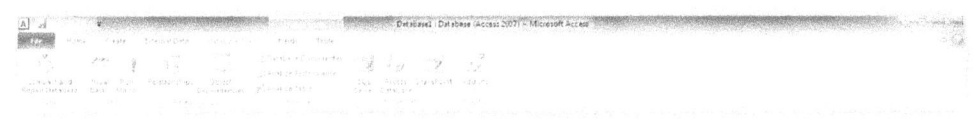

Figure 16.6: Database Tools Tab

The Table Tools: The Fields tab edits the properties of data fields in the table. You can set number and formatting options from this tab. You can also choose if a field is a unique primary key or if it is a required field.

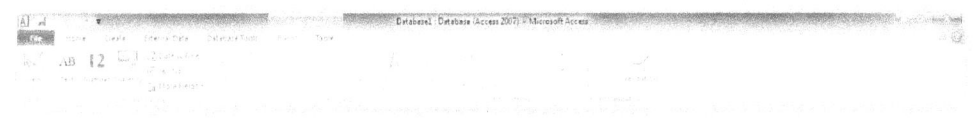

Figure 16.7: Table Tools – Fields Tab

The Table Tools: The Table tab lets you configure properties for the table, manage before and after events, and manage relationships and dependencies.

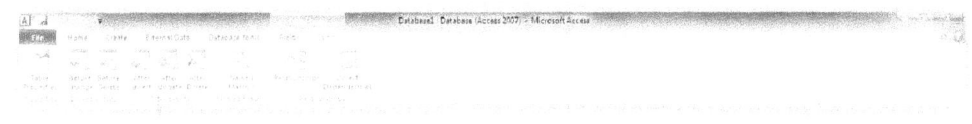

Figure 16.8: Table Tools – Table Tab

Clicking on the File tab will open the File Options screen. From this screen you can save, open, print, and publish your Access database.

The Info option allows you to use the Compact & Repair feature to resolve issues with the database file. You can also encrypt and password protect the database by using the Encrypt With Password feature.

Figure 16.9: Info Screen

The Recent option will list any recently opened or pinned database files. To pin an item to the list, click the pin icon on the right of the database file in the list.

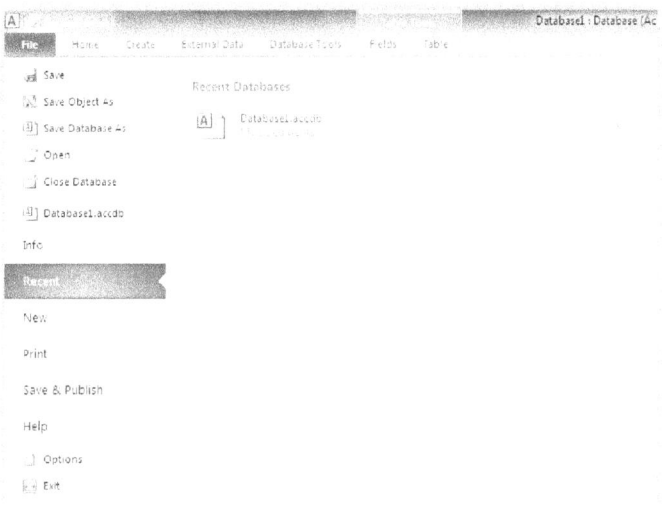

Figure 16.10: Recent Screen

The Print option can print the current object to the printer, allow you to configure print options, and view a preview of the print.

Figure 16.11: Print Screen

The Save & Publish option can be used to save the database for use with a previous version of Microsoft Access, save the database as a template, or save to a SharePoint server. You can also back up the database, apply a digital signature, or compile the database into an ACCDE executable only file.

Figure 16.12: Save & Publish Screen – Save Database As Option

The Save Object As option can save the current database object as a new object or as a PDF or XPS document.

Figure 16.13: Save & Publish Screen – Save Object As

Publish To Access Services is an option to publish the database to a business's SharePoint server.

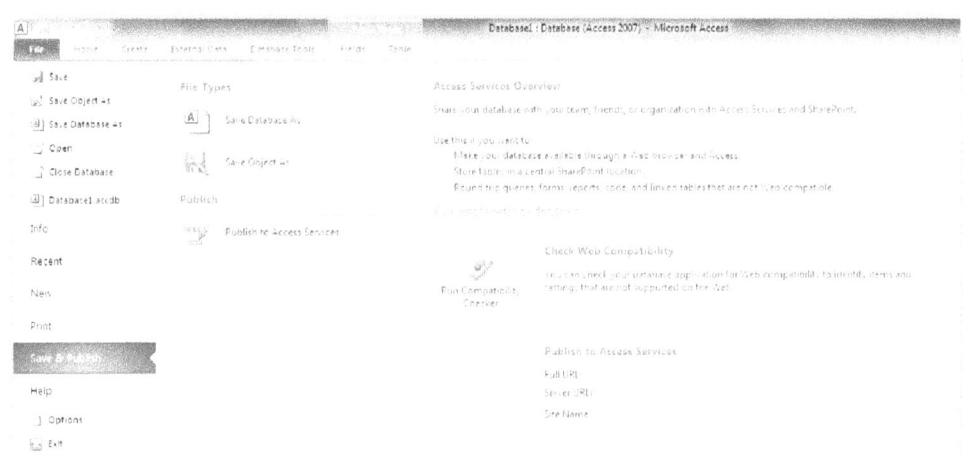

Figure 16.14: Save & Publish – Publish to Access Services

With the overview of the Microsoft Office 2010 Suite complete, you should have a basic understanding of how each program works and feel more comfortable performing many common tasks in each application.

Chapter Review Questions:

1. What is the best method for saving our database for use with a previous version of Microsoft Access?
2. What tab can be used to set a Primary Key?
3. What tool is used to minimize the size of a database file and to resolve issues with the file?

Conclusion

In this book you have learned about the three major components to Windows 7—the Start Menu, Windows Desktop, and the Windows Taskbar. You have explored desktop applications, internet browsers, and the Microsoft Office 2010 Suite. And you have also learned how to personalize and configure settings on the PC, manage the security of the computer, and how to stay safe online. I hope this book has helped create a solid foundation for continuing the Windows 7 and Microsoft Office 2010 learning process, and has helped to make you more comfortable working with the new operating system.

For more information and tutorial videos on Windows 7, Microsoft Office 2010, and other products, I encourage you to visit our website at www.comparecomputers.net.

KIEL EMERSON

ABOUT THE AUTHOR

Kiel Emerson received his degree in Computer Information Systems from Fort Hays State University. He is a co-owner and computer technician at Compare Computers L.L.C., a local computer repair business in Hays, KS. There he has provided support to thousands of businesses and individuals with their computing needs. He has also produced several tutorial videos to aid customers in learning Windows 8 and Microsoft Office 2013, and authored Beginning Windows 8 and Microsoft Office 2013.

www.ingramcontent.com/pod-product-compliance
Lightning Source LLC
Chambersburg PA
CBHW080400060326
40689CB00019B/4077